ACTS THROUGH REVELATION

# WITNESS

Other books by Jack J. Blanco:

*The Clear Word*
*The Clear Word for Kids*
*The Clear Word Psalms and Proverbs*
*The Clear Word—The Gospel of John*
*The Easy English Clear Word*
*Savior. Four Gospels. One Story.*

To order, call **1–800–765–6955**.

Visit us at **www.AutumnHousePublishing.com**
for information on other Autumn House® products.

ACTS THROUGH REVELATION

# WITNESS

*A fresh look at the New Testament church*

## JACK J. BLANCO

Autumn
House® Publishing
www.autumnhousepublishing.com
A Division of **REVIEW AND HERALD® PUBLISHING**
Since 1861

Published by Autumn House® Publishing, a division of Review and Herald® Publishing, Hagerstown, MD 21741-1119

Autumn House® titles may be purchased in bulk for educational, business, fund-raising, or sales promotional use. For information, please e-mail SpecialMarkets@reviewandherald.com.

Autumn House® Publishing publishes biblically based materials for spiritual, physical, and mental growth and Christian discipleship.

The author assumes full responsibility for the accuracy of all facts and quotations as cited in this book.

This book was
Edited by Steven S. Winn
Copyedited by James Hoffer
Designed by Trent Truman
Cover illustration: © Review and Herald® Publishing Association/Harold Sanden
Interior designed by Heather Rogers
Typeset: Bembo 11/13

PRINTED IN U.S.A.

13   12   11   10   09                    5   4   3   2   1

**Library of Congress Cataloging-in-Publication Data**
Bible. N.T. English. Selections. 2009.
 Witness : a fresh look at the New Testament church / Jack J. Blanco.
   p. cm.
 Includes bibliographical references and index.
1. Bible. N.T. Acts—Harmonies, English. 2. Bible. N.T. Epistles—Harmonies, English.
3. Bible. N.T. Revelation—Harmonies, English. I. Blanco, Jack J., 1929- II. Title.
 BS2617.8.A3B58 2009
 225.6'5—dc22

                                2009023003

ISBN 978-0-8127-0491-4

# Acknowledgments

*I wish to thank*
*Jolena King and Star Stevens*
*for their editorial skills in making this*
*a more readable manuscript.*

# Contents

# Contents

# Introduction

Witness is a harmony of the book of Acts and the Epistles, written for young adults of university age. Many students have found it difficult to follow the flowing historical narrative of the early Christian church as it occurred after the death and resurrection of Christ.

The purpose of this "harmony" is to make available to students a somewhat chronological narrative to deepen their understanding of the Holy Spirit's work. It was the Holy Spirit who guided believers to lay the foundation of the Christian church on which we stand today. Such history opens to view the struggles and victories of men and women who lived in a culture hostile to faith in Jesus Christ as Savior and Lord.

To make the narrative flow smoothly, lengthy sentences have been shortened, expressions chosen to meet the needs of current thinking, and verses within a passage have at times been transposed to create a flow of thought consistent with today's English. At appropriate times short sentences from various Epistles have been brought into the story to provide the reader with a more unified picture of how the early church handled theological issues, personality differences, and divisiveness that threatened to split the young congregations. An attempt has been made not to include every theological point from an Epistle, but to bring out principles to make clear the main thrust of the writer's concerns. Occasionally, historical information from commentaries has been inserted to make a smooth transition in sequence.

Witness covers approximately 70 years, beginning shortly after the death and resurrection of Christ in 31 A.D., extending to the deaths of Paul and Peter in 67 A.D., and to the arrest, release, and subsequent death of John, the last apostle, about 98 A.D. This spans the time of such notable Roman emperors as Tiberias, Caligula, Claudius, Nero, and Domitian.

Scholars are not in complete agreement regarding the dates of the Jerusalem Council, time of the writing of Galatians and other epistles, timing of the various mission trips and final imprisonment of Paul (followed by his execution), authorship of Hebrews, time of the arrest and death of Peter, and exile of the apostle John. It has been necessary, therefore, to exercise personal judgment in harmonizing the book of Acts and the Epistles to produce a flowing narrative.

While scholars differ on precise dates within the apostolic narrative, its setting in history is beyond dispute. The following A.D. timeline is assumed for this book:

| | |
|---|---|
| 31 | Crucifixion, Ascension, Pentecost |
| 34 | Stephen stoned |
| 35 | Paul converted |
| 35–38 | Paul at Damascus and in Arabia |
| 44 | James martyred, Peter imprisoned and set free |
| 44–45 | Barnabas brings Paul to Antioch and Jerusalem |
| 45–47 | Paul's first missionary journey |
| 49 | The Jerusalem Council |
| 49–52 | Paul's second missionary journey |
| 53–58 | Paul's third missionary journey |
| 58–61 | Paul's imprisonment and transfer to Rome |
| 61–63 | Paul kept as a prisoner in Rome |
| 63–66 | Paul's release and ministry |
| 67 | Paul's and Peter's arrests and executions |
| 70 | Destruction of Jerusalem |
| 81–96 | Persecution of Christians |
| 96 | John's arrest and banishment |
| 97–98 | John's release and eventual death |

one

# After Christ's Ascension

After His resurrection, Jesus spent 40 days with His disciples and about 500 other believers, proving in numerous ways that He was very much alive and telling them more about God's kingdom. When the disciples were alone with Him on the Mount of Olives, they asked, "Are You going to set up God's kingdom now?"

He answered, "No, but I want you to stay in Jerusalem and wait for the Father to send the Holy Spirit. The Spirit will empower you to be My witnesses and to preach the good news of the gospel, first in Jerusalem, then throughout Judea and Samaria, and on to the farthest corners of the earth."

Then Jesus began to rise off the earth, ascending into the sky until He disappeared in the clouds. As the disciples scanned the sky trying to catch another glimpse of Him, suddenly two angels in white robes stood among them and said, "Why are you men standing here gazing up to heaven? This same Jesus will come back the same way you have seen Him go."

### Choosing Another Disciple

So the disciples went back to Jerusalem, rejoicing. They assembled with 120 believers in the upper room where they had met before. They continued praying and waiting for the promise of the Father to send the Holy Spirit to empower them to carry out the mission Christ had given them.

Those present were Peter, James, John, Andrew, Philip, Thomas, Bartholomew, Matthew, the other James, Simon, and Thaddaeus. Also, some of the women believers were there, as were Jesus' stepbrothers and His mother, Mary.

Peter stood up and said to the group, "Brothers and sisters, the message of Scripture was fulfilled that the Holy Spirit gave to David, saying that a man would guide the priests and Temple guards to arrest Jesus. That man was Judas, who was one of us. With the 30 pieces of silver that Judas got for betraying Jesus and then in remorse gave back to the priests, they bought a field for him and turned it into a cemetery in which to bury the poor. After Judas had returned their money, he hanged himself. When the rope broke, his swollen body hit the ground and split open, and his blood and intestines spilled out. The people in Jerusalem know all this, so they call the cemetery 'The Field of Blood.'

"The Scripture says, 'Let another take his place.' So we need to choose someone who has been with us from the beginning of Jesus' ministry, who witnessed His baptism and saw Him after His resurrection until He went back to heaven."

The group proposed two names: Joseph and Matthias. They prayed, "Lord, You know the hearts of everyone. Show us which one of these men should take the place of Judas."

Then they cast lots, and the lot fell on Matthias. So he became one of the 12 apostles (Acts 1:1-26).

### Promise Fulfilled

At the time of the Feast of Pentecost, the believers were still meeting in the upper room, praying for the outpouring of the Holy Spirit as Jesus had advised them. They had been praying for 10 days.

Suddenly there was a sound like a violent wind, which filled the whole house. Then the presence of the Holy Spirit lit up the room and hovered over each head like a flickering flame. They were all filled with the Holy Spirit and were immediately given the ability to speak different languages as the Spirit directed.

When the people who had come from many countries to Jerusalem for the Festival of Pentecost heard the sound of a violent wind coming from the house where the apostles were staying, they gathered outside, wondering what was going on. Then the believers went out and began telling people about Jesus in their native languages. People were amazed that these uncultured, uneducated Galileans could speak their dialects so fluently. But the local people said, "These men must be drunk. Who can understand what they're saying?"

### Peter's Sermon

Then Peter spoke to the crowd in Hebrew, and those from other countries heard him in their own languages. He said to them, "Men, listen to me! We are not drunk! It's only nine o'clock in the morning. What you are witnessing is a partial fulfillment of Joel's prophecy when God spoke through him and said, 'I will pour out my Spirit on all flesh. Your

14

sons and daughters will prophesy, and your old men will be given dreams. I will pour out my Spirit on menservants and maidservants, and they will prophesy.'

"Listen to me! Jesus of Nazareth was a man sent by God, attended to by miracles and other wonders which, as you know, He did openly among us. But you took Him and had Him crucified, which God knew ahead of time you would do and let you do it for a greater purpose. Then God raised Him from the dead, as it was impossible for death to hold Him.

"David prophesied Jesus' words like this: 'I will keep God always before my face. He is at my right hand. I will not be shaken. My heart will rejoice and my tongue will speak Your praise. I will rest in hope. You will not leave Me in the grave, nor will You let My body see corruption. You have guided Me in life and will fill My heart with joy as You bring me back into Your presence.'

"I want you to notice the difference between David and Jesus. David is still dead and is with us to this very day. Yet, being a prophet, he held on to the promise that Christ, a descendant of his, would be raised from the dead to become king of Israel. This is one of the prophecies Christ fulfilled when He rose from the dead.

"We saw him after His resurrection and witnessed His ascension. Now He is sitting at the right hand of God, carrying out the promise of the Father to send the Holy Spirit, the results of which you see and hear today.

"David didn't ascend to heaven but wrote in the Psalms, 'God said to my Lord, "Come, sit at My right hand, and I will make Your enemies Your footstool.'"

"Let all Israel know without a doubt that God made Jesus, whom you crucified, your Savior and Lord."

## The Response of the People

When the people heard that, they were convicted and asked Peter and the disciples, "What should we do?"

Peter spoke up boldly, "Repent and be baptized in the name of Jesus Christ for the forgiveness of your sins, and you, too, will receive the gift of the Holy Spirit. The promise of the Father is also for you and your children, and to all those far and near to whom God extends the call to give their hearts to Christ."

Peter encouraged them to repent and be baptized in the name of Jesus and to be saved from this old sinful world. About 3,000 people believed and were baptized in just one day. And they were all faithful, holding firmly to what the disciples taught them, and meeting in small groups for fellowship, meals, and prayer.

## WITNESS: Acts Through Revelation

Many more miracles and other signs were done by the apostles, and all who believed shared what they had with each other. These early Christians sold their possessions and gave the money to help other believers. They were all focused on Christ. Every day they met in the Temple and in each other's houses, eating and fellowshipping together with gladness of heart and simplicity of faith. They praised the Lord and were favorably received among the citizenry. And every day the Lord added newly saved converts to the church (Acts 2:1-47).

# two

# Miracle and Arrest

One day Peter and John went to the Temple at three o'clock in the afternoon for the customary time of prayer. A man who had been lame from birth was being carried up the stairs to the Temple gate named "Beautiful," where he usually sat to beg.

When he saw Peter and John coming up the steps, he asked them for money. Peter stopped and said to him, "Look at us!" The man looked up, expecting to receive something. Then Peter said, "I don't have silver or gold, but what I have, I'll give you. In the name of Jesus, stand up and walk!"

Then Peter took hold of the man's right hand to help him stand up. Instantly the man's legs were healed! He jumped to his feet and began to walk. He followed Peter and John into the Temple, walking and jumping and praising God.

When the people saw this, they recognized the man as the one who usually sat by the gate, begging. They were amazed and could hardly believe that this same man was walking into the Temple, jumping and praising God. He kept holding on to Peter and John as they walked toward Solomon's Colonnade, and people came running from everywhere to see them.

### Peter's Sermon

When Peter saw all these people, he turned to them and said, "Men of Israel, why are you so amazed at this man's healing? Why are you looking at us as if we had healed him ourselves—by our own power? The God of Abraham, Isaac, and Jacob—the God of our fathers—has glorified His Servant, Jesus, after you had handed Him over to Pilate and refused to accept the governor's offer to release Him. You disowned the Holy One of Israel and asked that a murderer be released in His place. You killed the Giver of Life, whom God has now raised from the dead and taken back to heaven. We are witnesses of that fact.

"It's on the basis of faith in Jesus, the Messiah, and by using His name that this man whom you see was healed.

"I know that you and your leaders acted in ignorance, not realizing what you were doing. But God knew long ago that this would happen and told us through the prophets that the Messiah would suffer and die. Now these prophecies have been fulfilled.

"You need to repent and turn back to God so your sins may be wiped away and so the time of refreshing may come from the Lord. Someday Jesus will return from heaven to restore all things.

"God told us all this through Moses, who said, 'The Lord your God will raise up a Prophet and a Leader from among you. You need to obey Him and do everything He tells you to do. Anyone who does not obey Him will be removed from God's people.'

"All the prophets from Samuel on have said the same thing. You are the sons of Abraham and the descendants of these prophets. God made this covenant with our ancestor Abraham: 'Through your Seed all nations will be blessed.' This covenant also belongs to you. That's why God sent Jesus—to bless you and to help you turn from your sins" (Acts 3:1-26).

### Peter and John Arrested

As Peter and John continued speaking to the people, the priests, the Sadducees, and the captain of the Temple guards came to see what was going on. They heard Peter and John telling the people about Jesus and His resurrection. They had them arrested and put in jail to stand trial the next day, because it was already evening.

But many of those who had listened to Peter and John believed, becoming a group of about 5,000 men, not counting their families.

The next morning the rulers, elders, and experts in the law came together to question Peter and John. Annas, the retired high priest, was there, as was Caiaphas, who presided, along with John, Alexander, and other members of the high priest's family.

When Peter and John were brought in, the priests asked, "By what authority or power did you heal the man?"

Peter, filled with the Holy Spirit, answered, "Rulers of the people and elders of Israel, if we are being questioned about how this sick man was healed, you need to know that it was by the authority and power of Jesus Christ, whom you crucified and whom God raised from the dead. Jesus is the Stone which you nation-builders rejected, but God calls him the Cornerstone. There is no other name under heaven by which we must be saved."

When the council members saw the boldness of Peter and John, knowing they were uneducated fishermen, they were amazed and realized their fearlessness was because they had been with Jesus. Seeing the man who had been healed standing in front of them, they had nothing more to say.

Then they ordered Peter, John, and the healed man to step outside and began to confer with one another, saying, "What should we do with these men? It's obvious to the people that they worked a great miracle. That we can't deny. But we need to keep this news from spreading and to warn these men of the consequences if they continue telling the people how this man was healed." So they called them in and ordered them not to preach or teach in the name of Jesus.

Peter and John answered, "Whether it is right in the sight of God to obey you rather than God, you'll have to decide. But we can't stop talking about what we have seen and heard."

After warning the apostles again, they let them go, because they couldn't find a way to punish them without stirring up the people who were praising God for what had happened. Everyone knew that the 40-year-old man had been crippled from birth, but now he was healed and could walk (Acts 4:1-22).

### A Prayer for Boldness

After Peter and John were released, they went to where the believers were meeting and reported everything the rulers, chief priests, and elders had said to them.

When the believers heard that, they raised their voices to God and, in unity of heart and mind, prayed, "Lord, You are the God who made heaven and earth and everything in it. You are the One who spoke through David and said, 'Why do people and kings plot vain things? The rulers have come together and set themselves against the Lord and His Anointed.' It was against Jesus, Your Anointed, that Herod, Pilate, and the people in this city took their stand, which You knew ahead of time and allowed to happen. Now, Lord, take notice of the threats from our rulers and priests, give Your servants courage and boldness to present Your message, and stretch forth Your hand to heal and to perform other signs and wonders through the name of Jesus."

When they had finished praying, the place where they were meeting was shaken, and they were all filled with the Holy Spirit and began to speak the Word of God with boldness (Acts 4:23-31).

### Sharing

The believers were one in heart and mind. No one thought of the things he possessed as his own, but to be used for the good of all. So no one lacked anything. The apostles continued preaching about the resurrection of Jesus Christ, and the power of God's grace was with all of them.

Those who owned houses and properties sold them and gave the money to the apostles to distribute to the believers in need. Barnabas (whose name means "son of encouragement") also sold his property and gave the money to the apostles for those in need.

Now, one of the believers named Ananias, together with his wife, Sapphira, sold a piece of property and decided to keep some of the money, giving only a part of it to the apostles. When Ananias brought the money in, Peter asked, "Why did you let Satan control your heart and then come here and lie to the Holy Spirit about how much you received for your property? When you sold it, wasn't it up to you to do with the money whatever you wanted? Why did you decide to keep part of it and tell us you're giving the full amount? You're lying not only to us, but to God!"

When Ananias was confronted with the fact that he had lied to the Holy Spirit, he collapsed and died. The young men nearby came, wrapped him up, and carried his body out and buried it.

Three hours later his wife, Sapphira, came in, not knowing what had happened. Peter asked, "Tell me, did you and your husband sell your property for this much?"

She answered, "Yes, that's right."

Then Peter replied, "Why did the two of you agree to test the Holy Spirit, thinking that He might not know the difference? The young men who buried your husband are back. Now they can carry you out!"

Then she, too, collapsed and died. When the young men came in and found her dead, they took her body out and buried it next to her husband.

When word of what had happened spread among the believers, great respect for the Holy Spirit came upon all who heard about it (Acts 4:32–5:11).

## Miracles and Conversions

The Lord worked many miracles through the apostles. Believers often met together in the common area of the Temple known as Solomon's Portico. Even though people thought very highly of the believers, they were afraid to meet publicly with them. In spite of this, more and more people, both men and women, were added to the church.

People even carried their sick out into the streets and laid them on cots so that when Peter came by, his shadow would fall on them and they would be healed. Not only did those in Jerusalem do this, but people from the surrounding areas brought their sick and those troubled by evil spirits, and they were all healed (Acts 5:12-16).

## Arrested for Preaching

The growing number of believers enraged the high priest and the other Sadducees, so they ordered the apostles arrested and put in jail. But during the night an angel opened the prison doors, led the apostles out, and said, "Go and preach in the Temple and share with the people the words of life."

So first thing in the morning that's what they did.

That same morning the high priest and other members of his party called a meeting of the Jewish high council and ordered the jailed apostles to be brought in. But the officers found the jail cell empty. They reported back to the council, "The prison doors were locked with the guards standing outside, but when we unlocked the doors and went in to get the prisoners, no one was there!" When the captain of the guard and the members of the council heard this, they were puzzled and not sure what to do.

Just then someone came and reported, "The men you put in prison are in the Temple, preaching." Then the captain of the guard went with his men and brought the apostles to the high council without using force, because they were afraid the people would stone them if they did otherwise.

When the officers brought the apostles in, the high priest questioned them, "Didn't we give you strict orders not to preach in the name of Jesus? You are filling Jerusalem with your teaching and are trying to make us look guilty of this Man's blood."

Peter and the other apostles replied, "Sir, we must obey God rather than men. The God of our fathers raised Jesus from the dead, the same One you killed by handing Him over to Pilate to be crucified. Now God has exalted Him by having Him sit at His right hand as our Prince and Savior, to give our people the spirit of repentance and extend to them forgiveness for what they have done. We have witnessed these things, and the Holy Spirit has been given by God to those who obey Him."

## Gamaliel's Advice

When the members of the high council heard what the apostles said, they were ready to have them executed. But Gamaliel, one of the more important members of the council and highly respected by the people, stood up and asked that the apostles be taken out of the courtroom. Then he addressed the council: "Men of Israel, be careful what you decide to do with these men. Some time ago a man named Theudas claimed to be a special leader. About 400 men followed him. Eventually, he was killed and the men who had followed him scattered everywhere, and that was the end of it. After him came Judas from Galilee, who started a revolt against the Romans. He, too, was killed and his followers scattered. So in this case leave these men alone, because if their work is of their own doing, it will end in nothing, but if it is from God, you can't stop it and might even find yourself fighting against God."

The others agreed with him. So they called the apostles back in, ordered them whipped with 40 lashes minus one, told them not to preach about Jesus, and then let them go.

The apostles left, rejoicing, because they considered it a privilege to suffer for Jesus. And every day, whether in the Temple or in believers' houses, they never stopped preaching and teaching the good news that Jesus was the Messiah (Acts 5:17–42).

# three

# Stephen

As the believers increased, the Greek-speaking Jews who had accepted Jesus complained to the apostles that their widows were being neglected by the local believers in the daily distribution of food.

So the apostles called the believers together and said, "It's not good for us to spend our time supervising the distribution of food and neglect preaching the Word of God. We suggest that you select seven men from among yourselves who know the Lord, have a good reputation, and are filled with the Holy Spirit and wisdom to be in charge of the distribution. This will give us more time for prayer and the ministry of the Word."

The suggestion sounded good to the believers, so they chose Stephen—a man of faith and full of the Holy Spirit—then Philip, Prochorus, Nicanor, Timon, Parmenas, and Nicolas (a Jewish convert from Antioch). These men stood in front of the apostles, who placed their hands on them and prayed for them and their ministry.

The Word of God kept spreading, and the believers in Jesus greatly increased. Even a large number of priests obeyed and joined the faith (Acts 6:1-7).

### Stephen Arrested

Stephen preached the Word powerfully and performed many miracles among the people. Some men who listened to Stephen belonged to the "Synagogue of Freedmen," as it was called. These men were Jews who had been taken as slaves to Alexandria and other cities in the Roman Empire and had now gained their freedom. They argued with Stephen, but they couldn't resist the Holy Spirit and the wisdom with which he spoke.

Then they bribed some men to say, "We heard this fellow curse Moses and say blasphemous things against God." This stirred up the people, the elders, and the experts in the law, so they had Stephen arrested and brought before the Sanhedrin, the Jewish high council.

Witnesses were brought in who falsely testified, "This man never stops saying things against the law of Moses and the Temple. We heard him say that Jesus of Nazareth will destroy the Temple and change the traditions that Moses gave us" (Acts 6:8-15).

### Stephen's Sermon

The high priest asked Stephen, "Is it true what these witnesses are saying about you?"

Stephen answered, "Brothers and fathers, listen to me. The God of heaven appeared to Abraham, when he was still in Mesopotamia living among the Chaldeans, and said, 'I want you to leave your country and your relatives and go to the land I will show you.' So Abraham left and first moved to Haran because his father was not well. When his father died, he moved to the land where we are now.

"God didn't give Abraham even a foot of ground that he could call his own, but promised to give his descendants the whole country, even though Abraham had no children. God knew that Abraham's descendants would be treated as strangers and that they would be brought into bondage and be oppressed for over 400 years.

"God promised that He would judge the nation that enslaved His people. He would bring His people out of Egypt to Canaan where they could serve Him. To confirm His promise, He gave Abraham the rite of circumcision as a sign of His covenant. So eight days after Isaac was born, Abraham circumcised his son, and Isaac circumcised Jacob. Jacob had 12 sons, who became our patriarchs.

"These sons were jealous of Joseph and sold him into Egypt. But God was with him and delivered him out of his troubles, took him out of prison, and gave him favor with Pharaoh, who made him governor of Egypt.

"A famine came and covered all of Egypt and Canaan, causing great suffering, and our ancestors were running out of food. When Jacob heard that Egypt was selling some of its stored grain, he sent his sons to go and buy some, but they didn't recognize their brother Joseph. The next time they went, he told them who he was, and that's how Pharaoh got to know them. Then Joseph sent for his father and his relatives—all 75 of them. So Jacob moved to Egypt and died there, as did Joseph. (Their bones were taken back to Canaan and buried there.) When the time came for God to fulfill his promise to Abraham, our people had greatly increased in Egypt.

"Another Pharaoh came to the throne who did not know Joseph. He was very cruel to our people, even forcing them to kill their baby boys. About that time Moses was born. His parents hid him for three months and then placed him in a basket on the river. When the daughter of Pharaoh found him, she adopted him and raised him as her own. So Moses was trained in all the wisdom of Egypt and was mighty in word and deed.

"When he was 40 years old, he went to visit his people. Seeing one of them being mistreated, he defended him and killed the Egyptian. He thought the people would understand that God wanted to use him to set them free but they didn't.

"The next day he went to visit his people again and saw two of them fighting. He tried to stop them, saying, 'Don't fight each other! You're brothers!' One of them pushed Moses away and responded, 'Are you going to kill me as you did the Egyptian?'

"Moses then realized that word of what he had done had already spread and would soon reach Pharaoh. So he decided to leave the country to save his life. He fled to the land of Midian, got married, and had two sons. He stayed there for 40 years.

"One day as he was herding sheep near Mt. Sinai, the Lord spoke to him from the middle of a burning bush, saying, 'I am the God of Abraham, Isaac, and Jacob.' When Moses heard God's voice, he shook with fear and didn't dare look. Then the Lord said, 'Take off your sandals—the place you're standing is holy ground. I have seen the oppression of My people and heard their groaning. I have come to deliver them. And I will do it through you.'

"So it was that Moses, the one our people had rejected 40 years before, went back to Egypt and delivered our people by doing great signs and wonders. He led them through the Red Sea, guiding them through the wilderness for 40 years, taking them to the borders of Canaan.

"Moses said to our people, 'In the future God will raise up a Prophet and Leader like me. Listen to Him.' Yes, this was the same Moses to whom God gave the Ten Commandments, yet whom our people would not obey because they wanted to go back to Egypt.

"So they turned to Aaron, saying, 'Make us a different god, one who will lead us back to Egypt, because Moses has been up in the mountain so long we don't know what's happened to him.' Aaron was persuaded by their arguments. He made a golden calf, and the people offered sacrifices and danced for joy before it.

"God was not pleased but He forgave them and told Moses to build a sanctuary for our people, according to the pattern He showed to him. Our ancestors brought that sanctuary with them to Canaan under the leadership of Joshua. Our people worshipped there until the time of David, who decided that God should have a temple, which was later built by Solomon.

"But God doesn't need the Temple. Through the prophet Isaiah He said, 'Heaven is My throne and the earth is My footstool.'"

## WITNESS: Acts Through Revelation

### Stephen Is Killed

Having said that God doesn't need the Temple, Stephen sensed a change of attitude among the council members from interest to hostility. So he quickly came to the point and said, "You stubborn people, with your uncircumcised hearts. You're always resisting what the Holy Spirit is telling you. Which of the prophets didn't your forefathers persecute? They even killed those who told about the coming of the Righteous One whom you murdered. God gave you His law but you broke it."

Then the council members became furious and gritted their teeth. But Stephen, filled with the Holy Spirit, looked toward heaven and saw the glory of God, with Jesus standing at God's right hand. He pointed upward and said, "Look! I see heaven open and the Son of Man, the Righteous One, standing at the right hand of God!"

When the council members heard that, they covered their ears and, with a shout, ran toward Stephen. They grabbed him and dragged him out of the city. The false accusers took off their outer robes, laid them at the feet of a young man named Saul, and violently began throwing stones.

Stephen cried out, "Lord Jesus, into Your hands I commit my spirit!" As he sank to his knees, he said, "Lord, don't hold this against them!" Then he fell down and died (Acts 7:1-60).

# four

# Persecution

Saul had given his consent for the stoning of Stephen and was ready to persecute the whole church. He was born into the tribe of Benjamin and had been circumcised when he was eight days old. He grew up to be a "Hebrew of the Hebrews," a Pharisee blamelessly righteous in keeping the law of Moses. While still a comparatively young man, he advanced in Judaism to become a member of the Sanhedrin, the Jewish high council, because of his great zeal for the traditions of their forefathers (Phil. 3:5, 6; Gal. 1:14).

Though born in the Roman province of Cilicia in the city of Tarsus, he was educated in Jerusalem under the highly respected teacher Gamaliel, who taught him how to keep the law of Moses and be zealous for God. Everyone in Jerusalem knew that young Saul lived his life as one of the strictest Pharisees. The Jewish high council gave Saul permission to persecute the believers, arrest them, put them in prison, and even have them killed (Acts 22:3; 26:5; 22:4, 5).

Saul did this not only in Jerusalem but in other cities, as well. Full of rage, he persecuted them in every synagogue where he could find them and tried to make them curse Christ. He forced his way into every house where he suspected believers and dragged them off to prison, whether they were men or women (Acts 26:10, 11; 8:3).

## Philip

So the believers scattered everywhere, preaching the Word wherever they went. Philip, for example, went to the city of Samaria and preached. The people listened to what he said and saw the miracles he did. Many were set free from devil-possession, and those who had been paralyzed were healed. Joy filled the city (Acts 8:4-8).

## Simon the Sorcerer

A man named Simon lived in Samaria. He practiced magic and did things that really caught people's attention. He made great claims for himself, and many believed he had been given this power by God because of the amazing things he had done through the years.

When Philip came to town, preaching the kingdom of God in the name of Jesus, both men and women responded and were baptized. Simon said that he believed and he, too, was baptized. He followed Philip everywhere, awed by the power Philip had to work such miracles.

Word reached the apostles in Jerusalem that many people in Samaria were responding to the Word of God, so they sent Peter and John to check things out. When they got there and met the new believers, they could tell that they had not received the Holy Spirit, because they had been baptized in the name of Jesus only. The apostles laid their hands on these new believers and prayed for them, and they were filled with the Holy Spirit.

When Simon saw that by the simple laying on of hands people were filled with the Holy Spirit, he offered to buy that power from the apostles so he could do the same thing. Peter looked at him and said, "May you and your money perish because you think you can buy God's gift of the Holy Spirit! You cannot have a part in this work because your heart isn't right! You need to repent of your wickedness and ask the Lord to forgive you. You're jealous and a slave to sin!"

Simon replied, "Please pray for me so that nothing of what you said about me will happen." [Tradition has it that Simon never changed, but followed Peter wherever he went, stirring up trouble.]

After Peter and John preached the Word of God to the believers more fully, they went back to Jerusalem, preaching the good news of salvation to all the Samaritan villages along the way (Acts 8:9-25).

### The Ethiopian

An angel said to Philip, "Take the road going south from Jerusalem to Gaza." So Philip went. As he was walking along, an Ethiopian of great authority, and in charge of the royal treasury under Queen Candace, came by in his chariot. He had been to Jerusalem to worship and was reading from the book of Isaiah.

The Holy Spirit said to Philip, "Catch up with the chariot and run alongside it." When Philip did this, he heard the Ethiopian reading out loud. He called to him, "Do you understand what you're reading?" The Ethiopian answered, "How can I, unless someone helps me?" He then ordered his chariot driver to stop and asked Philip to come and sit next to him.

The scripture he had been reading was this: "He was led as a sheep to the slaughter; and as a lamb before the shearers is silent, so He opened not

His mouth. His life was taken from the earth." The Ethiopian asked, "Who is the prophet talking about, himself or someone else?"

Philip, using this scripture, told him all about Jesus and baptism. They talked for some time as they rode along. When they saw a small pond just ahead, the Ethiopian exclaimed, "Look, there's some water! Why can't I be baptized here?"

Philip said, "Sure, why not!"

So the two men got out of the chariot and went down into the water and Philip baptized him. After they came out of the pond, the Holy Spirit snatched Philip away, and the Ethiopian went on his way, rejoicing.

Philip found himself in the city of Ashdod (also called "Azotus") on the coast of southern Palestine. He preached the gospel there and in all the towns along the way to Caesarea, which is not far from Mt. Carmel (Acts 8:26-40).

# five

# The Conversion of Saul

Saul continued persecuting the believers, threatening them with death if they refused to deny their faith. He determined to expand his persecutions, so he asked the high priest for a letter to the Jewish leaders in Damascus, authorizing him to arrest any followers of Jesus, whether men or women, and to bring them to Jerusalem for trial.

As soon as he had the letter, he made his way north to Damascus. It was about noon on his last day of travel that he neared the city. Suddenly an extremely brilliant light from heaven surrounded him! Blinded by the brightness, he fell to the ground. He heard a voice saying, "Saul, Saul! Why are you persecuting Me?"

Fearfully, Saul answered, "Who are You, Lord?"

The Lord said, "I am Jesus, the One you're persecuting."

Saul asked, "Lord, what do You want me to do?"

The Lord answered, "Get up and go into the city, find a place to stay, and you will be told what to do."

The men who were with Saul stood there trembling, scared to death. They heard a voice but didn't see anyone, nor could they understand what was being said. Then Saul got up and when he opened his eyes, he couldn't see. They led him by the hand into the city and found a place for him to stay. For three days he refused to eat or drink.

### The Healing and Baptism of Saul

A believer named Ananias lived in Damascus. In a vision the Lord gently called, "Ananias."

He answered, "Here I am, Lord."

The Lord said, "Go down Straight Street to the house of Judas and ask for Saul of Tarsus. He's there praying. In a vision I gave him, he saw you coming and putting your hand on him so he could see again."

Ananias responded, "Lord, I've heard that this man has terribly persecuted our people in Jerusalem and that the high priest has given him permission to do the same thing here."

The Lord replied, "Go and do as I tell you. I have chosen him to be a special messenger for Me to take My name to the Gentiles, to kings, and to the scattered children of Israel. I will show him ahead of time all the things he will have to suffer for Me."

So Ananias went down Straight Street to Judas' house. When he met Saul, he said to him, "Brother Saul, the Lord Jesus, who appeared to you on the way here, has asked me to come to see you." Then he put his hand on Saul and said, "Receive your sight and be filled with the Holy Spirit."

Immediately a crusty layer peeled away from his eyes, and he looked up at Ananias and could see. Ananias said to Saul, "The God of our fathers has chosen you to be His witness to all men. What are you waiting for? Arise and be baptized and wash away your sins, calling on the name of the Lord."

Saul stood up, praised the Lord, and went with Ananias to one of the rivers in Damascus and was baptized. After that, he ate, his strength came back, and he spent a number of days with the believers in Damascus, who called him by his Roman name, Paul (Acts 9:1-19; 22:13-16).

### Paul's Self-analysis

"I would not have known the roots of sin in me if it had not been for the law. I would not have known the depth of selfishness if God's law had not said, 'Don't covet.' But my self-serving made me think I was keeping the law and, because I did, I thought that sin in me was dead and I was alive and spiritually well. But when the tenth commandment really hit home, my selfishness came to the forefront and in my heart I died. So the law that made me feel good about my zeal for God and that I had eternal life, condemned my pride and, in that sense, killed me. It's this that makes the law holy, just, and good.

"How could a good law condemn? Did the law change and become bad? Certainly not! It was my sinful nature that the law condemned and sentenced to death. It was my sinful nature that turned a good law against me. So, according to the law, my self-serving was extremely sinful.

"We know that the law is concerned about spiritual things, but I'm the one who is unspiritual, a slave to sin. I don't always understand myself and what I'm doing. I don't always end up doing what I really want to do. Instead, I end up doing what I don't want to do, actually doing what I hate. So if I don't want to do what's wrong, then in my heart I agree that God's law is good. It's that sinful nature in me that keeps pushing me to do wrong. There's nothing in this body to help me be good, because when

I want to do good of myself, I can't do it. Sometimes I do the very things I don't want to do! So if I do what I don't want to do, it's not me doing it, but my sinful nature.

"There is a law of life that even when I want to do good, sin is always there. Sin fights with my good intentions, against what I want to do, making me its slave. What a wretched man I am! Who's going to deliver me from this law of sin and death?

"Thank God that, through Jesus Christ and what He has done for me, I've been set free from the law of sin and death! Out of gratitude I do all I can for Him. With my mind I will serve the law of God, even though my sinful nature keeps pushing me to serve the law of sin.

"Therefore, there is no condemnation to those who have given themselves to Christ, because He has set us free from the law of enslavement to sin. What God's law couldn't do, God did by sending His Son to become one of us, to live a sinless life. Thus our sinful nature was condemned so that we might live according to the righteousness of the law. No longer must we follow our sinful nature, but we can now live a life of godliness through the power of the Holy Spirit" (Rom. 7:7-25; 8:1-4).

### Paul Begins His Ministry

Paul was not disobedient to the heavenly vision, but immediately began preaching that Jesus Christ is the Son of God. Those who heard him were amazed. They said, "Isn't this the man who persecuted those in Jerusalem who believe in the One he is preaching about? Didn't he come here to do the same thing—to arrest these believers and take them back to the chief priests?"

Paul continued preaching powerfully, confounding the Jews by showing from the prophecies that Jesus is the Messiah. He preached not only in Damascus, but later in Jerusalem, throughout Judea, and to the Gentiles that they should repent, turn to God, and show it by the way they live (Acts 9:20-22; 26:19, 20).

Before expanding his ministry, he felt his need of knowing Jesus better. So he went to the edge of the Arabian desert, not far from Damascus, and stayed there for three years. That's where he received the gospel—not from others, but from the Lord Jesus Himself. While in vision, he was taken up to heaven into Paradise (whether in body or in spirit he couldn't tell), and there he saw and heard things impossible to describe and put into words (Gal. 1:11, 12; 2 Cor. 12:1-4).

Then he returned to Damascus and preached even more powerfully than before and with great success. The Jews decided that the only way to silence him was to have him killed. So they made arrangements with the governor to guard the city gates day and night, to arrest Paul and have him executed for talking against people's religion and disturbing the peace. When Paul learned about the plot and told the believers, they prayed for him and decided to save his life by taking him at night to a small house on top of the city wall and, through a window, lowering him in a basket to the ground outside (Gal. 1:17; 2 Cor. 11:32, 33; Acts 9:23-25).

From Damascus he went to Jerusalem and spent two weeks with Peter. He saw none of the other apostles, but did stop to see Jesus' stepbrother, James. The churches in Judea didn't know Paul face to face. They had only heard that the one who had persecuted them was now preaching the faith he once tried to destroy. And they praised God for him (Gal. 1:18-24).

When Paul first arrived in Jerusalem, some were still afraid of him and didn't believe that he was a true disciple. So Barnabas took him to the apostles and told them the story of how the Lord had appeared to Paul on the way to Damascus, and that he had been baptized and now boldly preached in the name of Jesus. Then the apostles welcomed Paul and extended to him the right hand of fellowship. While he was in Jerusalem, he preached so powerfully in the name of Jesus that the Greek-speaking Jews, called "Hellenists" (who had debated with Stephen and were instrumental in having him stoned), decided to kill Paul.

One day when Paul was praying in the Temple, he had a vision. The Lord said to him, "Hurry and get out of Jerusalem as quickly as you can, because the Jews will not accept your testimony about Me."

Paul responded, "Lord, the Jews know that I love my Jewish brothers and was on their side. In every synagogue I beat those who believed in You and had them put in prison. I also consented to the stoning of Stephen and watched as they did it."

The Lord said, "They will not believe that I appeared to you on the road to Damascus. So leave here! I will send you far away to the Gentiles."

When the apostles heard about the plot and the vision that Paul had, they arranged a hurried escape from Jerusalem, asking some of the brothers to accompany him north to Caesarea and urging him to go on from there to Tarsus, his hometown in Cilicia.

Then the churches throughout Judea, Galilee, and Samaria had peace as they walked in the way of the Lord, comforted by the Holy Spirit and daily increasing in numbers (Acts 9:26-31; 22:17-21).

# six

# The Power of the Holy Spirit

Peter visited the believers in many places throughout Judea, encouraging them to be faithful to the Lord. When he came to Lydda, they took him to a man named Aeneas, who was paralyzed and had been bedridden for eight years. Peter greeted him and then said, "Brother Aeneas, Jesus heals you. Get up and make your bed!" Immediately Aeneas got up and made his bed. When those who had known him in Lydda and elsewhere heard about it and then saw him walking, they all believed and turned to the Lord.

Not far from Lydda, in the city of Joppa, was a woman believer named Tabitha, translated Dorcas. She was always doing good and helping those in need. It so happened that she got sick and died. The believers prepared her body for burial and took it to an upstairs room. When they heard that Peter was in Lydda, they sent two men to him, urging him to come without delay. Peter went with them and when he got there, they took him to the upstairs room. The widows stood around crying, showed him the clothes that Dorcas had made for the poor, and told him about all the other good things she had done.

Peter asked them to leave the room, and he knelt and earnestly prayed. Then he stood up, looked at the body and said, "Dorcas, get up!" She opened her eyes, and when she saw Peter, she sat up. He reached out his hand and helped her. Then he called the widows and the other believers to come back up, and he presented Dorcas to them alive and well. The news of what had happened spread through the city and beyond, and many believed in the Lord.

Peter decided to stay in Joppa for a while and accepted the invitation of Simon the Tanner to stay with him (Acts 9:32-43).

### Peter and the Roman Captain

A Roman captain named Cornelius was in charge of the Italian regiment stationed in Caesarea. He was a devout man who believed in God, as did his family. He was very generous, always helping the poor and praying regularly.

One day while praying, he had a vision. An angel appeared and called him by name: "Cornelius!"

This startled him and with fear in his heart he answered, "What is it, Lord?"

The angel said, "Your prayers, your pious life, and your generosity toward the poor have been noticed by God. Send some men south to the city of Joppa to find a man named Simon, whom people call Peter. He's staying with Simon the Tanner, whose house is by the Mediterranean Sea. Peter will tell you what God wants you to know."

The angel disappeared and the vision ended. So Cornelius called two of his personal servants and a trusted soldier from his staff and explained to them what had happened. Then he sent them on their way (Acts 10:1-8).

## Peter's Vision

The next day, just as Cornelius' men were nearing Joppa, Peter went up on the flat roof of Simon's house to pray. It was about noon and Peter was hungry. While lunch was being prepared, he had a vision. He saw the sky open and something like a large sheet being let down by its four corners. Inside the sheet were wild beasts, creeping things, and all sorts of birds. Then a voice said, "Peter, stand up, kill, and eat."

Peter answered, "No, Lord! I have never eaten anything that was unclean."

The voice responded, "Don't call unclean what God has said is clean."

This happened three times. Then the sheet with the animals was taken back to heaven.

While Peter was puzzling over the meaning of the vision, the men sent by Cornelius had found Simon the Tanner's house and were standing at the gate. They called for someone to come out and asked if a man named Peter was staying there.

The Holy Spirit said to Peter, "Three men are downstairs looking for you. Go down and meet them. Then go with them, because I sent them."

So Peter went down to meet the men and said, "I'm Peter. Why have you come? What I can I do for you?"

They replied, "Cornelius, the captain in charge of the Italian regiment, sent us. He's a good man, loves God, and is highly respected among the Jews. He wants you to come to his house so he can hear what you have to say about God."

Then Peter invited them in and they decided to stay for the night. Early the next morning, Peter and six brothers from the Joppa congregation left with the three men, arriving later that day in Caesarea (Acts 10:9-23).

Cornelius was expecting them and had called together his relatives and friends to hear what Peter had to say. When Peter arrived, Cornelius went out to meet him and fell at his feet in worship. Peter reached out to lift him up and said, "Come, stand up! I'm just a human being like you." Then they talked together and walked on into the house.

When Peter saw the group, he said to them, "You know that it's against Jewish law for me to visit a Gentile home. But God has shown me that I should treat no one as unclean. That's why I came. So may I ask why you sent for me?"

Cornelius spoke up and said, "Four days ago at about this time, three o'clock in the afternoon, I was in my house praying, when suddenly a man dressed in a shining white robe stood in front of me and said, 'Cornelius, God has heard your prayers and has seen your kindness to the poor. He wants you to send some men to Joppa to find a man named Peter. He's staying at the house of Simon the Tanner by the sea.' That's why I sent for you, and you were kind enough to come. So we want to hear what the Lord has told you to tell us."

Peter responded, "Without a doubt, God is not partial. Whoever looks up to Him and does what is right and good, He accepts. The word that God sent to the Jews through Jesus Christ was a message of peace. He is Lord of all. This was proclaimed throughout Judea, beginning in Galilee. At Jesus' baptism, God anointed Him with the Holy Spirit and power, and He went everywhere doing good and healing people, even those who were being harassed by the devil, because God was with Him.

"And we saw what He did throughout Judea and in Jerusalem. However, our leaders had Him arrested and crucified. Three days later God raised Him from the dead and did so openly. Not everyone was there the moment it happened, but we ate and drank with Him after He rose from the dead. He told us to take this good news everywhere and to tell the people that God had appointed Him to be judge over the living and the dead. All our prophets have told us that those who believe in Him will be forgiven of their sins."

While Peter was talking, the Holy Spirit came on all those present. When the six brothers from Joppa saw this, they were amazed that the Holy Spirit was being given to Gentiles, and that they were speaking in different languages, glorifying God.

Peter said, "How can we refuse to baptize these people when they're receiving the Holy Spirit the same way we received Him at Pentecost?" Then he authorized those with him to baptize the new converts in the name of the Lord Jesus. After they were baptized, Cornelius asked Peter to stay for a few days, which he did (Acts 10:24-48).

### Peter Defends His Actions

The apostles and elders of the church in Judea heard that through Peter's ministry some Gentiles had also become believers. When Peter returned to Jerusalem, those who held firmly to circumcision for everyone confronted him, saying, "You mean you went into the house of uncircumcised Gentiles and ate with them!"

Peter explained: "I was visiting our people in Joppa, and one day at noon as I was praying, I was given a vision. I saw a sheet being let down from heaven by its four corners, and inside were wild beasts, creeping things, and all sorts of birds. A voice said to me, 'Peter, stand up, kill, and eat.' I said, 'No, Lord! I've never eaten anything unclean!' The voice responded, 'Don't call unclean what God has said is clean.' This happened three times. Then the sheet with the animals was taken back to heaven.

"Just then three men came to the house where I was staying, looking for me. They had been sent by Cornelius, the captain of the Italian regiment. The Holy Spirit told me to go with them. I took six brothers with me, and we went to the man's house.

"He told me how four days before, an angel had come to his house and had said to him, 'Send some men to Joppa to find a man they call Peter, and he will tell you what you and your family need to know to be saved.'

"As I began to tell them about Jesus, the Holy Spirit came upon them as it came on us at Pentecost. Then I remembered what the Lord had said, 'John baptized you with water, but you will be baptized by the Holy Spirit.' If God poured out the Holy Spirit on the Gentiles after they believed in the Lord Jesus, who was I to stand up against God?"

When those supporting circumcision heard this, they were satisfied and glorified God, saying, "God has given the spirit of true repentance to Gentiles also so they, too, can be saved!" (Acts 11:1-18).

### Peter Arrested

Herod Agrippa, the grandson of Herod the Great, decided to persecute the church to please the Jews. He had James, the brother of John, beheaded and then he arrested Peter. This took place during the week-long Festival of Unleavened Bread, which is part of the Passover. Herod put Peter in prison and ordered four squads of four soldiers each to guard him until the Passover week was over. Then Herod would hold a public trial and execute Peter.

While Peter was in prison, the church earnestly prayed for him day and night. The evening before he was to be executed, Peter was sound asleep in his cell, chained to two soldiers, with two other soldiers right outside the cell door. This was in addition to the regular guards at the prison entrance.

Suddenly an angel stood next to Peter, lighting up the whole cell! The guards inside and outside the cell stood motionless, hearing and seeing nothing. The angel tapped Peter on the side and woke him up, saying, "Get up! Quick!" The chains fell off Peter's wrists and he got up. The angel said to him, "Hurry, put on your belt and sandals." Peter did. Then the angel said, "Now put on your outer robe and follow me." Peter put on his robe and followed him. The cell door opened and closed noiselessly, and the guards just stood there. Peter thought this was a vision. When they came to the big iron gate leading out of the prison, it quietly opened, and the guards heard and saw nothing.

Once outside, Peter and the angel walked down a narrow street, when suddenly the angel left him. All at once the cold night air woke Peter up to the fact that this was real, not just a vision. He said to himself, "The Lord has sent an angel to rescue me from Herod and the public execution the Jewish people expected."

He stood there for a moment, collecting his thoughts, then decided to go to the house of Mary, the mother of Mark. Peter didn't know it, but that's where the believers were praying for him. When he got there, he knocked on the door, and a servant girl named Rhoda went to see who could be knocking at that hour of the night. When she recognized Peter's voice, she got so excited that she forgot to open the door. Instead, she ran back to tell everyone that Peter was outside.

They said, "You're out of your mind! Peter's in prison!"

But she insisted it was Peter. Then they said, "Probably it's his angel."

Meanwhile, Peter kept knocking. So they finally opened the door and—sure enough—it was Peter! He came in and signaled with his hand for them to be quiet so as not to awaken the neighbors. Then he told them what had happened—how the angel had led him out of prison. He also told them to let James, the stepbrother of Jesus, and the other church leaders know that he was free. Then he quickly left town.

At the first sign of dawn, the soldiers checked on Peter but he was gone. They couldn't believe it! The whole prison was in an uproar, and they were now concerned for their own lives. When Herod heard about it, he called the guards in and cross-examined them. He ordered the whole prison searched. When Peter could not be found, he ordered the guards executed and left Judea for Caesarea (Acts 12:1-19).

## Herod and the Angel

Herod was angry with the people of Tyre and Sidon, so they sent a delegation to see him. They persuaded Blastus, the king's personal assistant, to help them ask for peace, because Herod could easily cut off their food supply by choosing other ports for his country's shipping.

The day Herod agreed to meet with them, he put on his best robes and took his seat as king and judge. He gave a splendid oration, so moving those present that they began shouting, "The voice of a god, not a man! The voice of a god, not a man!" At that moment an angel of the Lord touched Herod's side, and he was hit with such severe stomach pains that he doubled over and collapsed, and his attendants carried him out. Worms began to eat at his intestines, and a few days later he died.

But the word of God kept spreading, and believers continued to multiply (Acts 12:20-24).

# seven

# First Mission Trip

Those who had scattered because of the persecution that began with the stoning of Stephen went everywhere, as far as Phoenicia, Cyprus, and Antioch, sharing the Word of God with their fellow Jews. Some who had gone to Cyprus went to Antioch and began sharing the good news about Jesus with the Greeks also. The Lord was with them, and many of them believed and gave their hearts to the Lord.

The church leaders in Jerusalem heard what was happening in Antioch and sent Barnabas to check things out. When he got there and saw what the grace of God had done, he was overjoyed and encouraged them to stay true to the Lord and to love Him with all their hearts. Barnabas was a good man, full of the Holy Spirit, and a man of faith. Through his ministry many more were brought to the Lord.

Barnabas decided to go to Tarsus to find Paul, and when he found him, he brought him to Antioch. They worked together for a whole year, teaching the new members and reaching out to others. It was in Antioch where believers were first called Christians.

About this time several who had the gift of prophecy came to Antioch from Jerusalem, one of whom was Agabus. He stood up in a meeting and, in the power of the Holy Spirit, predicted that a severe famine would soon come on the whole Roman world. It happened under the reign of Claudius Caesar, just as Agabus had said.

So the believers decided to give what they could to bring relief to their fellow believers in Judea. They gave the funds to Barnabas and Paul and asked them to take their offering to Jerusalem (Acts 11:19-30).

After Barnabas and Paul had delivered the funds, they returned to Antioch and brought Barnabas' young cousin, John Mark, with them (Acts 12:25).

Now there were several prophets and teachers in Antioch: Barnabas, Simeon, Lucius, Manaen (who had grown up with one of the Herods), and

Paul. One day, as the believers were fasting and praying for a deeper spiritual experience with the Lord, the Holy Spirit spoke through one of the prophets and said, "Set apart Paul and Barnabas to do the missionary work for which I have called them." So after fasting and praying, the believers set these men apart, laid their hands on them, and sent them away (Acts 13:1-3).

## Island of Cyprus

Led by the Holy Spirit, Paul and Barnabas took along John Mark and made their way to the port city of Seleucia, and from there sailed to the large island of Cyprus. When they got to Salamis, they began preaching the Word of God in the synagogues.

Then they made their way across the island to the city of Paphos, where the Roman governor, Sergius Paulus, lived. When the governor heard about the preaching of Paul and Barnabas, he called for them, because he wanted to hear what they had to say.

Connected with the governor's staff was a certain Jew named Elymas, a false prophet who also practiced magic. Sergius Paulus had also invited him. Elymas challenged everything Paul said. Finally, Paul turned, looked at him intently and, in the power of the Holy Spirit, said, "You son of the devil, you're full of deceit and lies. You're an enemy of righteousness, always perverting the truth and ways of God. How long will you keep on doing this? The Lord is against what you're doing, so you will be blind for a while." Instantly, a dark mist covered his eyes and he began to grope his way along, asking for someone to lead him. When the governor saw this, he was astounded and believed Paul, rather than Elymas (Acts 13:4-12).

## Antioch in Asia Minor

From Paphos the three missionaries sailed to Perga, the seat of government for Pamphylia, one of the provinces in Asia Minor. That's when John Mark left and went back home to Jerusalem.

Paul and Barnabas decided to go on to Antioch in Pisidia. On the Sabbath they went to the synagogue. The elder stood up, read the Scripture for the day, then turned to Paul and Barnabas. "Brothers," he said, "if you have words of encouragement for us, let's hear what you have to say."

So Paul went up front, motioned a greeting with his hand, and said, "Fellow Israelites and you who worship the God of Israel, listen! God blessed our ancestors, even while they were aliens in the land of Egypt. When the time came, He used his mighty power to free them from slavery and bring them out of Egypt. For the next 40 years He put up with their ways in the wilderness and brought them into Canaan, giving them the land of the seven small nations who fought to destroy them. After that, God set up judges to govern His people, which they did for 450 years until the time of Samuel, the prophet.

"Now they wanted a king. So God gave them Saul, who ruled the country for 40 years. But because of Saul's disobedience, God chose David to replace him, saying, 'David is a man after My own heart. He will do what I ask him to do.' It is from the descendants of David that Jesus, the promised Savior, came.

"John the Baptist preached about Him and told the people to repent, change their ways, and be baptized. John's special mission was to point the people to the Messiah. He would say, 'Who do you think I am? Do you think I'm the One? Well, I'm not. Look for Him for He is due soon. I'm not even worthy to untie His sandals.'

"My brothers, sons of Abraham, and those of you who worship God, this message is for you, too. The people and rulers in Jerusalem didn't recognize the One they were expecting. He was innocent, but they turned Him over to Pilate to be crucified, fulfilling the very words of the prophets they read from every Sabbath. When what was written was fulfilled, His disciples took Him down from the cross and placed Him in a tomb. But God raised Him from the dead. He spent many days with the Galileans who had come with Him to Jerusalem. These men and women are witnesses of what we're telling you.

"This is the good news we've come to share with you. What God promised our ancestors has been fulfilled. By raising Jesus from the dead, God has given Him back to us. He had no intention that His Son should stay in the grave and decay. He gave a number of promises like this to David. After David had fulfilled God's purpose for him in his generation, he died and was buried among his ancestors and his body decayed. But not so with Jesus, whom God raised from the dead.

"Therefore, my brothers, I want you to know that because of what God has done for us through Jesus, the promise of forgiveness is sure. All those who believe in Him are made right with God, which the animal sacrifices under Moses could never do. So be careful that what the prophets have said does not happen to you: 'Scoffers will be amazed and will perish because they refuse to believe what God has done, even though someone shows it to them from Scripture.'"

The service closed and as Paul and Barnabas left the synagogue, people urged them to come back the next Sabbath. Many of the Jews and others who worshipped with them followed Paul and Barnabas, who encouraged them to hold on to what they had just heard.

The next Sabbath it seemed as if the whole city came out to hear what

Paul and Barnabas had to say. But when the Jews saw the large crowd of unbelievers listening intently, some of them became jealous and challenged Paul's message, even publicly slandering him. Paul and Barnabas responded by saying, "It was right that we first bring the Word of God to you. But since you've rejected the truth about God's Son and feel that you don't need eternal life as a gift, we'll work with the Gentiles. That's what the Lord told us to do when He said, 'I have appointed you to take the good news of salvation to the Gentiles, that it might go to the ends of the earth.'"

When the Gentiles heard this, they rejoiced and praised the Lord for His Word. Many were convicted by the Holy Spirit and chose to believe. So the Word of God spread throughout that whole province. But the Jews who rejected the truth incited the women of high social standing who worshipped with them and the prominent men of the city to turn against Paul and Barnabas and force them to leave.

So Paul and Barnabas left Antioch and went on to Iconium. The new believers who stayed behind rejoiced in the faith and were filled with the Holy Spirit (Acts 13:13-52).

### Iconium

In Iconium Paul and Barnabas went to the synagogue and were asked to speak. As a result, many Jews and Greeks believed. The Jews who refused to believe, however, stirred up the people and turned some of them against Paul and Barnabas. But they stayed and continued preaching about God's love and grace as long as they could, working miracles and confirming the new believers in the faith.

Soon the city was divided; some sided with the unbelieving Jews, and others sided with Paul and Barnabas. When told that a plot was being laid to attack and stone them, Paul and Barnabas quickly left town and headed for Lystra and Derbe. There they continued to proclaim the good news of salvation (Acts 14:1-7).

### Lystra and Derbe

In Lystra there was a man who had been crippled from birth, never able to walk. He was in the crowd listening to Paul preach. When Paul spotted him and noticed his childlike expression of faith, he looked at him and, with a loud voice, said, "Stand on your feet and straighten up!" The man jumped up and began walking.

When the people saw this, they shouted in their native language, "The gods have taken on human form to come and visit us!" They called Barnabas "Zeus" and Paul "Mercury." Then the priest of Zeus, whose temple was just outside the city, brought two bulls and wreaths of flowers to the city gates to offer sacrifices to them.

When Paul and Barnabas realized what was happening and what the people wanted to do, they tore their robes and pushed their way into the crowd, shouting, "Why are you doing this? We are human beings, not gods!"

When they finally got the people's attention, they said, "Our message is for you to turn from worshipping false gods to the living God, who created heaven and earth and everything in it. In the past God did not approve of the way you and other nations worshipped Him but He did not cut you off. He continued to be good to you by giving you rain, bountiful harvests, and plenty of food to make your hearts glad."

In spite of all Paul and Barnabas said and did, they barely kept the crowd from sacrificing the bulls to them.

Meanwhile, some unbelieving Jews from Antioch and Iconium had followed Paul and Barnabas to Lystra and stirred up the crowd against them. The people grabbed Paul, dragged him outside the city, stoned him, and left him for dead.

After the crowd left, Timothy and the other believers gathered around his body weeping, thinking he was dead. But Paul opened his eyes, got up, and praised the Lord. Then he walked with them back to the city. The next day he and Barnabas left for the city of Derbe (Acts 14:8-19).

### Return Trip

After preaching in Derbe where many believed, Paul and Barnabas retraced their steps, visiting the believers in Lystra, Iconium, and Antioch and encouraging them to keep the faith in spite of the persecutions they might have to face.

They fasted and prayed for the believers in each city and appointed local elders for their churches, committing them and the members to the care and protection of the Lord in whom they believed.

Then they made their way back to Perga, the port city from which John Mark had left them to go home, and sailed back to Antioch in Syria. This mission trip had taken them about two years. When they got home, they called the members together and gave them a report of everything that God had done for them and how He had opened the door of faith for other people as well. Paul and Barnabas continued their ministry in Antioch for some time (Acts 14:20-28).

# eight

# Questions to Be Settled

Some believing Jews went to Antioch from Jerusalem and told the Greek believers that they had to be circumcised as a covenant sign with God, and that they had to keep the laws of Moses in order to be saved. Paul and Barnabas strongly disagreed and argued with them about it. This threatened to divide the church, so the believers asked Paul and Barnabas and others to go to Jerusalem to meet with the apostles and elders to settle the question.

Along the way Paul and Barnabas passed through Phoenicia and Samaria. They told the Jewish believers there about the conversion of hundreds of Gentiles. The brothers and sisters were thrilled with the news and praised the Lord for what He had done.

When Paul and Barnabas got to Jerusalem, the apostles and elders warmly welcomed them, and although all the members did not know Paul personally, they rejoiced that he was now preaching the faith he once tried to destroy. The apostles and elders called a general assembly, and Paul and Barnabas told them what God had done through their ministry among the Gentiles. But some of the local leaders who had been Pharisees were very protective of their Jewish heritage. They stood up and said, "It is extremely important for these new converts to be circumcised and to keep the laws of Moses. We should require them to do so."

After the apostles and elders listened to the arguments on both sides, Peter stood up and said, "Brothers, you know that some time back God led me to share the good news of salvation with Gentiles, and they believed. God, who knows the heart, confirmed their faith by giving them the Holy Spirit, just as He did to us. He made no distinction between them and us, but cleansed their hearts through faith. So why should we continue to argue about what God's will is in this when we already know? Why should we put an extra burden on our Gentile converts, a burden that troubled not only us but our ancestors? We believe that we

Jews are saved through the grace of the Lord Jesus in the same way the Gentiles are."

Since no one had anything else to say, James spoke up, "Brothers, listen to me. Peter just told us how God is working among the Gentiles to bring them out of this world to be His people. The prophets, speaking for the Lord, told us the same thing when they said, 'I will rebuild the house of David that has fallen down so that others may find Me and Gentiles may be called by My name. The Lord will do all He says He will.' God knew all this from the beginning. Therefore, we should not make things hard for Gentiles who are turning to God. We should tell them not to continue identifying with paganism by eating things offered to idols, not to follow the sexual practices of the world, and to live healthfully by not eating meat filled with blood or meat from strangled animals. Also, they should familiarize themselves with the writings of Moses, which we read every Sabbath in the synagogue."

James' statement pleased the apostles and the delegates, so they decided to choose two leading brothers, Judas and Silas, to go to Antioch with Paul and Barnabas to deliver the letter. It read: "From the apostles and elders to our Gentile brothers and sisters in Antioch, Syria, and Cilicia: Greetings! We have heard that, without our permission, some Jewish believers from Jerusalem went to see you, giving you a different understanding of the gospel, which confused your thinking and upset your faith. So we called a general assembly and, after listening to both sides, decided to send Judas and Silas to go back with Paul and Barnabas, who have risked their lives for the Lord Jesus, to let you know what we decided.

"Since the Holy Spirit had already settled the question through Peter's ministry among the Gentiles, it seemed good to us also not to place any more burdens on you. Here, we believe, is a fair standard: Don't identify with paganism by eating meat offered to idols, for health reasons don't eat meat saturated with blood or meat from strangled animals that did not have their blood drained, and stay away from the sexual practices of the world. If you do these three things, you will do well. Blessings and farewell."

When Judas and Silas got to Antioch, they called the members together and read them the letter. The members were thrilled when they heard the decision of the apostles and elders, and their courage was renewed. Judas and Silas, who also had the gift of prophecy, confirmed what was in the letter, strengthening the believers in the faith. After spending some time in Antioch, the church decided to send Judas and some of the others back to Jerusalem to take greetings to the apostles and elders. But Silas decided to stay, and so did Paul and Barnabas, who, along with others, continued to teach and preach the Word of the Lord (Acts 15:1-35).

## Peter Visits Antioch

A short time later Peter came to Antioch and, in harmony with the decision made by the apostles and elders, ate and fellowshipped with the Gentiles as he had done before. But when certain men who had not accepted the decision of the apostles and elders came to Antioch from Jerusalem, he changed and held himself aloof from the Gentiles, because he was afraid of what they would say about him back home. Many Jewish believers followed his example; even Barnabas was influenced by him.

When Paul saw what was happening and that it was not consistent with the gospel, he confronted Peter in front of the whole church and said, "What you're doing is hypocritical. If you eat with Gentiles, you're not living like a Jew should, so why would you try to make the Gentiles live like Jews? We who are Jews, no matter where we were born, are not justified by works but by faith in Jesus Christ. No one will be justified by works, because we're all sinners. Does Christ encourage salvation by works? Absolutely not! If I uphold what I rejected, I'm turning against the gospel and become a lost sinner. But, no! I am dead to the law of works and live for Christ. Self has been crucified with Him and no longer lives, because Christ lives in me. And the life I live is a life of faith in the Son of God, who loved me and gave His life for me. I don't set aside God's grace, because if justification comes by works, then Christ died for nothing!" (Gal. 2:11-21).

Peter accepted Paul's rebuke and again ate with the Gentiles. Later he wrote, "Dear friends, look ahead to what God has in mind for us, and be at peace with one another when you come into His presence to worship. The Lord's patience with us is our salvation, just as Brother Paul wrote to you in all his letters, according to the insight given to him. Some things he wrote are hard to understand, which some people twist to their own hurt and destruction, as they do other portions of Scripture.

"You already know this, so be on your guard and you won't be led astray by the mistaken ideas of unprincipled men. But grow in grace and in your understanding of our Lord and Savior, Jesus Christ, to whom be honor and glory, both now and forever. Amen" (2 Pet. 3:14-18).

# nine

# Second Mission Trip

A fter spending some time in Antioch and having settled the question regarding which doctrines were essential for Gentile believers, Paul said to Barnabas, "Let's go back and visit the believers in the cities we worked before to see how they're doing."

Barnabas agreed, suggesting they take his young cousin, John Mark, along.

Paul vehemently protested, "Absolutely not! The last time we took him along, he left us and went home."

With such a strong disagreement between them, Barnabas chose to go to Cyprus, taking young John Mark with him. Paul decided to take Silas and they set out on foot to the cities in Cilicia. They wanted to see how the believers were doing who had been converted on Paul's first missionary trip. Before the four men left, the church members met and committed them to the care of the Lord (Acts 15:36-41).

Paul and Silas encouraged the believers in Derbe and then went on to Lystra, where young Timothy lived. His mother was Jewish but his father, Greek. Timothy was highly spoken of among the believers in both Lystra and Iconium.

Paul asked Timothy to join them. He suggested that Timothy be circumcised since the Jews in that region knew that his father was not a Jew. This would help the Jews accept Timothy. So Timothy agreed and was circumcised. Then he joined Paul and Silas as they visited the other cities where Paul had previously been.

Paul and Silas shared with the believers that the apostles and elders in Jerusalem had decided it was not necessary for Gentiles to be circumcised or to keep the ceremonial laws. When the members heard that, they rejoiced and were strengthened in the faith. So the gospel spread, and every day new members were added to the church (Acts 16:1-5).

### Timothy's Upbringing

Later, when Paul was in prison, he wrote to Timothy, saying, "I am thankful to God for you. I keep you in my prayers day and night. I remember how you wept for me after I had been stoned and you thought I was dead, and later when you heard that I had been arrested. How my heart would rejoice if I could see you again! How can I forget your simple and sincere faith, the same kind of faith like that of your grandmother, Lois, and your mother, Eunice! This same faith is in you. I want to remind you not to lose the fire for ministry which God gave you as a gift and which I acknowledged when I laid my hands on you in ordination. The Holy Spirit has not called you to be fearful, but to be loving and powerful for God, and to be faithful to the Lord Jesus and what He taught us" (2 Tim. 1:3-7).

### Expanding the Territory

After Paul, Silas, and Timothy had visited the churches where Paul had been before and encouraged the believers, they wanted to take the gospel north into new territory, but the Holy Spirit directed them to go west. Then they considered going northwest, and the same thing happened. So they bypassed Mysia and went west to Troas. That night Paul had a vision and saw a man from Macedonia in Greece, pleading with him, "Come over here and help us!" The next day they made plans to cross over from Asia Minor into Europe, knowing that the Lord was directing them to go there. It was about this time that Luke, a converted Gentile physician, joined them (Acts 16:6-10).

### Lydia

So they sailed from Troas, crossed the Aegean Sea to Samothrace, and then to Neapolis. There they disembarked and headed overland to Philippi, a city mainly populated by Roman citizens and one of the chief cities in that part of Macedonia. They stayed there for some time, teaching and preaching the Word of the Lord.

They could find no synagogue in town, so on the Sabbath they went out of the city to a place by the river where a devout group of Jewish women met for prayer, and he shared the gospel with them. One of them was a Greek woman named Lydia from the city of Thyatira, who had a business trading in purple cloth. She was a worshipper of the God of Israel. As she listened to Paul, the Lord opened her heart, and soon afterwards she and her family were baptized. Then she urged Paul and his friends to stay at her place, saying, "If you accept me as a believer, why are you so reluctant to stay at my house?" So they agreed to come (Acts 16:11-15).

# WITNESS: Acts Through Revelation

## Paul and Silas Imprisoned

Day after day Paul and his friends went to a place by the river to pray. One day a slave girl met them, who the people believed had the spirit of divination to tell the future. She brought her owners a good profit through fortune-telling. The young woman followed Paul and Silas and, with a shrill voice, kept crying out, "These men are servants of the Most High God and are proclaiming the way of salvation."

This went on for days and really bothered Paul because she said it in a tone that discredited the gospel. One day he turned to face the slave girl and said to the evil spirit, "I command you in the name of Jesus Christ to come out of her and leave her alone!" Immediately the spirit left the girl and she rejoiced to be free.

When her owners saw what had happened and realized that they had just lost a lot of business from her fortune-telling, they grabbed Paul and Silas and dragged them to the marketplace to see the authorities. They accused them of ruining their business and said to the magistrates, "These Jewish men are causing a lot of trouble. They're telling us Romans what to believe and what we can and can't do."

By this time a crowd had gathered, supporting the businessmen and demanding that something be done. When the magistrates heard their charges, they tore off Paul and Silas' robes and ordered them to be publicly whipped and thrown in prison. They said to the jail keeper, "Make sure that these men don't escape!" So the jailer put Paul and Silas into the innermost prison, sat them on the floor, and clamped their stretched-out feet in holes between blocks of wood (Acts 16:16-24).

## Earthquake

During the night Paul and Silas prayed and sang hymns to God, while the other prisoners listened. Suddenly at midnight an earthquake hit with such force that the whole prison shook, the doors flew open, and the prisoners' chains dropped off!

The jail keeper saw the prison doors open and assumed that all the prisoners had escaped. Rather than facing certain public execution, he pulled out his sword and was ready to kill himself when Paul shouted, "Don't! We're all here!"

The jail keeper dropped his sword, called for a torch, and went into the prison to see for himself. When he saw that all the prisoners were still there, he threw himself in front of Paul and Silas in gratitude. Then he took them out of the inner prison and asked, "Sirs, what must I do to be saved?"

They replied, "Accept Jesus Christ as your Lord and Savior, and you and your family will be saved." The jail keeper believed and took them to his house, and they shared the Word of the Lord with him and all in his house. In gratitude the jail keeper washed Paul's and Silas's wounds. Then he and his entire family went to the pool in the prison yard and were baptized. When they returned, the jailer fed Paul and Silas and rejoiced in his newfound faith, as did his family (Acts 16:25-34).

### Paul and Silas Released

In the morning the city magistrates sent officers to the prison to tell the jail keeper to let Paul and Silas go. So the jailer took the officers to the inner prison where Paul and Silas had returned after the events of the previous evening. The jailer said to Paul, "The magistrates think that one day in prison is enough for you and that I should let the two of you go. So go in peace and God be with you."

But Paul said to the officers and jail keeper, "The magistrates had us publicly whipped and thrown into prison without giving us a fair trial, to which all Roman citizens are entitled, and now they want us to just quietly leave? No! Let them come and release us publicly." Paul refused to leave.

The officers went back to the magistrates and told them what Paul had said. When they learned that Paul and Silas were Roman citizens, the magistrates went to the prison, apologized, and personally released the two men. They asked them to please leave the city peacefully, which they promised to do. Then Paul and Silas thanked them and left the prison to go to Lydia's house. There they encouraged the believers and then left Philippi to go to Thessalonica (Acts 16:35-40).

### Thessalonica

From Philippi, Paul and his fellow workers passed through Amphipolis and Apollonia, and then went on to Thessalonica. They found the synagogue and, as their custom was, went there on Sabbath to worship. For three Sabbaths Paul showed them from Scripture that the Messiah had to suffer, die, and rise again, and that Jesus was the promised Messiah. Some of the Jews believed, along with a large number of Greeks who worshipped the God of Israel, including quite a few prominent women.

But the Jews who didn't believe became jealous and went to the marketplace to get some worthless fellows to form a mob and start a riot. This they did, and the mob attacked Jason's house, looking for Paul and Silas. When they didn't find them, they took hold of Jason and a few other believers and dragged them to the marketplace to face the city officials, screaming on the way, "These men are causing trouble throughout the empire! Now they've come here and Jason has opened his home for this kind of people! They're saying there's a new emperor and His name is Jesus!"

When the people and the city officials heard this, they worried that Rome would hear about it and step in and take action against them. So they arrested Jason, made him promise to live peacefully, and set him free on bond until they could investigate the case. Then they let him and the others go (Acts 17:1-9).

### Berea

That night the believers took quick action and sent Paul and Silas off to Berea. When they got there, they immediately searched for a synagogue. The Jews were open-minded and eagerly listened to Paul, but every day they carefully examined the Scriptures to make sure that what Paul and Silas were saying was true. Many of them believed, including quite a number of prominent God-fearing Greeks, both men and women.

But when the Jews in Thessalonica heard about it, they went to Berea to stir up the people against Paul and his friends. So the believers urged Paul to leave, but they let Silas and Timothy stay. So Paul and those who were asked to accompany him headed for Athens. After they got there and Paul was situated, he said goodbye to them and asked them to tell Silas and Timothy to join him as quickly as they could (Acts 17:10-15).

### Athens

While Paul waited for Silas and Timothy, his heart was moved, because everywhere he went he saw idols. They were all over the city. So on Sabbaths he reasoned with the Jews and the Greeks, who also worshipped the God of Israel, and every day during the week he spoke in the marketplace to those who happened to be there. Some of the Epicurean and Stoic philosophers said, "What is this babbler trying to say? He seems to be talking about gods we've never heard of before." This was because Paul kept talking about Jesus and the Resurrection.

So they invited him to come to Mars Hill near the Acropolis. "We'd like to know more about what you're teaching," they said, "because what you're saying is so new to us that we want to know what it means." This was what the Athenians and the foreign students who came there did most of the time—listening to and discussing anything new.

Paul agreed to go, and from Mars Hill he spoke to the most respected council in Athens. He began, "Men of Athens, I see that in many ways your city is very religious. As I walked around, I saw many objects of worship. I even saw an altar with an inscription: 'To the Unknown God.' This is the God I have come to tell you about. He is the God who made the whole world and everything in it. He's the Lord of heaven and earth. He doesn't need a temple to live in, nor does He need people to give Him anything, for everything is His. He is the One who gives life, breath, and all things to everyone.

"He created one man, and from him came all other men, so all have the same blood, no matter what their nationality. Also, He decided where different people groups should live. He wants us to search for Him and find Him, even though He's not far from any of us. It is because of Him that we live and move and have our existence. As some of your own poets have said: 'We are His offspring.' Since that is true, we should not think that we can carve an image of Him out of gold, silver, or stone according to our own ideas.

"God has overlooked the times of our ignorance. But now He expects people everywhere to change their ways and come to Him. He has set a day when He will judge the world according to His standard of righteousness by the Man whom He appointed. He has given us proof of who this is by raising Him from the dead."

When they heard Paul talk about a man's being raised from the dead, some council members laughed at him and others simply said, "That's enough. We'll talk about this some other time." But a few believed and followed Paul back into the city, including Dionysius (a member of the council), a woman named Damaris, and some others (Acts 17:16–34).

# ten

# Concern for New Converts

By this time Timothy had come to Athens from Thessalonica, as Paul had asked him to, and told Paul that the believers there were doing exceptionally well. Paul was pleased and wrote a letter for Timothy to take back with him to Thessalonica:

"To the members of the church in Thessalonica: Greetings from Paul. Silas is there with you and Timothy is on his way delivering this letter. Grace and peace from God our Father and the Lord Jesus Christ.

"We thank God for you and constantly keep you in our prayers. How can we forget your faith, loving labor, and enduring hope in Jesus Christ?

"Brothers and sisters, God loves you and has selected you as His people to help save others. The gospel did not just come to you as information, but in the power of the Holy Spirit and with deep conviction. You know the kind of men we were when we came there. And when you heard the gospel, you embraced it with great joy and then modeled your life after us and the Lord's example, in spite of the persecutions you faced.

"You have become examples to the believers throughout Macedonia and Greece. Not just there, but everywhere we go people talk about your faith, so we don't have to tell them about you. They know how you welcomed us and turned away from your idols to serve God, and that you are now looking forward to the return of the Lord, whom God raised from the dead to deliver us from the destruction that is to come (1 Thess. 1:1-10).

"Our coming to you was worth it. Even though we were mistreated at Philippi and were opposed when we first came to you, we boldly preached the Word of God. We didn't deceive you, but shared the gospel with you just as God gave it to us. We never flattered you, nor did we demand things from you because we were apostles, although we could have. We were as gentle with you as a mother would be with her child and were ready to give our lives for you because you had become so precious to us.

"You remember how we worked day and night to support ourselves so we wouldn't be a burden to you. You and God are our witnesses that our conduct among you was blameless. We encouraged you as a kind father encourages his children to do what is right and to live to honor God, who has called you into His kingdom.

"We thank God that when you first heard the gospel, you accepted it, not as coming from us, but from God. You are like the believers in Judea who have suffered the same things from their countrymen as you have from yours. The radical Israelites killed prophets, crucified Jesus, and have persecuted us. They even tried to stop us from taking the gospel to others, because they believe that they alone are God's special people and will be saved. So they keep adding sin to sin and are already experiencing the rejection of God.

"Brothers and sisters, we may be separated by distance from you, but not in our hearts. We would love to see you again. Several times I intended to leave Athens and come to see you, but each time Satan stirred things up so I couldn't come. No matter what happens, you are our hope and joy in the Lord and our crown of glory when He comes (1 Thess. 2:1–20).

"I didn't want to be in Athens alone, but we asked Silas and Timothy to stay with you to strengthen you in the faith so you wouldn't be shaken by the troubles you were having, which come to all who believe. When I couldn't stand it any longer, I sent to find out how you were doing, because I was concerned that our work for you would be for nothing.

"But Timothy has come and brought us good news, telling us of your strong faith and love and that you're eager to see us again, just as we long to see you. When we heard that, we were relieved. Your strong faith in the Lord gives us courage and we feel like living again. How can we ever thank God enough for you! We pray day and night that God will open the way for me to come and see you, to help add to your faith whatever you feel is lacking.

"May our Father and the Lord Jesus open the way for us to come, and may the Lord help you to grow in love for each other and for all believers, just as we love you. That way we can grow together in holiness and be blameless before God when the Lord Jesus comes with all His holy angels (1 Thess. 3:1–13).

"In closing, let me urge you to live as we told you, to please God as you're doing, and to do so more and more. Remember what we taught you? It is God's will for you to live holy lives. He wants you to stay away from sexual immorality and other lustful passions that are so prevalent among the heathen. Your bodies belong to the Lord.

"I don't need to tell you to respect the rights of your brothers and sisters and not to take advantage of them or retaliate. The Lord knows everything, and that's all that matters. God did not call us to live impure lives and be an angry people, but a people of honor. Those who live as they please are not rejecting us, but God and the authority of the Holy Spirit.

"You don't need for me to tell you to love each other. Through the Holy Spirit, God has told you that, and it's what you're doing, for which we give thanks. You love all believers and that's good. Keep on living quiet, productive lives, minding your own business. That way you'll be good examples to unbelievers and not a burden to the community.

"Now, just a word about those who have died. I don't want you to grieve as those who have no hope. If we believe that Jesus died and rose again, which we do, then God will raise those who have died believing in Jesus, as He did His Son. And as we told you by the Word of the Lord, we who are alive when Jesus comes will not go to heaven ahead of those who are asleep. Jesus Himself will come back at the head of all the angels and, with His own voice like a trumpet blast, will raise the dead. Then those who are alive will be changed in the twinkling of an eye, and the two groups will be caught up together to meet Jesus in the sky to be with Him forever. So encourage each other with these words (1 Thess. 4:1-18).

"As to when this will happen, I don't need to tell you again, because you know that the day of the Lord will come as quickly as a thief at night. When everything is peaceful and people think that the world is finally safe, then sudden destruction will come like the pains of childbirth come suddenly on a pregnant woman and no one will escape. You're not in the dark on this, so that day won't take you by surprise.

"You are sons and daughters of the light. So stay wide awake and don't be sleepy believers. Nighttime is for sleeping and it's at night when people get drunk. But God's people love the light. So stay sober and put on the armor of faith and the helmet of hope. God has no intention of destroying us, but of saving us, because we belong to the Lord Jesus Christ. He died for us, so whether we're dead or alive, His plan is for us to live with Him forever. Encourage each other in this and continue to hold each other up as you're doing (1 Thess. 5:1-11).

"One final word and then I'll close. Respect your leaders and teachers; love them and honor them for the sake of the work. Live in peace among yourselves. Caution those who are careless and undisciplined. Comfort those who mourn. Encourage those who are discouraged. Help those who are weak. Be patient with everyone. Don't pay back evil for evil, but always do what's good for each other and for everyone else. Be happy. Keep on praying. Be grateful for what God has done for you. These are the things that God expects from His children. And don't stifle the Holy Spirit. Don't look down on prophetic gifts. Examine everything and hold on to what is good. Avoid every form of evil, no matter how small.

"May the God of peace make you holy, so that your whole body, mind, and spirit are kept blameless until Jesus comes. God is faithful and He will do it if you let Him.

"Brothers and sisters, pray for us. Greet all believers with a Christian hug. In the name of the Lord, I charge you to make sure that everyone reads this letter or hears it read. The grace of our Lord Jesus Christ be with you forever" (1 Thess. 5:12-28).

### Corinth

After strengthening the Athenian believers' faith, Paul left and went to Corinth. There he met a Jew named Aquila and his wife, Priscilla, who had recently come from Italy because Caesar had ordered all Jews out of Rome. They were tent makers, so Paul asked them for a job to support himself and they hired him.

On Sabbaths he went to the synagogue to speak to the Jews and God-fearing Greeks, trying to persuade them that Jesus was the Messiah.

When both Timothy and Silas came from Thessalonica, they attended the synagogue with him, and he gained courage and began preaching the gospel stronger than ever. But the Jews turned against him. So he shook the dust off his robe and said, "You're responsible for your own destruction, no one else. From now on I'm preaching to the Gentiles!"

Then he left the synagogue and went next door to the house of Justus, a Gentile who worshipped the God of Israel, and met with the believers there. Crispus, the one in charge of the synagogue, also believed. His whole family and many Corinthians believed and were baptized (Acts 18:1-8).

During this time Paul wrote another letter to the Thessalonian believers and sent it back with Timothy:

### Second Thessalonians

"To the members of the church in Thessalonica: Greetings from Paul, Silas, and Timothy, who are here with me in Corinth. Grace and peace to you from God our Father and from the Lord Jesus Christ. We thank God for you. You have really grown in your faith and in your love for one another, so much so that we tell all the other churches about your endurance and faith in the midst of persecutions and all the other troubles you're now facing.

"There is no doubt that God is using this opportunity to make you even more worthy of being citizens of His kingdom. God will repay your persecutors. When the Lord Jesus comes in flaming fire with all His mighty angels, He will destroy those who persecuted you, because they don't want to know God and have turned against the gospel. They will be destroyed by the glory of the Lord and His awesome power. But His glory and love will be seen in those of you who have believed what we told you about Him.

"We are always praying for you, that our God will make you worthy of the call that He has extended to you. May you do His will and carry on the work with power, so that the name of our Lord and Savior will be glorified through you. All this is only by the means of the grace of our God and the Lord Jesus Christ (2 Thess. 1:1-12).

"Now I want to clarify some things about the return of Christ, when He comes to gather His people to take them home. Don't let your faith be shaken or your minds be confused by letters that we supposedly sent to you telling you that Christ has already come spiritually. Don't be deceived. Before He comes, there will first be a falling away from the true gospel. Then the man of sin who thinks he can change God's law will be revealed, but he is destined for destruction. He will exalt himself and sit in a temple built for God, acting as if he were God.

"Don't you remember that I told you all about this when I was with you? This spirit of iniquity is already working, but is held in check until the time of the end when it will be fully exposed and then taken out of the way. When this man's goal has been achieved, the Lord will destroy him by the breath of His mouth and the brightness of His coming. Before that, Satan will give him great authority and power to work miracles. He will deceive those destined to perish who do not accept the truth and take it to heart. God will not stop them from being deceived, because they will turn against the truth and believe what is false.

"But you are not like that, for which we always thank God. You are loved by the Lord. From the beginning He wanted you to be saved and, by the power of the Holy Spirit, He has set you apart. You have believed the truth and accepted the gospel to the glory of our Lord and Savior Jesus Christ.

"Therefore, stand fast and hold on to what we've taught you, either by word or by letters. May the Lord Jesus Christ and God our Father, who loves us and through His grace has given us hope, comfort your hearts and strengthen you in all the good things you say and do (2 Thess. 2:1-17).

"Finally, brothers and sisters, pray for us, that the Word of the Lord may spread everywhere and be glorified in others, as it is in you. Also pray that we may be delivered from unreasonable and wicked men who don't know what faith is all about. But the Lord is faithful and can always be trusted. He will strengthen you and protect you from the evil one. We have confidence in the Lord that you will continue to do what you were told. May the Holy Spirit turn your hearts and minds toward the love of God and the steadfastness of Jesus Christ.

"In the name of the Lord, I warn you to stay away from any brother who is lazy and lives an unruly life, turning against what we have taught you. Imitate us. You know how we lived when we were among you. We didn't live off people's hospitality. We worked, earned money, and paid for our food. We never thought of living off the church, not because we didn't have a right to, but to be a good example to others. When we were still with you, we told you that if a man is not willing to work when he can, he doesn't deserve to eat. We've heard that you have some members who don't want to work, but spend their time meddling in other people's business. In the name of the Lord, I'm telling you that such people need to find a job and go to work to buy their own food.

"As far as you are concerned, don't get tired of doing good. If anyone among you doesn't do what we said and doesn't pay attention to what we wrote, don't keep associating with him and inviting him to your homes. We sincerely hope he'll get hungry enough to wake up and be ashamed of himself. Don't treat him as an enemy, but encourage him to do what is right, as you would your own brother.

"Now may the Lord of peace give you His peace and be with you always. I'm writing this final greeting with my own hand, which I do for all my letters, so everyone will know which letter is from me. The grace of God be with all of you" (2 Thess. 3:1-18).

### Paul Continues His Work

Then the Lord spoke to Paul in a night vision and said, "Don't leave Corinth yet and don't be afraid, but keep on preaching the gospel, because I have many people in this city who need to hear the gospel. No one will attack you or hurt you, because I'll be right beside you." So Paul stayed in Corinth for a year and a half, preaching and teaching the Word of God.

While Gallio was provincial governor, certain Jews grabbed Paul and dragged him to the city square in front of the courthouse. It was the day the governor was scheduled to hold public court. When he took his seat, the Jews spoke up, "This fellow is persuading people to worship God in a way that is contrary to what we believe!"

Just as Paul was about to open his mouth to defend himself, Gallio said to the Jews, "If this were a matter of some public misdeed or crime, I would listen to your charges, but since it has to do with your religion, you settle the matter among yourselves." Then he ordered the crowd to disburse. So the people grabbed Sosthenes, the head of the synagogue, and began beating him right in front of the governor, but Gallio could not have cared less (Acts 18:9-17).

### Paul Returns Home

So Paul stayed in Corinth for some time and finally said good-bye, leaving for Cenchrea, a port not far from Corinth, to sail for Syria. Aquila and Priscilla decided to go with him. Before boarding the ship, Paul had his hair cut short as a sign that he had taken the Nazirite vow of gratitude to God for deliverance from harm.

When they got to Ephesus, they disembarked and, at the first opportunity, Paul went to the synagogue to share the gospel with the Jews. They were encouraged and asked him to stay in Ephesus for a while. He said, "I have to get to Jerusalem in time for the festival but, God willing, I'll be back." So he said good-bye and left Aquila and Priscilla behind to carry on the work he had begun.

Then he boarded the ship and sailed from Ephesus to Caesarea, just south of Mount Carmel on the coast of Palestine. From there he made his way to Jerusalem. After greeting the believers and observing the festival, he headed north to Antioch, where he had started his second missionary journey three years before (Acts 18:18-22).

# eleven

# Third Mission Trip

After spending some time in Antioch resting from his second mission trip, Paul decided to go back and revisit the churches where he had been in order to strengthen the believers in the faith.

While he was resting in Antioch, a man named Apollos, a native of Alexandria, came to Ephesus. He was a highly educated Jew with a thorough knowledge of the Scriptures. He spoke powerfully about the coming Messiah, even though he knew only what John the Baptist had said. When Aquila and Priscilla heard Apollos speak in the synagogue, they invited him home and taught him God's plan of salvation more fully.

When Apollos decided to take the gospel to certain cities in Greece, the local elders encouraged him and wrote a letter of recommendation to the believers there to welcome him. He was a great help to those who had accepted God's grace, by refuting the Jews and showing from Scripture that Jesus was the Messiah (Acts 18:23-28).

## Rebaptism

While Apollos was in Corinth, Paul returned to Ephesus as he had promised. When he was introduced to 12 new members, he asked them what they believed and whether or not they had experienced the power of the Holy Spirit in their lives.

They said, "We've never even heard about the Holy Spirit."

Paul asked, "Then in whose name were you baptized?"

They answered, "We were baptized as a sign of the repentance that John preached."

Paul responded, "John indeed preached about repentance and a change of life, but he also told people to believe in the One who would come after him, that is, in Jesus, the Messiah." When they heard that, they believed, and all 12 were baptized in the name of the Lord Jesus. Then

Paul laid his hands on them, and the Holy Spirit came on them with power, giving them the gifts of languages and proclamation.

For the next three months Paul boldly preached in the synagogue, arguing persuasively with the Jews about the kingdom of God. But some were stubborn and refused to believe. They publicly insulted Paul and told the crowds that what he was preaching about the way of the Lord was not true.

So he decided to take those who believed to the school of Tyrannus and preached there every day for the next two years. This way, both Jews and Greeks throughout the province had a chance to come and hear the Word of the Lord (Acts 19:1-10).

### A Hurried Note

About this time Apollos returned to Ephesus from Corinth and gave Paul a report of what was happening there. So Paul quickly wrote a short note to the believers in Corinth, expressing his concern:

"Don't keep associating with sexually immoral people. I'm not referring to people in general, some of whom are greedy, cheats, idolaters, and immoral, because if you quit associating with them, you'd have to leave the earth. I'm talking about someone who is a church member. Don't even invite him to your house. It's not for me to judge those outside the church; God will do that. But it's your responsibility to judge those inside the church and, if you have to, remove such a wicked person from membership" (1 Cor. 5:9-13).

Paul urged Apollos to take his note to Corinth, but he declined to go back and went elsewhere to preach the gospel. So Paul asked Titus to take his note to Corinth to see what he could do to rectify the situation.

### Miracles

While Titus was gone, God worked some very unusual miracles through Paul. Even when believers took a handkerchief or a work apron that Paul had used and placed it on the sick, they were healed, and those possessed by evil spirits were set free.

During this time some itinerant Jews came to town, claiming to have power to cast out demons. After watching Paul, they decided to use the name of Jesus as he did. Among them were the seven Sceva brothers, whose father was a leading Jewish priest. When they used the name of Jesus to cast out an evil spirit from a man, the demon said, "I know Jesus and I know Paul, but who are you?" Then the possessed man attacked the brothers and overpowered all seven of them. He gave them such a beating that they left the house naked and bleeding.

Word of what happened spread throughout the city. Both Jews and Greeks got scared, and the name of Jesus became very highly respected. Many who had said they believed now confessed their sins and openly declared their faith. Those who had practiced magic brought their books and burned them publicly. When the value of these books was added up, it came to 50,000 silver coins, worth thousands of days of work. So the Word of the Lord spread far and wide and continued to grow in power (Acts 19:11-20).

### Visitors

About this time Stephanus, Fortunatus, and Achaicus came from Corinth, bringing a reply to Paul's note and asking his advice on a number of things, but said nothing of what was really going on. However, Paul got the facts from the family of Chloe, who had also come from Corinth. Immediately he sent Titus back to prepare the way for his visit. He then took time to carefully write his first letter to the Corinthians, answering their questions:

"Greetings from Paul, called to be an apostle of Jesus Christ by the will of God, and from Sosthenes, who has accepted Jesus Christ and is now the leader of our people here in Ephesus. This letter is to the believers in Corinth, who have been set apart by God for Jesus Christ and called to live holy lives. Such is true of all believers, no matter where they live, who have the same Savior and Lord as we have. Grace to you and peace from God our Father and from the Lord Jesus Christ.

"Every time I think back on how your church got started, I thank God for the grace He has given you through our Savior Jesus Christ. He has enriched your church with knowledge and the ability to communicate the gospel to others. Some of you were even given the gift of prophecy, so that you would not come behind in any spiritual gift as you look forward to the return of Christ. He will strengthen your faith until He comes and you stand blameless in His presence. God is faithful and has called you into fellowship with His Son, Jesus Christ (1 Cor. 1:1-9).

"I plead with you, brothers and sisters, in the name of the Lord Jesus, to stop dividing the church. Be of one mind and spirit, and make church decisions for the glory of God. Stephanus and his friends gave me your letter, and as I read it, I had a sense that you were not telling me everything. So when the family of Chloe came to Ephesus, I asked them to tell me what was really going on and they did.

"They told me about your rivalries over each group's favorite preacher. Some of you are saying, 'I'm with Paul!'; others, 'Apollos is my man!'; and still others, 'I'm for Peter!' or 'I'm with Jesus!' It was because of this that Apollos left Corinth and is now traveling with Zenas, the lawyer, spreading the gospel.

"Is Christ divided? Was Paul crucified for you? Or were you baptized in the name of Paul? I'm glad I didn't baptize any of you except Crispus and Gaius—oh yes, and Stephanus and his family. I don't remember baptizing anyone else. And I'm glad or it would only make these divisions worse. Jesus didn't send me just to baptize, but to preach—not with human wisdom, but by focusing on Calvary and what He has done (1 Cor. 1:10-17; Titus 3:13).

### Calvary

"The message of the cross—that a man's execution saves us from sin— is to those in the world nothing but foolish talk. They're on the road to destruction. But to those of us who are on the road of salvation, it makes sense, because the power of God has changed us. As God says in Scripture, 'I will turn the wisdom of the wise upside down and show the educated that their intelligence amounts to nothing.'

"So where is the wisdom of the wise? Where is the intelligence of the scholars and philosophers who love to debate? All the wisdom of the world did not bring us closer to God. But God in His wisdom used the preaching of the cross to save those who believe. The Jews demand miracles and the Greeks, logic; but we lift up Calvary, which is offensive to the Jews and foolishness to the Greeks. But those who respond to God's calling, whether Jew or Greek, see in Christ the power and wisdom of God. The so-called foolish message from God is wiser than human wisdom, and the meekness of Christ is stronger than the strength of man.

"So you can see, brothers and sisters, that when you responded to God's call, not many of you were considered wise by human standards, not many influential, and not many from the upper class. But God has chosen the humble to bring light to the wise and to the weak-minded, and to enlighten those who consider themselves intelligent. He is using those who are insignificant in the eyes of the world to expose those who think too highly of themselves. No one can boast of his wisdom in the presence of God.

"But you have given yourselves to Christ. He has become your wisdom, intelligence, righteousness, salvation, and sanctification. As the Scripture says, 'Let him who glories, glory in the Lord' (1 Cor. 1:18-30).

### My First Visit

"When I first came to you, I didn't try to impress you with my preaching or intelligence, because I decided to focus on nothing but Jesus Christ and Him crucified. I felt totally inadequate to lift up Jesus Christ and was trembling with fear that I might do Him injustice. That's why I didn't use impressive words, but let the Holy Spirit give the message power and focus. Your faith should not rest on human wisdom, but on God's power and what He has done for us in Christ.

"We don't base our message on the wisdom of this age or on what political experts say, for they will perish unless they turn to Christ. To them the gospel is a mystery, but to us it is our glory and joy. If the rulers of this world had known God as they should have, they wouldn't have crucified Christ. As the Scripture says, 'No eye has seen and no mind has thought of what God has revealed to those who love Him.' And He did that through the Holy Spirit, who knows that the deep things of God are hard for us to understand. We can't even know what's in another man's heart. So how can we know the deep things of God, except as the Holy Spirit tells us?

"That's why we don't use words of human wisdom, but only what the Holy Spirit has taught us. Spiritual things need to be spiritually understood. This sounds foolish to an unbeliever, because he can't understand what we're talking about. But those who are spiritually minded know exactly what we're saying. As the Scripture points out: 'Who knows so much that he can counsel God?' The Holy Spirit helps us think the way Christ thinks (1 Cor. 2:1-16).

"Brothers and sisters, when I first came to you, I could not talk about spiritual things as I could later. You were new babies in Christ, and I had to give you spiritual milk because you weren't ready for solid food. You're still not ready, because there is jealousy and fighting among you as we see in the people of the world. One says, 'Paul is my man!'; and another, 'I'm for Apollos!' Who is Apollos, anyway? Or who is Paul? We are only God's humble servants who have been sent to help you according to the ministry God has given us. I planted the spiritual seeds and Apollos watered them, but God made them grow. One plants and another waters. Both do their work and God rewards each one according to how well they do it. Apollos and I are workmen, and you are God's field.

"You also are God's building. According to the grace God has given me, I have laid a solid foundation as a good workman, and others will build on it. You need to be careful how you build your individual lives and the church. No one can change the foundation that I have laid, which is Jesus Christ. So some of you are using gold, silver, and precious stones to build on this foundation, and others are using wood or mud mixed with hay and straw. The day will come when the building you've built will be tested by fire to see if it will stand. If it stands, those of you who built well will be rewarded accordingly, but if the construction burns up, your reward will be less, even though you'll be saved.

"Don't you know that as a church you are a living temple and that the Holy Spirit is in each of you, bringing you closer to God? If anyone tears down this temple, he'll be destroyed, because the temple of God is holy, which you are.

"Don't let anyone fool himself. If he thinks he knows so much, let him admit how little he actually knows about God and he'll be a wise man. The wisdom that comes from the world means nothing to God. As the Scripture says, 'God catches the worldly wise in their own craftiness because He knows their purposes and thoughts ahead of time.' So let no one talk about how great someone else is, whether it's Paul, Apollos, or Peter. God is working everything to your advantage, whether it is life or death. We serve you, you serve Christ, and Christ serves God (1 Cor. 3:1-23).

"You need to think of us as servants who have been entrusted with the secret things of God. What is expected of servants? They must be faithful to their master. It doesn't matter what you think of me or what a human court decides about me. I don't even make decisions about myself. I let God do that. Even though I don't know of anything that I'm doing wrong, that doesn't justify me before God. That's why I leave everything about myself in the Lord's hands. He's the One who reads motives and brings everything to light. In time we will each receive praise from God, not from someone else.

"What I've said applies especially to Apollos and me. You need to learn from us to stay with what the Scripture says. That will keep you from becoming arrogant and proud, favoring one above the other.

"What makes you feel so superior and smart? What do you have that you didn't receive from God? Now, if you received it, why do you act so satisfied with yourselves, as if nobody ever gave you anything? You act as if you were kings. In one sense I wish the kingdom of God were already here and you were kings with Christ and we were kings with you.

"But God decided to put us apostles at the back of a military parade, as if we had been captured in war and condemned to die. So we are constantly on display for men and angels to see. Yes, we have been made fools for Christ, but you have been made wise. We are weak, but you have been made strong. You have been honored, but we are dishonored. We are often hungry and thirsty, poorly dressed, badly treated, and homeless. We work hard making a living with our hands. When we are cursed, we respond with a blessing. When we are persecuted and beaten, we don't complain. When people lie about us, we speak about them with kindness. Even now we are treated as scum of the earth.

"I'm not telling you these things to shame you, but to correct you as a loving father corrects his children. Even if you had 10,000 instructors in Christ, you have only one father. I'm the one who became your father when I brought you to Christ. So model your life after mine. That's one reason I'm sending this letter with Timothy, who is like a faithful son to me in the Lord. He will remind you of how I live in Christ and that I teach the same thing to believers everywhere.

"Some of you are arrogant and puffed up with pride, thinking I'm not coming to see you. But I will come to Corinth as soon as I can if that's what the Lord allows me to do. Then we'll see what these arrogant people are talking about and what makes them so powerful. The kingdom of God is not just talk, but action. How do you want me to handle the situation? With love and gentleness, or with discipline? It looks like it will have to be both" (1 Cor. 4:1-21).

# twelve

# Problems in the Church

## Incest

Paul continued his letter:

"Now I want to address some of the problems I've been told you're having. I hear that one of your members is having sex with his father's new wife. Two men, a father and a son, sleeping with the same woman! That's incest! Even the Greeks and Romans don't allow that! And yet you feel good about yourselves, proud of your church, when you ought to feel sick over it and weep before the Lord and remove this man from membership.

"I might not be there in person, but I am there in heart and spirit and have already decided what to do about this. When you come together in the house of the Lord Jesus to worship, kindly ask this man to leave, but do so firmly and tell him why. With my heart and soul I'll be there to help you. This will show your disapproval of what he's doing and will maybe wake him up so he'll change his ways and come back to the Lord.

"Don't you know that all it takes is a little yeast to go through a whole batch of dough? What this man is doing is like yeast. You need to become a new batch of dough in Christ without the yeast of sin. Christ gave His life for you. He's the Passover Lamb. Celebrate what He has done for you, and spiritually keep the Festival of Unleavened Bread by getting rid of the yeast of wickedness. Feast on Christ, who is without sin—the Bread from heaven, full of sincerity and truth.

"I don't want to repeat myself, but I've told you, in the short note that I sent to you before, not to keep company with sexually immoral members. You can't help associating with people like that in the world. But don't keep on inviting members to your house who claim to be Christians and yet live immoral lives, steal, cheat, are abusive, have foul mouths, and are drunkards. As I said, I'm not talking about people on the outside—God will judge *them*. I'm talking about people like that in the church. So remove this man from among you (1 Cor. 5:1-13).

## Lawsuits

"Also, I understand from the Chloe family that you go to court to settle your differences instead of going to the church. Don't you know that God's people will one day judge the world? If that's the case, why should we think that you can't handle differences among yourselves? Don't you know that one day we'll even judge angels? How much more should we be able to judge things in this life!

"When you decide to judge things, would you ask those least qualified to do the judging? If so, that's to your shame. It tells me that you can't even find one among you who is wise enough to counsel brothers who differ, and judge between them. Is that why you go to court and let unbelievers decide?

"It's not right to take a brother to court. Why don't you just accept the wrong that's done to you? Accept the fact that you were cheated and let it go at that. The reason you're upset and go to court is because you also cheat others, even your own brothers in the church.

"Don't you know that the dishonest will not inherit the kingdom? Neither will idol worshippers, adulterers, homosexuals, lesbians, thieves, extortioners, abusers, and drunkards. Some of you were just like that, but then you gave your hearts to Christ, were washed by His blood, born again by the Holy Spirit, justified in God's sight, and set apart to live for Him (1 Cor. 6:1-11).

## Sexual Immorality

"You have another problem. You think you can have sex with whomever you please. According to the law of the land, I could live that way, but some things in life are beneficial to me and some are not. While the law will not stop me, I'm not going to let myself be controlled by anything.

"For example, food is for the stomach and the stomach was made for food. But God didn't make either just so we can live to eat. It's the same with our bodies. We weren't made just to have sex. Our bodies belong to the Lord.

"God's plan is to raise us from the dead and take us to heaven as He did Christ. This means that our bodies belong to Christ and, through Him, to God. Now, if your body belongs to Christ, why should you give your body to prostitutes? Don't you know that when you give your body to a prostitute, you become one with her and the two of you become one body?

"We are one with Christ. We make up His body on earth and have the same spirit as He had. So stop this sexual immorality! Every other sin is outside the body, but sexual immorality has to do with the inside.

"Don't you know that your body is the temple of the Holy Spirit, who is in you as a gift from God? So it's no longer simply a body. It's a temple! God paid a high price for you. So honor God with your body (1 Cor. 6:12–20).

## Marriage

"Now let me respond to some of the things you wrote in your letter. You say that it's good not to be married. That may be so, but because of the immoral society in which we live, it's better to be married and fulfill each other's sexual needs. In one sense, neither one has a right to his or her own body. So don't deprive each other, unless you agree to do so for a short time for spiritual reasons. Then resume your normal relations so Satan doesn't take advantage of your lack of sexual control.

"This is not a command. If you can stay single as I am, that's good, but God leads each one differently. So to the unmarried and young widows I would say to stay single. But if they have a problem with this, let them get married, because it's better to get married than to live alone and be unable to control one's sexual needs.

"On the other hand, if you're married, don't get divorced. This is not my command, but the Lord's. But if you do separate, either stay single or get back together. Don't get divorced just to marry someone else.

"To those who are married, let me say this, even though it's not directly from the Lord: If a woman is married to an unbeliever and they're happy with each other, let them stay together. This way the unbelieving spouse is also considered by God as being set apart for Him, because in His sight they are one. This means that their children, too, are set apart for God. But if the unbelieving spouse wants a divorce, go ahead. Under those circumstances, the believing spouse shouldn't feel guilty. God wants people to live together in peace. Besides, how do you know whether or not your influence will win the unbelieving spouse to Christ? (1 Cor. 7:1-16).

## Don't Worry

"Whatever life situation you were in when the Lord called you, don't think you have to change it. If you came to the Lord after you were circumcised, don't worry about it. If you came to the Lord without being circumcised, don't think you have to be circumcised. What counts is living by God's commandments.

"If you gave your heart to the Lord after you sold yourself into slavery to pay your debts, don't break the agreement. But if you can work things out to be free, do so. In your heart and spirit you are free, because the Lord already paid for your freedom. On the other hand, if you gave your heart to the Lord as a free person, you agreed to serve Him. Don't forget that you were bought with a price, so don't let anyone take away your spiritual freedom and control you.

"In short, whatever your life situation when the Lord Jesus called you, keep holding on to Him (1 Cor. 7:17-24).

## Young People

"You asked about young people who are not married and what they should do. Though I have no direct command from the Lord, by His grace what I say is trustworthy.

"Because of the impending persecution of Christians, I think it's best for young people to stay single. If you're married, don't get divorced. If you're single, don't get married. If you do get married, it's not wrong. But under the present circumstances I would not advise you to get married, because I'm trying to spare you some pain.

"Brothers and sisters, because of the present crisis, some of us might not have many days left. So don't take on more care and responsibility than you have to, whether it has to do with marriage, buying and selling, or grieving over loss one moment and rejoicing over success the next. Think more about the Lord and how to please Him and not so much about the things of this world, or your affections will be divided. That's why it's easier to stay single. I'm not trying to tell you what to do, but I do want you to put the Lord first.

"If a young couple is engaged and each wants to get married, let them go ahead. I don't see any problem in this. But if they decide to hold off getting married, that will be better for now.

"You need to remember that a wife is tied to her husband as long as he lives. But if he dies, she's free to marry, as long as it's to someone who loves the Lord. That's true of the husband, too. But in this case, it's my opinion that a young woman will be better off if she stays single, because of the present crisis. And I think you can trust that I'm being guided by the Holy Spirit (1 Cor. 7:25-40).

## Conscience

"I now want to say something about following your conscience. You pride yourselves on your knowledge, like all Corinthians do. This just keeps feeding your pride and keeps you from knowing what you should— that love is more important than knowledge. God knows whether you really love Him or not.

"Let's apply this to buying food from a market where meat offered to idols is sold. We know that idols are not gods. There is only one God, the

Father in heaven who created all things, and there is only one Lord Jesus, through whom we live and move and have our being. But not everyone knows this.

"You have been accustomed to eating meat offered to idols, so your conscience doesn't bother you. Eating meat offered to idols is not the point. It has nothing to do with your relationship with God, one way or the other. It has to do with your relationship with your brother. So be careful not to make your freedom a stumbling block for others.

"If someone feels sensitive about this and sees you going into an idol's temple to eat, you're not helping him. You might know that idols are nothing, and eating there doesn't bother you, but are you helping your brothers and sisters? If you don't care what they think, you're hurting Christ. For this reason I wouldn't think of even touching the meat offered to idols, thereby weakening the faith of my brothers and sisters by having them think that, in addition to Christ, I still worship idols" (1 Cor. 8:1–13).

# thirteen

# Important Advice

Paul had questions:

"I think I have answered the questions you asked in your letter. Now, let me ask you some questions. Am I not an apostle? Am I not free to do what is best for you? Have I not met the Lord Jesus Christ and talked to Him? Are you not the fruit of my work for the Lord? Am I not an apostle sent by God to help others and you? And are you not the evidence of my apostleship? This is my defense against those who would like to cross-examine me.

"Don't we have a right to take a wife along with us as other apostles do, such as the Lord's stepbrother and Peter? Are Barnabas and I the only ones who have no right to financial support? Who ever heard of a soldier serving in the army at his own expense? Who has a vineyard and doesn't have a right to eat his own grapes? Who takes care of goats and cattle and isn't allowed to drink their milk? This is not just common sense, but the law.

"As the Scripture says, 'Don't put a muzzle on an animal while it's pulling the plow or the threshing wheel.' Does this apply only to animals? No, it applies to people, also! So if we sowed spiritual seed, don't we have a right to live off the harvest? Of course we do! And if you extend this right to others and support them financially, why not us? But we haven't demanded this right. We worked to support ourselves so no one could say that we preached the gospel for money. We want you to know that God's grace is free.

"Don't you know that the priests in the Temple were allowed to eat the holy bread, and those who served at the altar lived off the sacrifices and tithes and offerings? The Lord wants those who preach the gospel to live off the gospel. But I chose not to, nor have I ever asked you to support me. I would rather die than lose the satisfaction it gives me to preach the gospel for free. I don't have anything to be proud of, anyway, because God has given me the responsibility to preach the gospel, and woe to me if I don't! I do it, not because I have to, but willingly. The Lord has entrusted me with the gospel. So what is my reward? It's the thrill of preaching about Jesus Christ without pay—not being supported by you or anyone else.

"Even though I'm not controlled by anyone, I'm a willing servant to everyone, with the hope of winning even more to Christ. Trying to save Jews who keep the ceremonial laws, I go as far as I can to be like them. And when working among the Greeks who live by no law, I go as far as I can to be like them. To reach those who are poor, I too become poor. I become all things to all men, so that I might win them to Christ. And I do all this so I can live the gospel—not just talk about it.

"Don't you know that all who run in the Olympics run to win, but only one gets the prize? You too need to run to win, and all of you will get the prize. The Olympic runner's prize will fade away, but our prize will last forever. So I run to win. I don't fight like I'm beating the air or run like I'm chasing the wind. I keep my body disciplined in order to win, so that after preaching the gospel to others, I myself don't become disqualified (1 Cor. 9:1-27).

### Examples

"There are some things from the past that I need to point out to you, of which you're not aware. When God took our ancestors out of Egypt, He led them by a cloud and had them walk through the sea. In a spiritual sense, that's when Moses baptized them. They ate the food God provided called 'manna,' and they drank the water that flowed out of a rock, which points to Christ, our spiritual Rock.

"But God couldn't take our ancestors straight into Canaan because of their disobedience, and many of them died in the wilderness. This is an example of what can happen to people who want to do their own thing. Don't do what they did by worshipping idols and being sexually stimulated as a part of worship. The Scripture says, 'They ate and drank and indulged in heathen revelry.' Don't commit sexual immorality as they did. As a result, a plague broke out and thousands of them died in one day. Let's not put Christ to the test to see whether or not He will do something to stop our sinning.

"The people also complained about the manna and accused God of bringing them out of Egypt into the wilderness to deprive them of their needs and kill them. So God lifted His protection, and poisonous snakes came into the camp and bit them. Moses prayed for the people, and God told him to twist a piece of metal into the shape of a snake, put it on a pole, and hold it up. Whoever looked up to it in faith would be healed. This demonstrated that Christ's death on the cross would end the sting of Satan.

"These examples are recorded as warnings for us who live this side of the cross. Sexual immorality is quite common. Don't be overconfident and think that you cannot be tempted. Hold on to Christ. God, who is faithful, will not let you be tempted above what you are able to handle, but will make a way for you to escape the sinfulness of this world.

"Stay away from idol festivals. You're intelligent enough to know why. When unbelievers sacrifice to idols, they are sacrificing to demons. You can't have fellowship with the Lord and fellowship with demons. In ancient Israel, worshippers ate of the sacrifices they brought in order to fellowship with God and become one with Him. When we have communion and eat the bread and drink the grape juice, we fellowship with Christ and become one with Him and with each other. How can anyone sacrifice to idols when idols are nothing but wood and stone? Don't insult the Lord by thinking that you know more than He does.

"You are free to do anything you want, but is it helpful? Does it build your faith? Concentrate on being helpful to each other. As I said before, you can eat the meat sold at the pagan temple market. It's not going against your conscience, because everything belongs to the Lord. If someone who is not a believer invites you to his house for dinner, eat the meat that's set before you and don't ask questions. But if he tells you that the meat he's preparing was offered to idols, don't eat it. Respect his conscience and yours. And when you're in the presence of church members who see eating meat offered to idols as a sin, you need to respect their consciences.

"You say, 'If I asked the Lord's blessing on the food, why should I be judged?' Whether you eat or drink or whatever you do, do it to the glory of God. Don't offend people, whether Jew, Greek, or members of the church. I live for others, not for myself, because I want to save as many as I can. So follow my example as I follow Christ's example (1 Cor. 10:1–11:1).

## Women

"I want to thank you and praise you for trying to hold on to the things I taught you. But let me clarify some things. Man is the head of the family, Christ is the head of man, and the Father is the head of Christ. You ought to keep this in mind as you try to represent our faith to others. When a woman comes to church to worship and pray, she should cover her head. If she doesn't, she might as well disgrace herself by cutting off her hair and shaving her head. But when a man comes to church to worship and pray, he should uncover his head, for he is God's created glory, just like the woman is the glory of the man.

"All this is a symbol of our inward attitude toward God and the church, and that's how people understand it. Let's not offend them unnecessarily. Look at nature. A woman grows hair more easily than a man. If a man has long hair like a woman, it's not becoming to him, but if a woman has long hair, it's beautiful—it's like a covering for her.

"If some of you want to argue about this, let me just say that we have these same standards in all our churches (1 Cor. 11:2-16).

## Communion

"Now let me say something about the way you conduct your communion services. I'm not going to praise you for what you're doing, because after you have communion, you're worse off than before. They tell me you're still divided and I don't doubt it. To make it worse, those you look up to approve of what you're doing.

"When you come together for communion, is it not the Lord's Supper? But you've turned what you call a 'love feast for the Lord' into a feast like they have in pagan temples, where everyone gorges himself. You bring to church what you want for yourself and eat and drink, while others have hardly anything to eat. If you need more, can't you eat at home before or after you come to church? How do those feel who have little when they see you having so much? What you're doing is a disgrace to God's church. Do you expect me to praise you for what you're doing? I will not.

"The Lord told me how it was the night He was betrayed. So let me tell you again. He met with His disciples in the upper room, quietly took the bread, and said the blessing. He then broke it and gave each one a piece, saying, 'This bread represents My body, which I will give for you. Whenever you eat this bread, remember Me.' After they had eaten the bread, He quietly took the cup and said, 'This cup represents the new covenant of My blood. Every time you drink it, remember Me.' So when we get together for communion, we are celebrating what the Lord has done for us on Calvary until He comes again.

"That's why whoever eats the communion bread and drinks from the cup in the way you're doing is guilty of discrediting the body and blood of the Lord. Each one needs to examine himself to make sure his heart is right when he takes communion so he doesn't bring judgment on himself. Besides, the way you're eating and drinking before communion has made many of you sick, and some have even died before their time.

"Let's discipline ourselves before the Lord has to discipline us, so we don't end up being condemned with the world. When you come together for communion, wait until everyone gets there. And if you're hungry, eat at home before you come. If anything else needs my attention, I'll handle that when I get there" (1 Cor. 11:17-34).

# fourteen

# Gifts for the Church

Paul clarified another misunderstanding:
"Let me now share something important with you, brothers and sisters, because I don't want you to be ignorant about spiritual things. Do you remember that when you were pagans, you were led astray by voiceless idols and were always trying to figure them out? Now that you're Christians, one thing for certain is that no one can speak against Christ and claim to be led by the Holy Spirit. And no one can speak well of Christ except when the Holy Spirit is leading him. You can be certain of that!

"There are different spiritual gifts given by the same Holy Spirit. There are different ministries, but the same Lord Jesus. And there are different spiritual activities, but the same God. Whatever gifts there are, they are given for the benefit of everyone.

"To one is given the gift of wisdom, to another the gift of knowledge, and to another the gift of healing, all by the same Holy Spirit. To one is given the power to work miracles, to another prophecy, and to another the ability to detect false spirits, all by the same Holy Spirit. To one is given the ability to speak different languages, to another the ability to interpret accurately, and the Holy Spirit gives all these gifts as He decides.

"For example, we each have one body, but it has many parts. It's the same with the church, which is the body of Christ. We became part of that body when we were baptized and received the Holy Spirit, whether we were Jews, Greeks, slaves, or free. We all drank from the Holy Spirit's fountain.

"As I said, the body is not just one piece, but contains many parts. If the foot should say, 'Because I'm not the hand, I'm not part of the body,' is it not part of the body? If the ear should say, 'Because I'm not the eye, I'm not part of the body,' is it not part of the body? If the whole body were an eye, how would we hear? If the whole body were an ear, how would we smell things?

"God put the body together the way it is and there are many parts, but it is only one body. The eye can't say to the hand, 'I don't need you,' nor can the head say to the feet, 'I don't need you.' In fact, no matter how insignificant some body parts are, we need them all, especially those which are not as beautiful as others. That's the way God put the body together. So we need to take care of all parts of the body, even those we usually don't think about.

"It's the same with the church. As members, we should care about each other as we care about each part of our body. When one suffers, we all feel it. If someone is honored, we all rejoice.

"God assembled His church with different parts as He did for the human body. He has put apostles, prophets, and teachers in the church. He has also given power to work miracles, and gifts of healing, leadership, helping hands, and languages. Is everyone an apostle, a prophet, a teacher, a miracle worker, a healer, a leader, someone gifted in languages, and someone who can interpret correctly? Of course not! Do you want an important gift? Let me show you one (1 Cor. 12:1-31).

### Love

"If I can speak all the languages on earth and even the language of angels, but don't have love in my heart, as far as God is concerned, I am just a noisy gong or a clanging cymbal.

"If I can prophesy and am highly educated, having mastered all the sciences and understanding all mysteries, and if I have such strong faith to even move mountains, but don't have love in my heart, to God it means nothing.

"If I give away all my money to feed the poor or offer my body as a martyr for God to be burned at the stake, but don't have love in my heart, what good does it do?

"The love that comes from God is patient and kind, never jealous or proud, never rude, doesn't think about self, is never angry or resentful. Love rejects the pleasures of sin and rejoices in the truth. It never complains, it believes what is right, is full of hope, and endures to the end.

"There are no limits to love. Prophecies have their limits, as do languages and knowledge, because we don't know everything. When the Lord comes, all that was partially understood will be made plain.

"When I was a child, I talked and reasoned as a child. But when I became an adult, I abandoned childish thinking. The way we see things now is like looking in a cloudy mirror. But when the Lord comes, we will see things as they really are and will talk to Him face to face. Now I know only in part, but then I will understand things as clearly as God knows me.

"The things that really matter are faith, hope, and love. But the most important of these is love (1 Cor. 13:1–13).

## Spiritual Gifts

"First, walk in the way of love, then be eager for spiritual gifts, especially for the ability to proclaim the gospel. But if no one but God can understand what you're saying, what good is it?

"The gifts of the Holy Spirit are to strengthen faith and to encourage and comfort people. If people claim to speak a language the Holy Spirit gave them but no one understands it, it might make them feel good, but it certainly is no help to the church. If the Holy Spirit decided to give all of you the gift of languages, I would rejoice, but I would rather all of you had the gift of proclamation. The one who proclaims the truth is more important than the one who can speak many languages, unless someone interprets for him. It's for the building up of the church.

"Brothers and sisters, if I came and spoke to you in a language you didn't understand, what good would it do? But if I came and shared with you what God has shown me in vision, or if I helped you know more about God or studied with you, wouldn't that be better?

"Even with musical instruments, if a flute or a harp doesn't give distinctive notes, what good is it? If a trumpet gives uncertain sounds that no one recognizes, how will the troops get ready for battle?

"It's also true of you. If you speak a language no one understands, it's like talking to the wind. There are lots of languages in the world, and not one is without meaning. But if I don't know what you're saying, I might as well be a foreigner. So when you long for the Holy Spirit to give you a gift, ask for one that will help the church.

"If you pray in another language, you need someone to interpret. If there's no interpreter, it helps no one but you. When I pray, I pray from my heart and communicate with my mind. It's the same when I sing and praise the Lord. Otherwise, what good is it if people can't understand and say Amen! in agreement?

"I can speak many languages, more than any of you. But in church I'd rather speak five words you understand than thousands of words no one knows.

"Brothers and sisters, don't be childish in your thinking. Think like adults, but be as innocent as children in your living. The Scripture says, 'I give foreigners the gift of language and send them to speak to My people, but they still don't listen to Me.' The gift of languages is a sign from God to unbelievers, but the gift of prophecy is a gift from God to believers.

"If a visitor comes to church and hears everyone speaking in a language he doesn't understand, he will think you're out of your mind. But if he hears you proclaim a message that he understands, he might be convicted and fall on his knees, saying, Surely God is in this place (1 Cor. 14:1-25).

## Orderliness

"Why is it, my brothers and sisters, that when you come together for worship, each one sings, stands up to teach, speaks in a foreign tongue, tells about the vision he had, or interprets? This is nothing but confusion. Let everything be done decently and in order for the sake of the church.

"If someone starts to speak in a language no one understands, let someone interpret. If there are more who want to speak, it should be no more than two or three, and one following the other—not all at once. And if no one can interpret, let the speakers be quiet, and let the people talk to God in their hearts.

"The same is true for those who claim to have the gift of prophecy. Have them give their messages one after the other, and let the people evaluate what they say against Scripture. If one of them has a revelation from God, the one who is already speaking should sit down and let that one speak. And if there are others, let them take turns so the members can listen and learn and be encouraged. Remember that a prophet has to be subject to the prophets who have gone before. God is not the author of confusion, but of orderliness and peace in all the churches.

"Women should not take part in this confusion, but should quietly listen. If they want to make sense of what's going on, let them discuss it with their husbands at home. It's disgraceful for a woman to try to straighten out such confusion in church.

"Did the Word of God originate with you, or did it come only to you and to no one else? If anyone claims to have the gift of prophecy or is a spiritual leader, he should accept what I have written as from the Lord. If he does not, his prophecy should not be accepted and he should not be a leader.

"Brothers and sisters, long for the gift of prophecy, and don't stop those from speaking who have the gift of languages, as long as what they say is being interpreted. Let all things be done in good taste and in an orderly way (1 Cor. 14:26-40).

## Clarification

"Brothers and sisters, let me remind you of the gospel I preached to you, which you received, and on which you now stand. You're saved through the gospel, but only if you hold on to it; otherwise, your faith is good for nothing.

80

"The heart of the gospel is that Jesus Christ died for our sins, according to the Scriptures. He was buried and rose from the dead, according to the Scriptures. He was seen by Peter, by the 12 disciples, and by over 500 followers at one time, many of whom are still alive today. After that He was seen by His stepbrother, James, and again by all the apostles.

"Last of all, He was seen by me when I was not worthy to be an apostle because I was persecuting the church. It is by the grace of God that I am what I am. And He didn't extend His grace to me in vain. In fact, I've worked harder than anyone, yet it isn't me, but the grace of God in me. Whether the preaching of the gospel comes through others or me doesn't matter. What's important is that you took hold of it by faith, not having seen the Lord yourself.

"So how can some of you say there is no Resurrection? If that were true, then Christ was not raised from the dead, our preaching is empty, and your faith is useless. We would be false witnesses if we had told you God raised Christ from the dead when it wasn't so. If God didn't raise Christ, your faith means nothing and you're still in your sins—and those who have died in Christ are gone forever. If there is hope only for the living, we are to be pitied above all people.

"But Christ did rise from the dead, like the first fruit of a great harvest. By Adam came death, but by Christ came life. First is the resurrection of Christ, then the resurrection of believers when He comes again. After that He will turn the kingdom back over to the Father. But first He will put an end to all human power and authority, because He's been put in charge until He defeats all His enemies. The last enemy to be destroyed is death. When the Scripture says, 'in charge of everything,' it does not include the Father, because He was the One who put Christ in charge originally. And when Christ completes His work, He Himself will be subject to God, who gave Him this responsibility, that the Father may be all in all (1 Cor. 15:1-28).

## Questions

"Why would some of you get baptized for those who are dead if there is no Resurrection? That's strange. Why do we risk our lives by preaching the gospel? Not a day goes by that I'm not in danger of being killed. Do you think I'd risk my life if I didn't care about you and believe in the Resurrection?

"Here in Ephesus I feel like I'm in an arena fighting off wild beasts. Do you think I'm doing this for my own benefit in some way? If there's no Resurrection, then we might as well eat, drink, and party, because tomorrow we'll die.

"Don't be deceived. You know that keeping bad company corrupts good behavior. I'm ashamed to tell you this, but some of you act as if you don't know God. So wake up to the righteousness of Christ and stop your sinning (1 Cor. 15:29-34).

## Answers

"There are still some skeptics among you saying, 'Is there really a resurrection? If the body is dead, how can people get another body? That's impossible.' That's faulty logic. Look at nature. When you sow seeds, they must die before there can be a harvest. And you don't harvest the same seeds that went into the ground. That's how God planned it.

"All bodies are not the same. People have one kind of body and animals, birds, and fish have different kinds. So in God's plan there are earthly bodies and heavenly ones. You see the same in the sky. There's the glory of the sun, the moon, and the stars, each with its own kind of glory.

"That's also true of the resurrection. Earthly bodies die, but heavenly bodies will not. Here we have a natural body, but in heaven we'll have a supernatural one. Our present bodies are weak, but our future bodies will be strong and powerful. Our natural bodies are like seeds sown to give us supernatural spiritual bodies.

"As the Scripture says, 'Adam was created from the dust of the ground and became a living being.' But the second Adam was conceived by the Holy Spirit and is the Giver of Life. The natural man was created first, then the spiritual man. Like Adam, our bodies are made of dust, but now we have been born again. We came into the world in the likeness of Adam, but now that we have been born again, we reflect the image of Jesus Christ.

"Brothers and sisters, in our sinful bodies of flesh and blood we cannot enter the kingdom of heaven. What is perishable cannot live where nothing perishes. Let me share with you a mystery. We will not sleep in death forever; we'll be resurrected. In the blink of an eye we'll be changed. God's trumpet will sound, and those who have died in Christ will be raised and given bodies that never perish. We will put on immortality! When that happens, then the Scripture will be fulfilled: 'Death has been swallowed up in victory! Where is the triumph of the grave? Where is the sting of death?' The sting of death is sin, and sin is the breaking of God's law. But thanks be to God, who gives us victory over sin and death through the Lord Jesus Christ.

"So, my dear brothers and sisters, stand firm in the faith. Don't be moved! Do the work of the Lord, knowing that what you do for Him will not be lost (1 Cor. 15:35-58).

### A Visit

"Before I come, collect the donations you want me to take to our destitute members in Jerusalem who need help. The other churches throughout Galatia are doing the same thing.

"After you announce this in church on Sabbath, let each one sit down on the first day of the week and set aside what he can give, according to how God has blessed him. I don't want this done after I come. As soon as I get there, I want to write a letter to our people in Judea, explaining the purpose of these donations. We'll send the money, together with letters from the other churches, to Jerusalem. You pick the men who should go, and if I have to go with them, I will, although I'd rather go later.

"From Ephesus I have to go through Macedonia first; then I'll come to see you. I might spend the winter with you—we'll see. If I do, you can then send me on my way when the Lord asks me to go. I don't want my visit to be just a short one. Lord willing, I want to spend some time with you. But for now I need to stay in Ephesus a little longer. An opportunity has just opened for the gospel to be preached more fully, which I can't pass up, even though I'll be facing some strong opposition.

"In the meantime, I'll be sending Timothy to see you. When he comes, welcome him with open arms. Don't turn against him—listen to him. He's doing the Lord's work, just as I am. Then send him back to me. Others will probably be coming with him.

"I strongly encouraged Apollos and those with him to visit you also. He's not willing to go just yet, but he'll come when the Lord opens the way (1 Cor. 16:1-12).

### Closing Thoughts

"Take courage, stay awake, and be strong. I urge you to listen to men like Stephanus. He and his family were the first converts of mine, and from the beginning they have been doing all they can for God's people. And there are others like him with whom you need to work.

"I was so glad to see Stephanus, Fortunatus, and Achaicus. It was like fellowshipping with you. They refreshed my spirit, and I'm sure they do the same for you. Look up to people like that and respect them.

"The churches throughout Asia Minor send their greetings, especially those affectionate brothers and sisters meeting in the house of Aquila and Priscilla. When you come to church, show this same affection by greeting each other as is appropriate.

"These last few lines are in my own handwriting so no one can say this letter is not from me.

"If anyone scorns the Lord Jesus Christ, let him go his way. He's not one of us, not one of you. Maranatha!—Christ has come and will come again. The grace of the Lord Jesus be with you. I love you all in Christ" (1 Cor. 16:13–24).

# fifteen

# Troubles

After Paul wrote to the Corinthians, he stayed in Ephesus a little longer, because an opportunity had opened for him to preach the gospel more fully. But soon the opposition became so strong that he decided to leave and visit the churches in Macedonia again, go on to Corinth, and travel from there to Jerusalem. After that his plans were to go to Rome and also to Spain.

Paul had sent Timothy and Erastus on to Corinth by way of Macedonia with his letter to remind the churches of the collection for the poor in Jerusalem. He would follow later. It was not long after Timothy had left that opposition began over what was called the "Christian Way."

A craftsman named Demetrius made little silver shrines housing the love goddess Artemis, also called Diana. Because he was losing a lot of business, he called the craftsmen of similar trades together and said to them, "Listen, men, you know that we prospered because of Diana. But this man Paul has convinced people everywhere that Diana is not a god. He is not only ruining our local business, but our tourist trade as well. At this rate we'll not only lose our business, but Diana and her temple will mean nothing, and people everywhere will stop coming here to worship."

When the craftsmen heard this, they became angry and started chanting, "Great is Diana!" Soon a crowd gathered and the whole city was in confusion about what was going on. The people grabbed Gaius and Aristarchus from Macedonia and shoved them into the arena. Paul wanted to rush in to help his friends, but the believers held him back. Even some city officials sent him a note telling Paul to stay away.

In the arena the people were shouting one thing and another. It was utter confusion. Some didn't even understand what it was all about. Then the Jews in the crowd pushed Alexander, one of their leaders, up front to tell the people that the Jews had nothing to do with Paul. Alexander motioned to the crowd and was ready to defend the Jews, but when the people saw who he was, they began shouting, "Great is Diana of the Ephesians! Great is Diana of the Ephesians!" This went on for almost two hours.

Finally, the city clerk quieted the crowd by saying, "People of Ephesus, who doesn't know that our city has been made the guardian of the temple of Diana and that her image fell like a meteor from heaven as a gift from Zeus, the chief of the gods? These facts can't be denied. So you need to calm down before you do something reckless. You brought Gaius and Aristarchus here, who have done nothing against Diana. They haven't blasphemed her or desecrated her temple. If Demetrius and the craftsmen have a complaint to make, they can bring it to court. There are always judges available to hear the case. If you want anything settled, let's do it legally. If word gets to Rome that we've had a riot without a cause, what can we say?" Then he dismissed the crowd and the people went home.

This was when Paul decided it would be best for him to leave Ephesus. He called the leading disciples together to encourage them. After praying for them, he hugged each one and then left for Macedonia.

He was hoping to meet Titus in Troas and take advantage of the opportunity that had opened there to preach the gospel more fully. When Titus didn't come, Paul went on to Philippi. That's where Titus caught up with him and gave him a preliminary report of how things were turning around in Corinth. Later Timothy arrived to give Paul a more complete report. That's when Paul decided to write this second letter to the Corinthians:

"Greetings from Paul, an apostle of Jesus Christ by the will of God, and from Timothy, who is here with me. May the grace and peace of God our Father and Jesus Christ our Lord be with all of you in Corinth and with all the churches in Asia Minor.

"Praise be to God, the Father of our Lord and Savior, who is merciful and comforts us in all our troubles so that we can comfort others using the same help we have received from God.

"Just as Christ suffered for us, we share in His sufferings for you. It is for your salvation that we are enduring all this. If God helps us, it is so we can help you. Our hope and faith in you is strong, for we know that as you suffer for the Lord, you will receive the help and comfort you need.

"Brothers and sisters, we want you to know that the persecutions we endured in Asia Minor were terrible. We gave up all hope of making it through alive. On top of that, we were very worried about you. All this taught us not to rely on ourselves, but to put our total trust in God. He delivered us in the past, is delivering us in the present, and will deliver us again.

"We thank you and others for helping us with your prayers. Many of you have thanked God for our ministry. God will not forget this, and He will bless you for it.

"We served you in good conscience, with pure motives, and in godly sincerity. We did not rely on human wisdom, but on God's grace, working for people everywhere and especially for you. The things I wrote to you in my first letter are things you needed to understand, and you did, for which I'm grateful. I hope this mutual trust we now have will continue. Just as you are proud of us, we are proud of you. It will be that way when the Lord Jesus comes and we'll be together in heaven (Acts 19:21-41; 20:1; 2 Cor. 1:1-14).

### Changed Plans

"I intended to come to see you before visiting the churches in Macedonia so I could personally help you. Then I had planned to go back to Macedonia and return to you so you could help me get ready to go to Judea. That way we could have two visits.

"I was not planning this trip with a yes-or-no attitude as you might think, deciding whether to visit you or not. God doesn't work that way and neither do we. When He says yes or no, He means it. That's the way Silas, Timothy, and I first brought the gospel message to you, with a positive yes, not with a yes-no, or maybe it's so. All of God's promises are given with a reliable yes, never with an uncertain no. Amen!

"We give all the glory to God, because He is the One who strengthens us in Christ, as He does you. And through the gift of the Holy Spirit He has given us His seal of approval as a guarantee of what is to come.

"God is my witness that I decided not to come to you to straighten you out, because I'm not your lord and master. We're just God's workers, doing all we can to make you glad about your faith. I didn't want to come and confront you in your sins to make you sad. That's why I wrote to you first so that when I did come, we could greet each other with joy. I was troubled and heartbroken, and I wrote to you with tears in my eyes. I'm not telling you this so you'll feel sorry for me, but so you'll know how much I love you (2 Cor. 1:15—2:4).

### Forgiveness

"In my first letter I asked you to discipline the man who was having an incestuous relationship with his father's new wife. He has saddened all of us by doing this. Now that you've disciplined him, don't overdo it. You need to forgive him and love him so he doesn't feel like he's been totally rejected. This will test the other side of your Christianity. Whom you forgive, I forgive as well. For your sake I've already forgiven him in the spirit of Christ. We need to do this so Satan won't push us into being a strict, unforgiving people.

"When I left Ephesus and got to Troas, I saw a great opportunity to further the gospel there again. I expected to meet Titus there, but he wasn't able to come. I was so concerned about you that I decided to leave Troas and cross over into Macedonia, and from there go on south to see you. Finally, Titus came with the good news that you're making progress. What a relief! (2 Cor. 2:5-13).

## Gratitude

"Thanks be to God, who always causes us to triumph in Christ and works through us to spread His love wherever we go. This is the fragrance of life to those who are being saved and the scent of death to those who are perishing. Who is adequate for such an awesome ministry?

"We are not like some who are peddling the Word of God for profit, but we preach the Word of God in sincerity as if in the presence of Christ—messengers sent by God. Does this sound like we're recommending ourselves to you? We don't need letters of recommendation. You are our letters of recommendation, which everyone can read. You are living epistles written by Christ, not with ink, but by the Holy Spirit, not on stone tablets, but on the tablets of your hearts.

"Our confidence is totally in God because of what Christ has done. We have no confidence in our own qualifications as if we were heroes, but in Him who qualified us. We are servants of God, ministers of His renewed covenant with the human race. These qualifications are not based on letters of recommendation, but on the life-giving power of the Holy Spirit (2 Cor. 2:14–3:6).

## The Holy Spirit

"If the commandments written on stone were surrounded by the glory of God at Sinai, what about the ministry of the Holy Spirit? If the face of Moses reflected the glory of God so the people couldn't look at him until that glory faded away, what about the glory of the Holy Spirit and His ministry?

"The law can only condemn—it cannot give life. So if the giving of the law was a glorious event, the giving of the gospel far exceeds it. The glory of Sinai has passed away, but the glory of the gospel remains.

"This is what gives us hope and boldness. We don't have to put a veil over our faces as Moses had to do because the people were blinded by the light. The people of Israel who read the Old Testament today have a veil over their hearts. However, once we give our hearts to Christ, the Holy Spirit removes the veil, and we can see and understand.

"Where the Holy Spirit is, there is freedom. Our eyes are uncovered and we see the face of the Lord reflected as in a mirror. As we look at Him, we are transformed into His image, and through the power of the Holy Spirit we reflect His glory (2 Cor. 3:7-18).

## The Gospel

"God has been merciful by calling us into the ministry, so we too are merciful and never lose heart. We will not shame the ministry, nor will we distort the Word of God. Deceit and craftiness have no place in the ministry. We preach the truth and, in the sight of God, commend ourselves to people's consciences.

"If our preaching is hard to understand, it is made this way by those whose minds have been blinded by the god of this world. That's why they can't see the light of the glory of the gospel and of Christ, who came in the likeness of God.

"We're not here to preach about ourselves and what we have done, but about what Jesus Christ has done. He is the Lord and we are His servants. It is the God of Creation who said, 'Let there be light,' and He lets His light shine in our hearts to give us a knowledge of Himself as seen in Jesus Christ.

"We have this treasure of knowledge in these clay bodies of ours, but the power of our preaching does not come from us—it is from God. We are never in doubt or despair, never crushed. We are persecuted, but never without Jesus as our Friend. We are knocked down and beaten, but not dead, carrying in our bodies the marks of death as a reminder of the death of Jesus Christ. While death is our lot, life has come to you.

"But we all have the same faith. As David says in Scripture, 'I believe, therefore I speak.' We know that God, who raised Jesus from the dead, will also resurrect us and, together with you, take us to be with Him. All that God has done in Christ is for your sake. And His grace is offered to everyone so that more and more people may be saved, and our thanksgiving swells into a mighty chorus to the glory of God.

"So let's not lose heart. *We* don't. Even though our physical bodies are wearing out, our inner selves are being renewed day by day. Compared to eternity, our present suffering is but a moment. There's no comparison between our present condition and the glory that will follow. We don't look at the things we can see, but at the things we can't see—not at what is temporary, but at what is eternal (2 Cor. 4:1-18).

## WITNESS: Acts Through Revelation

### Assurance

"We know that even if our bodies are killed, we have new and glorious bodies waiting for us in heaven. We long to be there. We feel like we're not dressed and wish we could have such bodies now and that our earthly mortality could be swallowed up by eternal life.

"It is God who is preparing us for these heavenly bodies and who has given us the Holy Spirit as a guarantee of what He has in mind for us. That's why we're always full of courage, even though we're not in heaven. We live by faith, not by sight. It would be great to be out of this body and with the Lord.

"Our purpose in life is to please the Lord, whether we're here or there, because we all must appear before Christ, our Judge, to be rewarded for what we have done while in this body of ours, whether it was good or bad.

"That's why we try to persuade people to give their hearts to Christ. God knows what we're doing, and I hope that deep in your conscience you know that too.

"We're not thinking about ourselves, but about you. You have a right to be proud of our ministry and what we're doing. It will help you to answer those who like to talk about themselves and what they're doing, but don't have Christ in their hearts. If we sound like we're too zealous, it is for the Lord and you.

"It is the love of Christ that motivates us. He died for everyone because we're all doomed to die. He died for our sins and we should not live for ourselves, but for Him who rose from the dead and is living for us.

"At first we thought of Christ as just another man, but not anymore. And it's the same with other people. No longer do we look at them from a human point of view. Anyone who has accepted Christ is a new creation! What is old has passed away, and what is new has come!

"This new creation comes from God, who through Christ brings us to Himself. This is what our ministry is all about—bringing people to God. This means that God is not holding our sins against us, but is extending to us His love and friendship.

"We are ambassadors for God, who is pleading with you through us. And we plead with you on behalf of Christ, to let God change you. Give yourselves completely to Him. He's your Friend! God put all our sins on Christ, who knew no sin, so we would become righteous through Him (2 Cor. 5:1-21).

### Purpose

"As workers together with God, we beg you to not waste the grace He has given you. As He says in Scripture: 'When the time came for me to help you, I did. I heard you and came to save you.' Look, now is the time for you to respond and make sure of your salvation.

"We try not to offend you or anyone else so no one will have an excuse to turn against our ministry and the gospel. As God's servants, we have recommended ourselves to you by enduring persecutions, hardships, endless troubles, beatings, imprisonments, riots, mobs, overwork, and often going without sleep and food. We have shown you that we are God's servants by our moral purity, patience, kindness, love, and honesty, all through the power of the Holy Spirit. Righteousness is our weapon to defend the gospel and attack evil.

"We continue our ministry, whether honored or dishonored, praised or slandered. We are accused of lying while telling the truth. We are unknown, yet well known; constantly in danger of being killed, yet still alive; scourged, yet rejoicing; poor and destitute, yet making many rich; and having nothing, yet having everything" (2 Cor. 6:1-10).

# sixteen

# An Appeal

Paul continued his second letter:

"Brothers and sisters in Corinth, listen to me! We have opened our hearts and spoken frankly to you. Our love for you has no limits. Why would you limit your love for us? You're our children in the Lord! Open your hearts to us!

"Don't partner with unbelievers. What connection does righteousness have with lawlessness? Are light and darkness the same? Does Christ work together with Satan? What does a believer have in common with unbelievers? What does God have to do with pagan idols?

"You are the temples of God! Just as He said in Scripture: 'I will live in you and walk among you. I will be your God and you will be My people. So come out from the world; be separate and don't touch what is unclean. I will be a Father to you and you will be My children.'

"Because we have such promises, let's stop doing things that defile our bodies and kill our spirits and faith. Let's live holy lives out of respect for God and what He has done for us.

"Please make room in your hearts for us. We haven't wronged, cheated, or taken advantage of anyone. I told you before that we have you in our heart; we live for you and are willing to die for you.

"I love you and am proud of you. But in the midst of our suffering we were still worried about you, wondering how you would take what I said in my first letter. Even after we left Ephesus and came to Macedonia, we had troubles on the outside and fear on the inside. But we were comforted when Titus came and gave us a good report. He told us how well you treated him, how you took my first letter to heart, and how you had changed your ways. Also, he told us that you are eager to see me and are sorry for what you did. When I heard that, I was thrilled. I was so happy, more than I can tell you.

"I do not regret writing that letter, even though I worried that it would hurt you. But I'm glad I wrote it, because even though it hurt, it did make you change your ways and live for God. So we didn't actually hurt you—we helped you.

"Being truly sorry brings on a godly sorrow which produces a repentance that turns you away from sin and ends in salvation. This leaves no regrets, because it's different from human sorrow. Look at what godly sorrow did for you—how eager and earnest you are now to serve the Lord and how determined you are to be a pure church. You really became alarmed—and rightly so—when I told you that you needed to do something about the man who had relations with his father's new wife, and you took care of it. You disciplined him, which was necessary. You truly have proven yourselves.

"And even though I wrote to you, asking you to do something, it wasn't because I had in mind the father who was wronged or the son who did the wrong. What I had in mind was to show your devotion to God.

"We've really been encouraged by what Titus has told us, and we rejoice to see how happy he is. He is so excited over the way you've helped him. You have put his mind at ease. I had told him what good people you are and you didn't disappoint me. We have always been honest and straightforward with you. We've told others about our faith in you, and according to Titus, what we said has been proven true. His love for you keeps growing every time he thinks back on how warmly you welcomed him and how eager you were to do what he asked you to do. I'm so happy about all this and have total confidence in you (2 Cor. 6:11-18; 7:1-16).

### Helping Others

"Brothers and sisters, I want you to know that the grace of God has been poured out on our churches in Macedonia. They have gone through a lot of suffering, yet they're full of joy and, in their extremity, have given beyond their means to help our poverty-stricken members in Judea. They not only gave more than we expected or hoped for, but gave their hearts to the Lord all over again.

"That's why we urged Titus to finish what we started—to make sure you have a part in this offering, also. You are so much better off than the other churches. You're strong in faith, in your ability to share the gospel, in knowledge, and in your love for the Lord. So we want you to excel in generosity, also. I'm not commanding you to do this, but am testing the genuineness of your love for God by asking you to do something for others.

"Christ is our example. Although He had all the riches of heaven, for our sake He became poor so you could become rich. It's to your spiritual advantage to finish what you started a year ago. You were the first ones to respond to help our members in Judea, so I appeal to you to finish what you started and give what you can. What's important to God is not how much you give, but your willingness to give.

"I don't mean that you should try to outdo all the other churches and have this offering become a burden, but give according to what you have. If the time should come when you're in need, they will help you. As the Scripture says about collecting the manna: 'Those who gathered much didn't have more, and those who gathered less had all they needed' (2 Cor. 8:1-15).

### Collecting the Offering

"I praise the Lord for putting the same love that I have for you into the heart of Titus. He'll be going back to deliver this letter, not only because we have asked him to, but because he wants to go.

"We're sending a brother with him who is well respected among the churches for his work in spreading the gospel. Also, he has been chosen to go with us to take this offering to Judea. This is good, because we want to avoid any idea that I'm handling the money or using any part of it for myself. We want to do what's right, not only in the sight of the Lord, but also in the eyes of others. Many times we have tested the honesty of this brother whom we are sending with Titus and his fellow worker. He is eager to meet you because of what we've told him about you and has the same confidence in you that we have.

"If there are some who have questions about Titus himself, he is my partner in the work. And if there are questions about the other two, they've been chosen by the churches. So receive them with open arms and show your love for them, so that when they return, their church will know what we said about you is true (2 Cor. 8:16-24).

### Generosity

"It's not necessary for me to write to you about the importance of this offering, because I know how willing you are to help. I keep telling the churches here in Macedonia about your zeal and how eager you were to have a part in this project even a year ago.

"That's why we're sending these brothers ahead of us to help collect your offering, so when I and some believers from Macedonia come, they'll find everything ready, just as I told them it would be. We're sending these brothers not only to collect your offering, but so you can give without pressure from me. I am confident you will show these Macedonian visitors how generous you are.

"But one thing is for sure: those who sow sparingly will reap sparingly, and those who give generously will reap generously. So let each one give from his heart as he has decided, not because he has to, but because he wants to. God loves it when you give cheerfully. He will bless you for it and will help you to continue to give.

"As the Scripture says, 'God scatters His blessings widely. His goodness never ends.' He gives seed to the sower and provides bread for the hungry.

"This is true spiritually also. As you sow unselfishly, you will produce a harvest of gratefulness. Those whom you help through your offering will thank God for your generosity, obedience, and faith in the gospel of the Lord Jesus Christ. They will pray for you and in their hearts reach out to you, because they will see what God's grace has done for you.

"Thanks be to God for His indescribable gift of love and grace!" (2 Cor. 9:1-15).

## Comparisons

"I plead with you in the meekness and gentleness of Christ to listen to me. Some think that I'm bold and courageous only in my letters when I'm away from you, and that all this confidence and boldness is gone when I have to face you. You conclude that I'm no different from any other human being. In one sense you're right. But when it comes to spiritual things, we don't function on a human level. We're empowered by God and use spiritual weapons to tear down every false argument and arrogant attitude against the gospel to bring people into obedience to Christ.

"If any of you are so confident of yourselves and boast that you belong to Christ, you need to think again, because we belong to Christ too. I don't want to say too much about the authority God has given me, lest I be misunderstood. But God has given me authority to build you up—not to lord it over you and tear you down.

"Some of you still say that while my letters are powerful, my physical presence is weak and that my personality and speaking are not very impressive. Let me assure those of you who think this way that I can be just as bold when I'm with you as I have been in my letters.

"We don't keep recommending ourselves to you as some do. They're always comparing themselves to others and measuring themselves by themselves. By doing this, they show they're not as intelligent as they think they are.

"We know our limitations. But let me tell you what God has put in our hearts to do for you. This is not about our authority, even though we need to remind you that we were the ones who brought the gospel to you.

By saying this, we're not trying to take credit for what others have done for you. The important thing is that your faith continues to grow and that our work of spreading the gospel continues to expand. There are many places that need to be reached. So we can't just concentrate on you alone.

"As the Scripture says, 'He who glories, let him glory in the Lord.' It is not those who keep recommending themselves that the Lord approves, but those whom He recommends (2 Cor. 10:1-18).

### Deception

"This may sound foolish, but bear with me. I'm concerned because I gave you in marriage to Christ. But I'm worried that the serpent might deceive you (as he did Eve) and lead you away from the simplicity of the gospel.

"If someone comes and tells you things about Jesus that are different from what we have told you, it's a false gospel. It's not the gospel you got from us. Why would you listen to such a person and put up with him?

"I'm not inferior to these so-called great apostles. Even if, as they say, I'm not the best speaker, I'm not dumb. Did I do wrong by humbling myself to make you look good? Or was it wrong for me to bring the gospel to you free of charge? Other churches gladly supported me so I could help you.

"When I was in need, I said nothing, because I didn't want to be a burden to you. Brothers from Macedonia came and brought me what I needed. My motive has not changed. I still don't want to be a burden to you. Christ is working through me to help you, and I'm not ashamed to say so. Why do I say this? Is it because I think highly of myself? God knows that isn't true.

"I will continue to serve you. This will put a stop to those who want to take my place because they claim to be sent by Christ, which isn't true. They're deceitful and masters of disguise. This shouldn't surprise you, because Satan himself is deceitful and a master of disguise, transforming himself into an angel of light. Don't be surprised if his followers do the same thing. The day will come when they'll be judged according to their works (2 Cor. 11:1-15).

### Suffering for Christ

"You may think that what I'm going to say next is foolish of me because it will look like I'm proud. But I'm going to say it anyway, even if it sounds like I'm not lifting up the Lord, but talking about myself as human beings usually do.

"You have some of these false apostles among you who like to talk about themselves, and you put up with it. They treat you as if you were their servants. They exploit you and even slap you in the face when you don't agree with them. Maybe I've lost your respect by not acting as they do, and that's why people think I'm a weak leader.

"Let me mention some things to you, even though it's foolish for me to say so. Are these false apostles Hebrews? So am I. Are they committed Israelites? So am I. Are they descendants of Abraham? So am I. Are they servants of Christ? It's foolish for me to say, but I'm more of a servant of Christ than they are.

"I've worked harder to spread the gospel than they have. I've been imprisoned, beaten, and have faced death many times. Five times I was whipped by the Jews and given 40 lashes minus one, which is their custom. Three times I was beaten with rods by the Romans. Once I was stoned and left for dead. Three times I was shipwrecked, and once I was adrift in the open sea for a whole day and night.

"On my missionary journeys I've crossed swollen rivers, faced dangers from robbers, and been attacked by my own countrymen or nonbelievers. These were some of the dangers I had to face from false apostles wherever I went, whether in the city, in the country, on ships, and even in churches. There were days of weariness, hard work, sleepless nights, hunger, thirst, and not enough clothing to keep warm. In addition to all this, there was the everyday concern about the churches.

"Does this sound like I'm a weak leader? Do I not face sin with courage? If I have to talk about things that make me sound weak and lack courage, I can do that too. God the Father and the Lord Jesus know that I'm not lying when I tell you that while preaching in Damascus, I escaped by climbing into a basket. The brothers helped me get in and then lowered me through a window over the city wall (2 Cor. 11:16-33).

### Honored by Christ

"It's been foolish for me to tell you all this, but you forced me into it. So I might as well tell you about the revelations and visions I've had. About 14 years ago I was taken up to the highest heaven. Whether it was bodily or only in spirit, I don't know. God knows. I was taken to Paradise and heard many things.

"Let me talk about this as if it had happened to someone else, because I don't want to be so foolish as to keep talking about myself. I need to keep reminding myself that I'm just a weak human being. For me to do this is best for everyone. I will always tell you the truth. But I don't want people to have a higher opinion of me than they should.

"To keep me from becoming proud, God gave me what you might

call a 'thorn in the flesh,' which Satan is using to get me discouraged. Three times I've asked the Lord to give me back my full eyesight. All He said was, 'My grace is all you need, because My power is seen through your weakness.' I would rather be weak so the power of Christ can be seen in all that I do. That's why I can be happy in the midst of slander, hardships, and persecutions, all of which I endure for His sake, because when I'm weak and surrendered to Him, then I'm strong.

"It was foolish for me to tell you all this about me. I wish I hadn't. But you forced me into it because of these false apostles of whom you speak so highly. I gave you evidences of true apostleship by what I endured for you, by the miracles I performed, and by the success of the gospel in changing your lives. The only thing I didn't do for you, which I did for other churches, is give you an opportunity to help me financially. If that was wrong, forgive me (2 Cor. 12:1-13).

### Another Visit

"Now for the third time I'm ready to come to see you. I have no plans to be a financial burden to you, because I don't want what you have—I want *you*. Parents pay for their children, not children for their parents. And you are my children. So I will most gladly be spent for you, even though the more I love you, the less you seem to love me.

"Be that as it may. What's important is that I caught you with the gospel net and pulled you in. I have not used you to my advantage, nor will Titus and the other brother I'm sending, because we think the same and have the same interest in you.

"If this sounds like we're defending ourselves, let me assure you that's not so. Everything we do is for you. We're telling you this in the sight of God and the Lord Jesus Christ.

"In spite of the good reports, I'm still afraid that when I come, I won't find you the kind of people I wish you were. I'm afraid I'll find you arguing among yourselves, angry, jealous, selfish, ambitious, gossiping, conceited, arrogant, criticizing each other, and with your church worship in total disarray. And I'm afraid God will humble me in your sight by letting me weep over your continued sexual immorality, instead of being the strong leader you want me to be (2 Cor. 12:14-21).

### Settling Things

"When I come this time, we will settle some of these things once and for all. As the Scripture says, 'Everything is to be settled by at least two or three witnesses.' I told you this before and now I am putting it in writing, that I will not be easy on those still living in sin. If you want proof that

Christ is speaking through me, you shall have it. Christ is not a weakling, even though He submitted to die on a cross. He chose to become weak, but is now alive with the full power of God. We too are weak but will not hesitate to exercise the power of God for your own good.

"So examine your hearts and take a good look at your actions to see if you're still in the faith. If you fail the test, do something about it. I'm praying for you. But I don't want you to focus so much on the test, but on doing what's right, even though it may look as if you've failed.

"We can't destroy the truth. The gospel will win out, no matter what we do. So we're glad to be weak if it can make you strong. We pray that you will grow to be mature in Jesus Christ. I'm telling you these things before I come so that when I do, I won't have to be hard on you. God has given me authority for building you up, not tearing you down (2 Cor. 13:1-10).

### Greetings

"Finally, brothers and sisters, let me close this letter and give it to Titus to take it to you. Be of good courage. Set things right. Live in peace. May God's love and peace be with all of you. Give each other a hug for me. The church members here send their greetings.

"Now may the grace of our Lord and Savior Jesus Christ, the love of God, and the companionship of the Holy Spirit be with you" (2 Cor. 13:11-13).

# seventeen

# Future Plans

After Titus left with Paul's second letter to the Corinthians, Paul and his friends finished going through Macedonia encouraging the churches. They finally arrived at Corinth. It was a joy to see that most of the church members had changed for the better and were loyal to Christ, but some still rejected Paul's leadership and continued their immoral lifestyle. Though Paul loved them, he had to take action and discipline them, no matter how painful it was to him.

Paul and his friends stayed in Corinth for three months. He had planned to stay longer, but when the Jews plotted against him, he decided to leave and not bring unnecessary trouble on the members. His long-range plans were to take the funds collected from the churches, including Corinth, to Jerusalem first, then visit the church in Rome, and from there take the gospel to Spain.

At first he thought of taking a ship and sailing directly to Syria, from there making his way to Jerusalem. Then he changed his mind and decided to backtrack through Macedonia, catching a ship at Philippi, and sailing to Troas. Eight men accompanied him: Sopater, Aristarchus, Secundus, Gaius, Timothy, Tychicus, Trophimus, and Luke. When they got to Philippi, Paul decided to stay there to keep the Festival of Unleavened Bread. Luke stayed with him, but the rest went on to Troas. Five days later Paul and Luke joined them at Troas and stayed there for a week (Acts 20:2-6).

### Romans

Before Paul and his friends left Corinth for Jerusalem with the offerings, Paul wrote this letter to the church in Rome:

"From Paul, a willing servant of Jesus Christ, called to be an apostle to take the good news about God everywhere. This good news has to do with Jesus Christ, His Son, who came to save us, according to God's promise in Scripture. Jesus Christ was born from the lineage of David and powerfully showed Himself to be the Son of God by living a holy life and by His resurrection from the dead.

"Through Him we have received grace, and I was called to be an apostle to take the gospel to all nations for His name's sake. It is this gospel to which you have been called and which you have accepted.

"So this letter is to all believers in Rome who also are set apart to serve Christ. Grace and peace to you from God our Father and from the Lord Jesus Christ (Rom. 1:1-7).

## The Gospel

"I thank God for all of you, because we hear about your faith wherever we go. God is my witness that I never stop praying for you. And I'm praying that He will let me come to visit you. I really want to see you. I can help you spiritually and you can be an encouragement to me. That way we can help each other.

"A number of times I planned to come to see you, but something always came up. I would like to bring people to Christ in Rome also, as I have done in many other places. This is my gift to the Lord for what He has done for me. I'm accountable to Him because He asked me to take the gospel to the Greeks and Romans, to pagans and barbarians, and to the wise and the foolish. That's why I'm also eager and ready to preach the gospel in Rome.

"I'm not ashamed of the gospel. Why should I be? It's the good news of God's love and power to save all who believe. It came to the Jews first and now is going to the Gentiles. It is through the gospel that the goodness of God is revealed, so that by faith we stand righteous before Him. As it is written, 'The just shall live by faith' (Rom. 1:8-17).

## The Problem of Evil

"God is displeased with those who suppress the truth and live unrighteously. He is against all sin and ungodliness. He has put a sense of right and wrong in every heart. His goodness and tenderness can be seen in the beauty of nature, and His power can be seen in the forces of nature. This way people have no excuse.

"Even though people knew God, they didn't accept Him or thank Him. As a result, they didn't think right and their hearts were darkened. They thought they were wise, but they became fools. They carved out human images, birds, animals, creeping things, and even cobras and worshipped them as God. So He let them do what they wanted. They ended up worshipping their own bodies and, by their immorality, dishonored

Him. They exchanged the truth of God for a lie and became slaves of things, rather than serving the Creator and being a blessing to Him.

"They gradually became worse and were soon caught up in all kinds of passions. Women did what was unnatural and had sexual relations with women, and men did what was against their nature and had sexual relations with men. So they reaped the consequences of such shameful acts with many diseases.

"Because they turned against God, their minds were filled with all kinds of wicked thoughts. They became greedy, selfish, heartless, and cruel; and they lied, cheated, stole, fought, murdered, became arrogant, hated God, disobeyed parents, broke agreements, and had no pity.

"They knew these things were wrong and that those who did them deserved to die, but they did them anyway. And not only did they do them, but they approved of others doing them, also (Rom. 1:18-32).

## Judging Others

"Those of you who know better should be careful not to condemn people, because you're doing some of the same things. So you're condemning yourselves too. We know that God judges everyone the same. He measures by what is right and in no way condones wickedness. Do you think He's going to make an exception when you do some of the same things you condemn in others?

"Have you forgotten the kindness of God, His mercy, goodness, and patience? If you would focus on these things, you would repent and change your ways. But because you're so stubborn and unwilling to change, you're adding to God's displeasure. As the Scripture says, 'God will reward everyone based on what he has done.' Those who continue to do good will be given immortality, but those who are arrogant and continue their sinful ways will feel the displeasure of God and be destroyed.

"God will make no difference between Jews and Greeks, but will treat everyone alike. He will bless those who do good with His peace, but will withhold His peace from those who do evil. They will reap the consequences of what they have done, for God is not partial.

"Those who sin without knowing God's law can't be judged by it. And it's not those who know about the law who are considered righteous, but those who actually live by it. If the Greeks who don't have the law live by what they know, it shows that God is working on their hearts. They are better off than those who have the law and know what's right and don't do it.

"The day is coming when God will judge everyone by Jesus Christ, according to the gospel which I have been preaching (Rom. 2:1-16).

## Pride

"If you as a Jew depend on your law-keeping to be right with God and pride yourself in your knowledge of what God wants you to do because you have the Scriptures, be careful. If you become so confident that you think you're the light of the world and the great teachers of truth, how about teaching yourselves?

"You tell people not to steal, but do you steal? You tell people not to commit adultery, but what about you? You tell people not to worship idols, but aren't you robbing God of His honor by worshipping His Temple and turning it into an idol?

"You're so confident of your relationship with God, yet you're constantly breaking His law. As the Scripture says, 'The name of God is cursed among unbelievers because of your behavior.'

"Being circumcised doesn't mean a thing if you're not living according to God's law. If those who are not circumcised keep the law, they're better off than you, and God accepts them as His people, circumcised or not. They will judge you, even though you have a written copy of the law. It's not circumcision of the flesh that's important, but circumcision of the heart. That's what makes a man a real Jew—not what's on the outside, but what's on the inside; not what is physical, but what is spiritual. It's not the praise of fellow Jews that's important, but praise that comes from God (Rom. 2:17-29).

"So what is the advantage of being a Jew? Much in every way, but most of all because we have the Scriptures. What if in the past some of our people did not believe as they should have? Did their unbelief change what God said? Absolutely not! What God said is still true, no matter what man says. As the Scripture points out, 'When you go to court and stand before a judge, the law does not change. You will be tried by what you have said and done.'

"If our sinfulness makes God's grace look good, wouldn't this make God unjust if He took His stand against sin? Absolutely not! Then God would have no right to judge anyone, much less the whole world. For example, if my dishonesty brings glory to God, why should He judge people? Forget such nonsense! If that were true, why not say, 'Let's all go out and sin to make God look good?' And if I'm a liar, as some say I am, why condemn me as a sinner? Let those who think this way about God be condemned (Rom. 3:1-8).

## Righteousness

"Are Jews better than Gentiles? No way! We are all sinners, Jews and Gentiles alike. As the Scripture says, 'No one is righteous, not even one.

No one understands, no one seeks God or feels his need of Him. They have all turned away from Me. No one is good, not even one. They lie, curse, are quick to kill, and wherever they go there's nothing but trouble. They don't know real peace and have no respect for God.'

"We know that whatever the law says, it says the same thing to everyone. So the whole world is guilty of breaking the law. This ends all arguments of self-righteousness.

"No one is declared righteous by keeping the law, either. The only thing the law can do is to point out sin and tell us that we need a Savior. This is what the gospel is all about, which Moses and the prophets have been telling us.

"Righteousness comes by faith in Jesus Christ, because all have sinned and fallen short of the glory of God. It is through God's grace that we are justified because of what Jesus has done for us. By His death He sprinkled, as it were, His blood on God's mercy seat and made atonement for our sins. This is why God is just when He declares sinners righteous, which He did even before Jesus came. He declared people righteous on the basis of their faith that He would send His Son to come and die for them. This justifies His previous forgiveness.

"So what should we boast about? What we did for God? Absolutely not! Salvation is based on faith, not on works. God is not only God of the Jews, but also God of the Gentiles. There is one God, and He will justify all who have faith in Christ, whether they're circumcised or not.

"Does this mean that keeping the law is not important? No way! On the contrary, because we love Him, we uphold the law (Rom. 3:9-31).

### Examples

"Look at Abraham! If anyone could have been justified by works, he could have. What does the Scripture say? 'Abraham *believed* what God said and this was credited to him as righteousness.'

"Does this mean that because our faith is to our credit, it doesn't matter what we do? It matters a great deal! Our good deeds are done, not to gain God's favor, but are based on our debt of gratitude to Him. That's why Abraham was not declared righteous by what he did, but because of his faith.

"Let's look at David. He talks about how blessed a man is who is declared righteous apart from what he does. Notice what he says: 'Blessed are those whose sins are forgiven. Blessed is the man whom the Lord will not charge with sin.'

"Is this blessedness available only to those who are circumcised and not to the uncircumcised? We just said that Abraham was credited with righteousness because of his faith. Was he circumcised? Not yet. Circumcision came afterward as a sign of faith. So this makes him the father of both the circumcised and the uncircumcised who have faith in God (Rom. 4:1-12).

## Promise

"God's promise to Abraham that he and his descendants would inherit the world is not based on keeping the law, but on faith. If it were based on obedience only, then faith is out and God's promise means nothing. The law tells us what sin is. If there were no law, there would be no sin. So the law is good. But salvation is by grace, which puts God's promise on solid ground. And His promise is to all who have the kind of faith that Abraham had. That's why the Scripture calls him the father of many nations.

"He believed what God said. He knew that God can raise the dead and create things out of nothing. His life was filled with faith and hope. He's the father of many nations, because God's promise included his descendants.

"Abraham showed his faith by believing when God said that he and Sarah would have a baby, even though Abraham was 100 years old and Sarah was 90. As time went on, his faith grew stronger because he knew that God keeps His promises. That's why he was declared righteous.

"This is recorded not only to show that Abraham was righteous, but also for our sakes. It is written to help those whose faith is anchored in God, who raised Jesus from the dead. Jesus not only died for our sins, but was raised from the dead so we, through Him, can stand in God's presence as righteous" (Rom. 4:13-25).

# Peace and Hope

Paul continued his letter:

"Therefore, through Jesus Christ we stand before God as if we had never sinned, and we are at peace. We have access to God's grace through faith, and our hearts thrill in anticipation of seeing Him in His glory. Even in the midst of suffering we are full of courage, because suffering develops perseverance, perseverance strengthens character, and character witnesses to our hope in Christ. That hope will never disappoint us. You see, the love God puts in our hearts comes through the Holy Spirit, whom He has given us as a gift (Rom. 5:1-5).

### Christ

"When we were weak and helpless, Christ came and died for us. He died for sinners, not for those who think they are righteous. Rarely will a man die for someone else—for a good person, maybe. Yet God showed how much He loves us by sending Christ to die for us while we were still His enemies.

"Now that we have been declared righteous because of Christ, we will be saved from the destruction to come. If we were made right with God by the death of His Son when we were sinners, how much more will we be helped by Him now that we have been declared righteous! Not only is this good news, but we are overjoyed that through Jesus Christ we are now God's friends again (Rom. 5:6-11).

### Grace

"One man brought sin into the world and death came in with it. As a result, everyone sins and everyone dies. And where sin is, there has to be a law, because without a law, there are no lawbreakers. But people died because of sin, even though they had not deliberately disobeyed and sinned against God like Adam did. This proves that the law was in effect even before it was written down and given to Moses.

"As strange as it may seem, Adam points to Christ. One man brought in sin and death, and one Man brought in forgiveness and grace. Grace is much stronger than sin. It also extends to everyone, not to condemn as sin does, but to redeem and cover sin. So if through one man sin came in and ruled, how much more will righteousness rule through Jesus Christ in the lives of those who accept God's gift of grace! Just as condemnation came through one act of a disobedient Adam, so abundant redemption came by one act of an obedient Jesus Christ.

"God wrote the law with His own finger and gave it to Moses so there would be no question about what sin is. But where there is a greater increase of sin, there is a greater outpouring of grace. Just as sin brings eternal death, so grace brings eternal life through Jesus Christ our Lord (Rom. 5:12-21).

### Freedom

"So what should we do? Should we continue sinning to make God's grace and forgiveness more evident? Absolutely not! How can we say we've died to sin if we continue sinning?

"Don't you know that when you were baptized in the name of Christ, you died to sin just as He died for you? You were buried in a watery grave and then raised from spiritual death to live a new life, just as Christ was buried and raised from the dead and lives to the glory of the Father.

"If we are made one with Him through baptism, we will continue to be one with Him by living a resurrected life. Our old life of sin was crucified with Him, so we're no longer slaves of sin. We are set free through Jesus Christ our Lord. If we died with Christ, we will also live with Him. He died one time and will never die again. Death has no control over Him. He died once for us—now He lives to the glory of God.

"So don't let sin rule your body. You are no longer under its power, but under the power of grace. Does this mean that if we sin, we shouldn't worry because we are under God's grace? No way! Don't you know that when you give in to sin, you become its slave? You are slaves to whomever you obey, whether it is sin, which leads to death, or righteousness which leads to life.

"But thanks be to God that, even though you were slaves to sin, you listened to the gospel and obeyed. Now you are freed from sin and have become servants of righteousness. Let me speak in human terms so you can understand what I'm trying to tell you. There was a time when you lived as if there were no law, but now you're living lives of obedience and righteousness. Before this, one sin led to another, but now you're becoming more and more like Christ.

"When you were slaves of sin, you felt no obligation to live righteously. Did it help you? Looking back, you're now ashamed of what you did. The end result would have been eternal death. But now you're a free people and servants of God, living for Him, the end result of which is eternal life. The wages for sinning is death, but the *gift* of God is eternal life through Jesus Christ our Lord (Rom. 6:1-23).

### Personal Experience

"Don't you know that people are under the law as long as they live? For example: a married woman is united with her husband as long as he lives—only if he dies is she free to marry someone else. If she marries someone else while her husband is still alive, she has broken the law and is considered an adulteress.

"Let's apply this spiritually. Your old life of sin has died, so now you are free to marry. Marry Christ, who has been raised from the dead. Then bring forth fruit to God as He did.

"Before this, we listened to our bodies and were controlled only by what we wanted. But the law set boundaries, showing that the fruit of our former lives would be death. Now things have changed. We are free from the law that leads to death, because we have died to our old lives. We now live new lives controlled by the Holy Spirit.

"So what should we say? Is the law bad? Absolutely not! I would not have known that I was selfish if the law had not said, 'Thou shalt not covet.' Sin produced in me all kinds of selfish desires and ambitions. Before the law convicted me of my selfishness, as far as I was concerned, I wasn't sinning. I was alive and well and zealous for the Lord. But when the commandment convicted me, self died. I had thought since I was keeping the law, I would be given eternal life, but the law actually condemned me. My sinful nature had deceived me and tried to kill me, so the commandment was actually for my own good. So there is no doubt that God's law is holy, just, and good.

"You asked how that which is good can kill me. Well, it wasn't the law that did it—it was my sinful nature. All the law did was to point out sin. The law has to do with what's spiritual. I am the one who's sinful.

"When I want to do what's right, sin urges me to do what's wrong, which I don't want to do, but sometimes I end up doing it. That's my sinful nature coming through. I love God's law, but there's this other law in my sinful nature which takes hold of me and gives me all kinds of trouble. Oh, wretched man that I am! Who is going to deliver me from this body of death?

"I thank God that through Jesus Christ I'm delivered from myself! So with all my heart and mind I serve the law of God, even though my body continues to serve the law of sin (Rom. 7:1–25).

## No Condemnation

"Therefore, there is no condemnation to those who are in Christ, who no longer live according to their sinful nature, but in harmony with the Holy Spirit.

"Jesus Christ has set me free from the law of death, and through the power of the Holy Spirit the law has now become a law of life. What the law couldn't do for me God did, by sending His Son to live a holy life as a human being and to overcome the power of sin. Christ fulfilled the requirements of the law for those of us who walk according to the Holy Spirit and not according to our sinful nature. To follow our sinful nature means death, but to be spiritually minded and follow Christ means life. Our natural self does not want to obey God and keep His law. Even if it wanted to, it couldn't do it by itself.

"However, you're no longer controlled by your natural self, but by the Holy Spirit who lives in you. If anyone does not have the Holy Spirit in his heart, he does not belong to Christ, no matter what he says. On the other hand, if Christ is in you, then the power of sin is dead and the power of righteousness is alive! And if God, who through the Holy Spirit raised Jesus from the dead, empowers you, He will also raise you from the dead and give you a new body (Rom. 8:1–11).

## A Glorious Future

"You're not in debt to your sinful nature—you owe it nothing. If you did, you would have to die. But you're indebted to the Holy Spirit, and when you stop doing what your sinful nature tells you to do, you will live.

"Those who are guided by the Holy Spirit are sons and daughters of God. They do not live in fear, because through the Holy Spirit they have been adopted by God and call Him their Father. The Holy Spirit, along with us, testifies that we are children of God. And if we are God's children, then we are His heirs along with Christ.

"If we are willing to suffer for Christ, we will certainly share the glories of heaven with Him. The suffering I'm going through at the present time is not worth mentioning compared to the glory that is to follow.

"All nature is suffering, not by choice but because of our sin. But according to God's plan, nature also has hope, looking forward to being free from decay and enjoying with us God's glorious freedom.

"This is the kind of hope that saves us. If we already had what we hope for, then we would have nothing to look forward to. But we tenaciously look toward to the time when our hope will be fulfilled.

"And the Holy Spirit helps us, since we don't even know how to pray as we should. The Spirit feels our pain and entreats God on our behalf. Our loving God knows our hearts and understands what the Holy Spirit has in mind as He intercedes for believers everywhere.

"We know that God will work out all things for the good of those who love Him, who are called to fulfill his purpose. His purpose is for us to be like His Son and to have all the rights a firstborn has among his brothers and sisters. This is God's plan, and that's why He called us, justified us, and will glorify us (Rom. 8:12-30).

### God's Love

"So what else can we say? God is not against us, He is *for* us. If He sent His Son to give His life for us, won't He generously also give us all the help we need?

"Who is going to condemn God's people? God Himself has declared us righteous. Christ died for us—and is alive! He is seated at the right hand of God to speak to God on our behalf.

"Who can separate us from God's love? Will trouble, distress, persecution, hunger, homelessness, violence, or threat of death? Absolutely not! As the Scripture says, 'We are willing to face death every day. Like sheep we are ready to be sacrificed.'

"No, in all these things we are more than conquerors through Christ who loves us. The battle is over! I am confident that neither life nor death, angels nor rulers, height nor depth, things present nor things to come, not even demonic powers—*nothing* can separate us from the love God has for us as seen in Christ Jesus our Lord" (Rom. 8:31-39).

# nineteen

# Israel

Paul's heart went out to his fellow Israelites:

"I'm telling you the truth—I am not lying. My conscience and the Holy Spirit are witnesses that I anguish over Israel. If I could save my people, I would give up my eternal life for them.

"Who are the Israelites? They are God's people! God has adopted them, shown them His glory, made a covenant with them, and given them His law, the Temple, and His promises. The patriarchs belong to them, and from these ancient Hebrews Christ is a descendant. He is the promised Messiah! As the Son of God, He is in charge of everything. Praise His name forever! Amen!

"Because Israel as a nation has failed, that does not mean the Word of God has failed. Not all Israelites are part of God's true Israel. Neither are all the descendants of Abraham his true descendants. Look at the supernatural birth of Isaac. To be true descendants of Abraham we need to be born again by the power of God.

"All of Abraham's natural descendants are not the children of God—only those who are born according to the promise God made when He said to Sarah, 'It is through My power that you will have a son.'

"This same decision by God applies to the twin sons of Isaac and Rebecca before they were born. God said, 'The one who comes out last is the one I have chosen. His older brother will serve him.' God loved Jacob but was displeased with Esau (Rom. 9:1-13).

## Questions

"Does this mean God is unfair? Of course not! He made this clear when He said to Moses, 'I will have mercy and compassion on whom I will.' Our standing with God does not depend on human effort, but on His mercy and grace. God said to Pharaoh, 'I did not interfere with your rule over Egypt, but the time came for Me to display My power and to spread My name throughout the earth.' God decided on whom to have mercy and who was too stubborn to be saved.

"You say to yourself, 'Why does God find fault with us if He makes all the decisions?' Are you challenging God? Does the clay say to the potter, 'Why are you making me this way and not some other way?' Doesn't the potter have a right to decide what kind of vessel to make?

"God is the potter. If He wants to have mercy or, after showing great patience, reveal His power and glory, that's His right. He decided to extend His call of salvation not only to the Jews, but also to the Gentiles.

"Through the prophet Isaiah He said, 'I will call them My people who were not My people and will love those who were not loved. And where it was said of them, "You are not God's people," they will be called the sons and daughters of God.'

"Isaiah continues, 'Though the number of Israelites be as the sand on the beach, only a comparatively few will be saved. The Lord will finish the work on the earth, and when the time comes, He will cut it short and will do so quickly.' Isaiah further says, 'If the Lord did not watch over us like a farmer watches over his seed, we would disappear like Sodom and Gomorrah.'

"What should we say when the Gentiles, who were not interested in living righteously, are declared righteous because of their faith in God? Or when the Israelites, who had the law and tried so hard to keep it, have not been declared righteous?

"Why is this? Because they didn't put their faith in what God could do for them, but in what they could do for themselves. Christ became a stumbling block to them. As the Scripture says, 'I will place in Israel a Rock. It will be a stumbling block to some, but to those who put their faith in Him it will be salvation' (Rom. 9:14-33).

### The Gospel

"My heart's desire is for everyone in Israel to be saved. They are zealous for God but don't understand that righteousness comes from Him. They try to make themselves righteous without humbly accepting God's righteousness.

"Christ came and kept the law for us, which means His righteousness is available to all who believe. Yes, Moses talked about keeping the law— if we could keep it perfectly. But he also talked about the righteousness that comes by faith, which has to do with the heart. Faith doesn't keep looking for the Messiah to suddenly come down from the sky or up from the sea. Christ has already been here and can live in our hearts by faith.

"If you believe that He's alive and are not afraid to say so, you will be saved. It all has to do with the heart. The Scripture says, 'Those who believe in Him will not be disappointed.' There's no distinction between Jews and Greeks, because all of us have the same Lord, who blesses everyone who comes to Him in faith. The Scripture also says, 'Whoever calls on the Lord will be saved.'

"But how can people believe in Someone they've never heard about? How will they know about Christ if no one tells them? And who will tell them unless someone is sent? The Scripture says, 'How beautiful are the feet of those who go and preach the gospel of peace, who share the good news about what Christ has done for us!'

"But all who hear the good news do not respond. As Isaiah says, 'Who has believed me?' Faith comes by hearing, and hearing by listening to what the Word of God says. Haven't the Jews heard about Christ? They have! The Scripture also says, 'The good news is going everywhere. It's going to the whole world!'

"How can the Israelites say they don't know? Moses himself said, 'God will make you jealous of those who are not Israelites, whom He is blessing.' Isaiah is even more pointed. Speaking for God he wrote, 'Day after day I stretched out my hands of love to a disobedient and stubborn people, but they would not come to me' (Rom. 10:1-21).

### God's Mercy

"Does this mean God has rejected His people? Absolutely not! I'm a Jew, a descendant of Abraham, belonging to the tribe of Benjamin. God has not turned against His people. Notice what the Scripture says about Elijah when he prayed, 'Lord, they have killed Your prophets, torn down Your altar, and I'm the only one left who is faithful to You. And now they're after me!' What did the Lord say to him? 'There are 7,000 men in Israel who refuse to worship Baal and are loyal to Me.'

"It's the same today. Many Israelites are faithful to God and have responded to His grace. And if salvation is by grace, then it's not by works. If it is by works, then it could not be by grace.

"As a nation, Israel did not fulfill God's purpose. The Israelites acted as if they were blind. The Scripture says, 'They have eyes but can't see. They have ears but can't hear.' And David says, 'Their stubbornness has become a snare to them, a trap to catch them. They have become blind so they cannot see, and their backs are bent from the spiritual load they have put on themselves.'

"Does this mean the end of Israel because its people have stumbled and fallen? Absolutely not! The gospel has now gone to the Gentiles in order to wake up Israel. And if Israel's stubbornness has enriched the Gentiles, how much more will Israel's response to God's grace enrich them! (Rom. 11:1-12).

## God's Kindness

"I have been called to be an apostle to the Gentiles, and I want to expand my ministry to them. I hope that God's work among them will wake up many in Israel when they see what's happening. If their rejection as a nation is blessing the world, their acceptance of God's grace will be like a resurrection to the world.

"Let me use two examples of what I mean. If you offer God the first slice of a loaf of bread and say it's holy, then the whole loaf must be holy. If you dedicate the sprout of a tree with its roots to God, then the whole tree belongs to Him. And when the tree grows bigger and some of the branches have to be cut off and some wild branches grafted in, those wild branches are not more important than the original tree.

"If you Gentiles say, 'Those branches were cut off for our sake so we could be grafted in,' that's only partially true. The real question is: Why were some branches cut off? They were cut off because of their unbelief. And you were grafted in because of your faith, not because you were so righteous. So don't be proud, but be humble and grateful. You, too, could be cut off.

"God is extremely kind. But He will cut off any branches that don't have the fruit of faith. And if an old branch shows signs of faith, God can graft it back into the tree. If you were cut from a wild tree and grafted into a cultivated tree, how much more can the natural branches be grafted back in?

"I'm telling you this because I don't want you to think you're better than the Israelites. The things that have happened to Israel were to your advantage and to make Israel complete. The Scripture says, 'The Deliverer will come from Israel to fulfill God's covenant to take away the sins of the world.'

"Israel's rejection of the gospel was to your advantage. But as far as God's purpose and love for them is concerned, that hasn't changed. God's gifts and purposes can't be taken away.

"There was a time when you were disobedient, but God was kind to you. It's the same for those Israelites who have disobeyed. God doesn't force people to obey. When they disobeyed, He still loved them. This shows how merciful and kind He is.

"How deep is God's wisdom and how knowledgeable He is! Who can explain everything He does? The Scripture says, 'Who can read God's mind? Who is going to counsel Him? Who has given Him anything so that God has to repay him?' All things were made by Him and continue to exist because of Him. To Him be honor and glory forever and ever" (Rom. 11:13-36).

# twenty

# Living for God

Paul continued his letter to the Romans:

"God is so merciful! I urge you, brothers and sisters, to live for Him! Dedicate yourself to His service and please Him in all you do. Be a living sacrifice, not a dead one. This is important and reasonable, considering all that He has done for you.

"Don't give in to the world, but let God transform you and change the way you think. Then you'll be able to test yourself to see if you're doing God's will. You will know what pleases Him and whether or not He approves of what you're doing.

"Don't think too highly of yourself, but be humble and modest in your thinking. Measure yourself by the faith God has given you and what you have done with it. Just as your body has many parts with different functions, that's how it is with us as we make up the body of Christ here on earth. We belong to one another but have different functions. Whatever gift God has given you, whether it's preaching, teaching, helping, encouraging, correcting, or sharing; being kind, merciful, and compassionate; or providing leadership, use your gift to strengthen the body of believers. Do it cheerfully and sincerely from your heart (Rom. 12:1–8).

## Christian Love

"Love each other sincerely. Don't be hypocritical. Hate what's evil and hold on to what's good. Be kind to each other as a loving family in the faith. And honor each other above yourself.

"Be zealous for the Lord. Serve Him with your whole heart. Thank God for the hope you have. Keep up your prayer life. Hold on to God when troubles come. Take care of your fellow believers, be hospitable, and don't curse those who persecute you, but bless them. Be happy with those who are happy and weep with those who weep. Live in harmony with each other. Don't be proud or think you're wiser than others. Accept everyone, whether they're rich or poor.

"Don't take revenge; even if people have done something bad to you, do something good for them. Do your part to live in peace with everyone. Don't take revenge on those who have hurt you. God says, 'I will take care of all that. If your enemy is hungry, feed him. If he's thirsty, give him something to drink. This is the way you should repay him.' Don't let hate control you, but do good no matter how you feel (Rom. 12:9–21).

### Obeying the Government

"Everyone should be a good citizen and obey the government. The idea of human government came from God. So those who oppose it have to answer to God. If you're good, you don't have to be afraid of the law—only if you're bad. Conduct yourselves properly and the authorities will speak well of you.

"In one sense they're God's servants to keep order and to arrest those who break the law. God didn't give them this authority for nothing. So stay within the law, not only to keep from being punished, but to be true to your own conscience. Pay your taxes as required by law, and respect those in charge as you're expected to do (Rom. 13:1–7).

### Loving Your Neighbor

"Owe no one anything, except to love them. This is included in the law when it says, 'Don't kill. Don't commit adultery. Don't steal. Don't be envious.' All these commandments can be summed up in one statement: 'Love your neighbor as yourself.' This means you should not do anything to harm him. To show love like this is the way to keep the law.

"And don't be spiritually asleep, but wake up and live for the Lord. The times in which we live tell us that the end is nearer for some of us than when we first believed. The night of spiritual darkness is over, and the day of truth is here. Let's put on the armor of light. Let's live good lives, without wild parties, sexual immorality, drunkenness, fighting, and jealousy.

"Instead, put on the Lord Jesus Christ, and don't do anything to arouse your sinful nature and follow its leading (Rom. 13:8–14).

### Don't Judge

"Accept those who have newly come to the faith, and don't argue over little things. One person believes they can eat almost anything, and another believes in eating only vegetables. Let the first not judge the second, and the second not judge the first. You both belong to God. Don't judge your neighbor's servants, because they're accountable to their master, not to you. God is our Master and will help those on both sides of such issues.

"It's the same with the festival Sabbaths. One thinks we ought to keep them, and another doesn't. Each one has to decide for himself. The one who keeps these Sabbaths does it for the Lord. That's all that matters. It's the same with eating. One is very careful what he eats, and another doesn't worry about it. But they're all thankful to the Lord for what He has done for them.

"No one lives apart from others. We all live for the Lord and are ready to die for Him. So whether we live or die, we belong to the Lord. Christ's death and resurrection means He is Lord of the living and the dead.

"Why judge others? Why look down on your brothers and sisters who differ from you? Everyone will have to stand before God to answer for himself. As Scripture says, 'Every knee will bow before the Lord and every tongue will praise His name.' Each one will have to give an account for their actions.

"So don't judge one another, but determine not to be a hindrance or a stumbling block to your brother's faith (Rom. 14:1-13).

### Be Considerate

"I know from the Lord Jesus Christ that no food created to be eaten is unclean. But if someone thinks that certain foods are ceremonially unclean, he shouldn't eat them. On the other hand, if your brother or sister is hurt when they see you eating what they think you shouldn't, out of love for them, don't eat it. Don't weaken their faith in the gospel by insisting on doing what you think is right. Christ died for them, too. Don't turn what you consider good into something evil.

"The kingdom of God is about more than food. It is about righteousness, peace, and joy in the Holy Spirit. Those who serve God in this way please the Lord and are accepted by others.

"Let's do what brings peace and what builds each other up. Don't destroy what God is doing by making an issue over food. Even though you're eating what's clean, it's wrong to cause others to stumble by your determined independence. It's better not to eat or drink anything that offends your brothers and sisters.

"Keep your convictions to yourself. Don't parade them around. Happy is the one who has the right attitude—he is not to be condemned. But he who believes that eating a certain thing is wrong but eats it anyway is condemned already. Whatever does not build faith in God is sin (Rom. 14:14-23).

"Those of us who are stronger ought to help those who are weaker and not just live to please ourselves. Let each one help their neighbor and strengthen them in the faith. Christ didn't live to please Himself. The Scripture says, 'The troubles that were aimed at you I took on Myself.' Everything in Scripture has been written to teach us how to live and to give us hope and courage to endure.

"May God, who is the source of our courage and comfort, bring you together in unity and in harmony with the Lord Jesus Christ. With one voice let us praise and glorify the Father of our Lord! Accept each other to the glory of God, as Christ has accepted you (Rom. 15:1-7).

### The Gentiles

"Jesus became a servant to confirm and fulfill the promises God gave to our forefathers. So now even the Gentiles praise God for His kindness and mercy. David said, 'I will hold up Your name and sing Your praises among the Gentiles.' And Moses said, 'Let the Gentiles rejoice together with God's people.' David added, 'Let Jews and Gentiles praise His name.' And Isaiah said, 'A descendant of Jesse will come and be Lord of the Gentiles, and they will put their hope in Him.' So may the God of hope fill you with joy and peace as you put your faith in Him. And may your faith continue to grow by the power of the Holy Spirit.

"I have confidence in you, my brothers and sisters, that there is a lot of goodness in you and that you know enough of the gospel to teach others. I have been quite bold in reminding you of things. God has called me into the ministry and, by His grace, made me an apostle to the Gentiles. I'm like a priest who wants the Gentiles to be an acceptable offering to God through the powerful working of the Holy Spirit.

"I can talk about my work for Christ without being proud, because I'm excited about all those who have accepted the gospel and have been baptized. This wasn't accomplished by me, but by Him. He made the Gentiles listen and obey through the power of the Holy Spirit with signs and miracles.

"From Jerusalem all the way to the wild country of Illyricum the gospel has been preached. My goal is to take the gospel to those who have never heard of Christ and not to build on the work that someone else has done. The Scripture says, 'Those who didn't know about Him will see and hear and understand' (Rom. 15:8-21).

### Rome

"For some time I've been wanting to go to Rome, but the mission work here kept me from coming. Now that this part of my work is done, the way is finally open for me to come to see you. I've been looking forward to this for some years. My plan is to eventually go on to Spain, but first I'd like to stop and see you and stay a while to enjoy your company. Then you can help me on my way.

"But first I have to take the donations that the churches in Macedonia gave for our needy believers in Jerusalem. The Gentiles have been given a share in the spiritual riches of Israel, so now they feel indebted to share some of their material riches with their fellow believers. As soon as I complete this mission, I'll be on my way to Spain and will stop by to see you. When I come, it will be with the full blessing of Jesus Christ.

"I urge you, brothers and sisters, in the name of the Lord Jesus and in the love the Holy Spirit gives us, to join me in prayer that all will go well. Pray that those in Israel who have turned against the gospel won't oppose my ministry there, and that the believers will accept me so I can come to see you with joy in my heart. May the God of peace be with all of you (Rom. 15:22-33).

### Greetings

"Phoebe, a deaconess from the church in Cenchrea, is on her way to Rome. So welcome her in the name of the Lord, and give her whatever she needs to carry on her work. She has been a great blessing and has helped a lot of people, including me.

"And give my greetings to Priscilla and Aquila, who have risked their lives to save me. All the churches in this area are grateful to them for what they have done. Also, give my greetings to the members meeting in their house, especially Epaenetus, who was my first convert in Asia Minor.

"Greet Mary, who has done so much for me, and Andronicus and Junica, fellow Jews who were arrested and spent some time in jail with me. They are well-known among the apostles, for they accepted Christ before I did. Greet my good friends, Amplias and Stachys; and Urbanus, a fellow worker in Christ.

"Give my greetings to Apelles, whose ministry Christ approves, to the family of Aristobulus, also to Herodion, a relative of mine, and to the family of Narcissus. Greet Tryphena and Tryphosa, who are great workers for the Lord, as is my friend Persis; and Rufus and his mother, who has been like a mother to me.

"Give my greetings to Asyncritus, Phlegon, Hermas, Patrobas, Hermes, and the group of believers meeting with them. Oh, and Philologus and Julia, Nereus and his sister, as well as Olympas and the group of believers meeting with them.

"Always greet each other warmly when you meet. All the churches send you greetings (Rom. 16:1-16).

## Be Careful

"I urge you, brothers and sisters, to notice those who are unsettling people's faith and causing division in the church by going against what you've been taught. Stay away from them. They are not serving the Lord Jesus Christ, but are only interested in themselves and their own authority. They deceive people by their smooth talk and flattering speeches about their concern for the church.

"Your faithfulness to Jesus Christ and the gospel is known everywhere. I'm happy for you and praise the Lord. But I don't want you to be gullible. I want you to be wise as to what is evil and what is good. The grace of the Lord Jesus will help you. And the God of peace will shortly crush Satan under your feet (Rom. 16:17-20).

## Additional Greetings

"Timothy, my fellow worker, sends his greetings, as do Lucius, Jason, and Sosipater, my fellow countrymen. Gaius, in whose house I'm staying, sends his greetings. And Erastus, the city treasurer, together with our good brother Quartus, send their greetings. (I, Tertius, who am writing this epistle for Paul, send my greetings, too.) The grace of Jesus Christ be with all of you (Rom. 16:21-24).

## Benediction

"Now to God, who is able to strengthen your faith in the gospel of our Lord Jesus Christ and in the truth that has now come to light, to Him be all the glory and honor. What was not previously known by the world has now, through the fulfillment of the prophecies of Scripture by Jesus Christ, been made known to people everywhere to help them believe and obey.

"To God alone, who is all-wise, be glory and honor forever through Jesus Christ our Lord. Amen" (Rom. 16:25-27).

# twenty-one

# Trip to Jerusalem

After Paul wrote his letter to the Romans and told them his plans, he was ready to sail from Corinth to Syria and from there make his way to Jerusalem. But when he heard that the Jews were forming a plot to kill him, he decided to first head north to Macedonia on foot and catch a ship in Philippi.

He didn't go alone. Sopater, Aristarchus, Secundus, Gaius, Timothy, Tychicus, and Trophimus went with him. I, Luke, had joined Paul earlier. When we got to Philippi, Paul decided to keep the Passover and the Festival of Unleavened Bread, while Timothy and the others boarded a ship and sailed for Troas.

After the festival, Paul and I boarded a ship, and five days later we arrived at Troas, where we stayed for a week.

Sabbath evening after sundown the believers got together for a fellowship meal and to say good-bye to us. Our plan was to leave in the morning. After eating, Paul talked to the people until midnight. Because of all the burning torches to light the large upstairs room, the place got quite warm. A young man named Eutychus was sitting on the sill of a large open window to catch the cool night breeze. As he was listening to Paul, he fell asleep, lost his balance, and fell down three stories. The believers rushed down to help him, but when they tried to pick him up, he was dead. Paul came down, hugged him, and earnestly prayed for him. Then Paul turned to the believers and said, "Don't cry. God just gave him back his life."

We all went back upstairs, held communion, and talked until dawn. Then we left and they took the boy home, praising the Lord for what He had done.

Paul decided to go from Troas to Assos on foot, while we boarded a ship and later picked him up there. From Assos we sailed to Mitylene, the next day we got to Chios, the next to Samos, and on the third day we arrived in Miletus. Paul purposely chose a ship that didn't stop at Ephesus, because he was in a hurry to get to Jerusalem for Pentecost. But we had sent a message to the elders at Ephesus to come and meet us at Miletus, which they did (Acts 20:1-17).

### Paul's Counsel

After visiting with the elders and inquiring about the church there, Paul said to them:

"You know the kind of person I was when I was with you. From the first day I set my foot in Asia Minor, I served the Lord with humility and tears, facing all kinds of death threats from the Jews.

"I didn't keep back anything that was helpful to you. I taught the gospel publicly and from house to house. I urged both Jews and Gentiles to repent and put their faith in the Lord Jesus Christ.

"On this trip we didn't stop at Ephesus because, in obedience to the Holy Spirit, we needed to go to Jerusalem in time for Pentecost. I have no idea what I'll face when I get there, except that the Holy Spirit has told me several times along the way to expect persecution and imprisonment. But my life is not the important issue. The only important thing is for me to finish the course the Lord laid out for me when He called me into the ministry to preach the good news of God's grace.

"I know I won't see you again. But I thank the Lord for the privilege of bringing the gospel to you. I told you all about God's plan and purpose. If any of you are lost, it's not because I held anything back from you. Watch out for yourselves and for God's sheep, like good shepherds should. God paid for His church by the blood of His Son, and the Holy Spirit has called you to care for it.

"I know that after I'm gone false teachers will come and attack God's sheep like wolves. Even from among your own members, men will say they have the truth and will twist the gospel to draw people to themselves. So be on guard and remember how I worked with you for three years, pleading with tears for you to be faithful to the Lord.

"Now I turn you over to the care of God and to the Word of His grace, which will build you up and give you all that you need to inherit the kingdom, together with all those who have set themselves apart for Him.

"When I was with you, I never asked for money or clothes for myself, but worked with my own hands to provide for all my needs and for all those with me. I gave you an example that we should always help those in need. As the Lord Jesus said, 'It's more blessed to give than to receive.'"

Then we all knelt and prayed together. The elders cried, hugged Paul, and kissed him on the cheeks. It really hurt when they realized they would never see him again. They walked him to the ship and watched as we sailed away (Acts 20:18-38).

## The Rest of the Trip

From Miletus we sailed to Cos, arriving the next day at Rhodes, and the day after that, at Patara. There we caught a ship going southeast past Cyprus to Syria. When we landed at Tyre, the men had to unload the cargo. So we disembarked and, after locating the believers, decided to stay for a week before going on.

During that week the believers repeatedly told Paul through the Holy Spirit about the dangers he would face in Jerusalem. But he was determined to obey the leadings of the Holy Spirit, even though the Spirit had warned him what would happen. So they accompanied us to the port, together with their wives and children. We knelt on the beach and prayed for each other. Then we said good-bye and boarded the ship, and they returned home.

The next day we arrived at Ptolemais and visited with the believers there for a day. Then we sailed to Caesarea, where we stayed with Philip the evangelist, who was one of the original seven deacons chosen by the apostles. He had four unmarried daughters who had been given the gift of prophecy.

While we were there, a prophet named Agabus from Judea came to see us. He went up to Paul, untied the rope belt around his waist, wrapped it around his own hands and feet, and said, "The Holy Spirit says, 'This is what the Jews will do to the man who owns this belt, and then they will turn him over to the Gentiles.'"

When we heard this, we cried and begged Paul not to go to Jerusalem. Paul said, "What are you trying to do to me? Break my heart? I'm ready to go to Jerusalem and face whatever I have to—even to die there for the Lord Jesus Christ." We tried but couldn't change his mind. So we said, "The Lord's will be done" (Acts 21:1-14).

## Jerusalem

We packed and took off for Jerusalem on foot. On the first day, some of the believers from Caesarea went with us. That night we stayed with a man named Mnason, who was one of the first converts in Cyprus before he moved back to Judea.

When we got to Jerusalem, we were warmly welcomed by the believers. The next day Paul went to see James, the stepbrother of Jesus, and some of the leading elders in Jerusalem who happened to be there. Paul told them all the things God had done for the Gentiles through his missionary work the last five years. Then, as evidence of the Gentiles' love for their Jewish brothers and sisters, he gave them the donations he had brought with him.

When they heard what God had done through Paul's ministry and saw the large donations the Gentiles had sent, they praised the Lord. Then they told him what God had done through them in Judea and about the thousands of Jews who had accepted the Lord Jesus Christ and were true to the laws of Moses.

After expressing their appreciation, they said to Paul, "We've heard that you're advising Jews living in other countries to forget the laws of Moses, telling them not to be circumcised and otherwise downplaying our traditions. We would win more of them to the faith if we could show them that this is not true. So this is what we would like you to do: We have four men who have taken the Purification Vow. We'll introduce you to them. Join them and at the end of the week go through the purification rituals with them. You can do this by paying the Levite barber to shave their heads and also by paying for their offerings and other Temple expenses. This way the people can see for themselves that you uphold our traditions.

"As far as the Gentiles are concerned, we have sent them a letter, as you know, telling them they don't have to live like Jews. But they shouldn't eat meat sold in the markets that has been offered to idols. That would be a wrong witness. Nor should they eat any raw meat still filled with blood, like the pagans do. And they should uphold the sacredness of marriage and keep themselves sexually pure."

Against his better judgment, but hoping to gain back the confidence of the people, Paul agreed to take part in the Purification Vow. So the next day he met the four men, and together they went to the Temple to let the priest know when the seven days of purification would end so they could come and offer the required sacrifices (Acts 21:15-26).

## Paul Arrested

Every day Paul went to the Temple to pray. When the seven days were almost over, some Jews from Ephesus, who had come to Jerusalem for the Festival of Pentecost, saw Paul in the Temple, grabbed him, and started shouting, "Help! This is the man who tells everyone wherever he goes that our laws are not important. He says that our Temple has no more significance than any other temple! He even brought Gentiles into the courtyard reserved for Jews and made it unclean for us!"

These Ephesian Jews had seen Trophimus, whom they knew from Ephesus, with Paul earlier and supposed that Paul had brought him into the Temple.

This not only stirred up the crowd of worshippers, but word spread from the Temple into the city. The people grabbed Paul, dragged him out of the Temple, and shut the doors. They were ready to kill him. When the Roman commander in charge of keeping peace in the city heard about it, he immediately went with his officers and troops to the Temple to see what was going on.

When the people saw them coming, they stopped beating Paul. The commander arrested Paul and had him bound with chains. He asked Paul what he had done and what this was all about. Some in the crowd began shouting one thing and others something else, so that the officer couldn't tell what was true. He ordered his men to take Paul to the fortress. When they got near there, the mob became violent and started shouting, "Kill him! Kill him!" The soldiers had to carry Paul on their shoulders to protect him.

Partway up the stairs into the fortress, Paul asked the commander in Greek for permission to speak to the people. The surprised commander said, "You speak Greek? You're not the suspected terrorist leader from Egypt who, with 4,000 men, escaped into the desert, are you?"

Paul answered, "No, I'm a Jew, born in Tarsus in Cilicia. Please let me speak to the people." The commander gave him permission, so Paul motioned to them and when they calmed down, he spoke to them in Hebrew (Acts 21:27-40).

## Paul Explains

"Brothers and fathers in Israel, listen to me." When they heard him speak in Hebrew, they grew very quiet.

"I am a Jew, born in Tarsus of Cilicia. I came to Jerusalem for my education and studied under that great teacher Gamaliel. He was strict and taught me the laws of our fathers and how to keep them. I became as zealous for the law as you are today. I even persecuted those who didn't believe like we do and had both men and women arrested and thrown into prison to be killed if they did not conform. You can ask the high priest and the council and they'll tell you that is true. They even gave me authority in writing to do the same in other cities, beginning with Damascus. I was to arrest such people and bring them back to Jerusalem in chains to be tried and executed.

"Then this is what happened: As I traveled toward Damascus, suddenly a beam of light came down from heaven and surrounded me. It was so bright that it blinded me, and I fell to the ground, trying to shield my eyes. A commanding voice said, 'Saul, Saul, why are you persecuting Me?'

"I was shocked and asked, 'Who are You?'

"He answered, 'I'm Jesus—the One you're persecuting.' (Now, those with me saw the light and were very frightened, but they didn't hear anything.)

"I asked Him, 'Lord, what do You want me to do?'

"He said, 'Go on into Damascus and you will be told what to do.' Then the light disappeared.

"When I got up and opened my eyes, I was blind. So they had to lead me into the city and help me find a place to stay.

"A few days later a man named Ananias, a very committed and highly respected Jew, came to see me. He said, 'Brother Saul, God has given you your sight back. Look up and you'll be able to see.' I did, and I could see!"

"Then he said, 'God has chosen you to do His will. You have seen the Lord Jesus Christ and talked with Him. You are to be a witness for Him to all kinds of people, telling them what you have seen and heard. So what are you waiting for? Get up and let me baptize you as a sign that your sins have been washed away and that you now belong to the Lord.' So I went ahead and was baptized.

"After that I returned to Jerusalem, and while I was praying in the Temple, I was taken off in vision. The Lord said to me, 'Quick! Get out of Jerusalem, because they will not accept what you say about Me.'

"I answered, 'Lord, they know I arrested those who believe in You. I beat them in their houses and in the synagogues and sent them to prison to be killed. That's what happened to Stephen. I approved the council's decision to stone him to death and even watched as I stood by the pile of robes of those who did it.'

"He said firmly to me, 'Leave Jerusalem and take My message to the Gentiles'" (Acts 22:1-21).

### Paul Questioned

The crowd respectfully listened to him until he talked about going to the Gentiles. Then they screamed and shouted: "Away with him! Kill him! He's not fit to live!" They even tore their robes and threw dust into the air to show their hatred.

The officer quickly ordered his men to take Paul up into the fortress and closed the doors. He was determined to find out from Paul the cause for such hostility and anger. So he had Paul stripped, tied to a post, and ordered him whipped until he talked.

Paul said to the officer standing next to him: "Is it legal for you to have a Roman citizen beaten before he is found guilty?"

When the officer heard that, he went to the commander and told him what Paul had said and suggested they be careful what they did to a Roman citizen. Immediately, the commander got up and went into the guard room to talk to Paul. He asked him, "Are you really a Roman citizen?"

Paul answered, "Yes, I am."

The commander said, "I'm a citizen and paid a good sum of money for it."

Paul replied, "I was born one."

As soon as the guards heard that, they backed off, and the commander himself got scared when he realized he had taken a Roman citizen into custody and ordered him whipped. He untied Paul and decided to order a meeting of the Jewish Council, hoping they would find out what he had done to cause such a public reaction. The next day he took Paul to the council, untied him, and let him speak in his own defense (Acts 22:22-30).

### Paul Defends Himself

Paul stood before the council and said, "Brothers in the faith, all my life I have lived with a clear conscience in serving God."

When Ananias, the high priest, heard that, he ordered those nearby to slap Paul across the mouth for making such a claim.

Paul looked at the high priest and said, "How can you judge people according to the law when you yourself break it by ordering them to hit a defendant because you disagree with what he says? That's illegal. God will punish you for this!"

Those standing nearby said, "How dare you talk to the high priest that way!"

Paul immediately apologized: "I didn't know the chairman of the council was the high priest. I'm sorry. The Scripture says, 'Don't speak evil of the spiritual ruler of God's people.'"

As Paul looked around, he noticed that some members of the council were Sadducees and others were Pharisees. So he spoke up loud enough for everyone to hear: "Brothers! I'm a Pharisee and the son of a Pharisee. I'm being tried because of the hope I have that there will be a resurrection from the dead!"

Suddenly things changed. The Sadducees, who don't believe in the resurrection, and the Pharisees, who do, started arguing among themselves. Some of the Pharisees even stood up and said to the council, "We find nothing wrong with this man. Maybe an angel did speak to him on the way to Damascus."

The uproar became so violent that the commander was afraid that if they got hold of Paul, they would pull him apart. He ordered his troops to take Paul back to the fortress and, if necessary, to use force to do so.

That night the Lord appeared to Paul and said, "Take courage, Paul.

Just as you have testified about Me in Jerusalem, you will testify about Me in Rome" (Acts. 23:1-11).

## Paul's Nephew

The next morning, 40 men got together and took an oath to not eat or drink anything until they had killed Paul. They went to the chief priests and told them about the oath they had taken and suggested, "We would like you to call another meeting of the council and ask the commander to bring Paul back one last time for questioning. When he does, we'll break through the ranks of the Roman guard and kill Paul before he gets here."

When the young son of Paul's sister heard what was being whispered on the street, he quickly went to visit his uncle to tell him what he had heard. Paul was glad to see his nephew and listened to what he had to say. Then he called one of the officers and said, "You need to take this young man to the commander. He has something to report."

So the officer took Paul's nephew to the commander and said, "The prisoner, Paul, asked me to bring this young man to you because he needs to report something."

The commander took the young man by the hand to a private area and asked, "What is it that you want to report?"

The young man said, "Tomorrow the chief priests will call for another meeting of the council and will ask you to bring Paul one last time for questioning. Don't do it, because 40 men have taken an oath not to eat or drink anything until they kill Paul. They'll be waiting for you to bring him to the council, and then they will break through your guards and kill him."

The commander thanked the young man and said, "Don't tell anyone you came to see me" (Acts 23:12-22).

# twenty two

# Paul Taken to Caesarea

As soon as Paul's nephew left, the commander called two officers in and said, "I want you to take 200 regular troops with swords, 70 horsemen, and 200 men with spears, and take Paul to Governor Felix in Caesarea. I want you to leave by nine o'clock tonight. Also, take two horses for Paul, because it will be a long trip. We need to get him there quickly."

Then he sat down and wrote this letter:

"From Claudius Lysias, commander in Jerusalem, to His Excellency, Governor Felix. Greetings:

"A couple of days ago the Jews attacked a man named Paul and were ready to kill him. When I got word that he was a Roman citizen, I quickly went with my officers and men to rescue him. I needed to know what the Jews had against him. So I took him to their council and found out that the problem was over different interpretations of their laws, which certainly was not something that deserved prison or execution.

"When I learned that some of them were waiting for the first chance they had to kill him, I decided to get him out of Jerusalem as fast as I could and send him to you for protection. Those who want to kill him need to come into a Roman court of law and state what charges they have against him. Farewell."

That night the soldiers took Paul and got as far as Antipatris. The next morning the horsemen and Paul went on to Caesarea, while the regular troops went back to Jerusalem.

When the horsemen got to Caesarea, they gave the letter to the governor and turned Paul over to him for custody. Felix read the letter and then asked Paul where he was from. Paul answered, "The Roman province of Cilicia." Felix said, "In that case, you'll be kept in Herod's old palace until your accusers come and I hear what they have to say" (Acts 23:23–35).

### Accusations

Five days later Ananias, the high priest, along with some of the members of the council, came to see the governor. They brought with them a well-known lawyer named Tertullus to present the case against Paul.

Tertullus began: "Governor Felix, it's because of your leadership and foresight that we have peace and enjoy a time of prosperity. We are most grateful, Your Excellency, for what you have done.

"We don't want to impose on your time, but because you are so gracious, we know you will hear us out.

"This man Paul is a troublemaker. He's the ringleader of a fanatical religious group called Nazarenes. He even desecrated the Temple—that's why we arrested him and wanted to judge him according to our laws. But Commander Lysias came and, with great violence, took him out of our hands and told us to come to you to present our case. When you examine him, Your Excellency, you will see that what we are saying is true."

The high priest and those with him spoke up and confirmed everything that Tertullus had said (Acts 24:1-9).

### Paul Defends Himself

The governor then nodded to Paul to speak. Paul said, "I know, Governor, that you have judged many cases over the years. So I'll gladly make my defense.

"About 12 days ago—and you can verify this—I went to Jerusalem to worship. I didn't go to the Temple to argue or cause a disturbance, nor did I cause trouble in the city synagogues. They can't prove their accusations against me.

"But this much I would like to say: I do worship the God of our fathers according to what people call 'The Way,' believing what the prophets have said. I have the same hope my accusers do that there will be a resurrection and judgment of the righteous and wicked. This being so, I have always done my best to live with a clear conscience toward God and others.

"After being gone from Jerusalem for some years, I came back to bring offerings to God and donations for the poor. That's why I was in the Temple. Also, I was going through the steps of purification. I was not there to stir up a crowd or to cause trouble.

"But some Jews from Asia recognized me, and they stirred up the crowd and caused an uproar. These are the men who should be here facing charges and telling you what they have against me and why they think I'm guilty. They are the ones who should have been judged by the Jewish Council.

"There is one thing that I probably shouldn't have done when I stood before the council. I spoke up loudly for all to hear: 'I'm being judged because I believe in the resurrection of the dead!'"

By now Felix better understood what it meant to worship according to "The Way." So he dismissed the court, saying, "When Lysias, the commander in Jerusalem, comes, I'll look into this matter more carefully and make my decision."

Then he ordered the officer in charge to take Paul to Herod's old palace and put him under guard, but to give him some freedom and let his friends come to see him and bring him what he needed (Acts 24:10-23).

## A Private Conversation

A short time later Felix and his wife, Druscilla, who was Jewish, sent for Paul to talk to him privately about his faith in Christ. Paul told them about God's love, righteous living, the need for faith and self-control, and the judgment.

Felix listened and became somewhat frightened at the thought of judgment. So he said, "Paul, when I have time for another visit, I'll call for you."

He was hoping that during one of these private conversations Paul would offer to buy his freedom. That's why he sent for him so often.

Two years afterward Festus became governor and Paul was still in prison. Festus too wanted to get along with the Jews so he kept Paul locked up (Acts 24:24-27).

## Paul Appeals to Caesar

Three days after he took office, Festus decided to visit Jerusalem. The chief priests and some of the prominent council members went to see him to present their charges against Paul. They urged Festus to bring Paul to Jerusalem to stand trial. Their plan was to ambush the guards along the way and kill Paul before he got there. Festus sensed that something wasn't right, so he said, "In a few days I'll be going back to Caesarea. Why don't you come with me and present your case?"

About a week or so later he left Jerusalem and went back to Caesarea. The next day he took his seat as judge and ordered the guards to bring in Paul. The priests and council members brought all kinds of charges against Paul, none of which they could prove. Then Paul spoke up and said, "Their accusations are not true. I have done nothing against the Jews or against Caesar."

Festus still wanted to please the Jews, so he asked Paul, "Are you willing to go to Jerusalem to stand trial?"

Paul answered, "I'm a Roman citizen, standing in a Roman court, and that's where I should be tried. I have broken no Jewish laws. If I had done something that deserved death, I would be willing to die. But these charges are false. To be handed over to them is against the law. I appeal my case to Caesar!"

Festus talked with his advisers about the appeal and then said to Paul, "You have appealed your case to Caesar—to Caesar you will go" (Acts 25:1-12).

### King Agrippa's Visit

Soon after Festus had become governor, King Agrippa and his wife, Bernice, came to visit and congratulate him. Near the end of their extended visit, Festus told Agrippa about Paul and said, "I have a man left in prison by Felix, the former governor. Recently I visited Jerusalem. While there, the chief priests and prominent council members told me that this man deserved to die and that I should have him executed. I told them that it was against Roman law to execute a man or to hand him over to anyone before he had a chance to face his accusers and defend himself.

"So they accompanied me to Caesarea, and the next day I ordered the prisoner to be brought into court to hear what his accusers had to say. Their charges were not about some terrible crime as I had expected, but about different interpretations of their religion, especially about a man named Jesus, who had died but whom Paul said was now alive.

"I asked him if he would be willing to go to Jerusalem to defend himself, but he appealed his case to Caesar. So I have kept him locked up until I can find a ship going directly to Rome."

Agrippa said, "I'd like to hear for myself what this man has to say."

Festus replied, "We'll do it tomorrow."

The next day King Agrippa and his wife, Bernice, were ushered into the courtroom with great pomp and ceremony, together with top military officers and prominent city leaders. Then Paul was brought in.

Festus stood and said, "King Agrippa and all of you here, this man standing before you is a Roman citizen, whom the Jews want me to execute. I heard their charges, but they had nothing to do with a crime deserving death. When I asked the prisoner if he wanted to defend himself before the Jewish Council, he appealed to Caesar. But I have nothing specific with which to charge him.

"So I have brought him before you, King Agrippa, for a preliminary hearing, hoping you can help me find something to put in my letter to Caesar. I can't send him to Rome without charging him with something" (Acts 25:13-27).

## Paul Allowed to Speak

King Agrippa said to Paul: "You are allowed to speak."

Paul stretched out his hand in a gesture of respect and replied, "King Agrippa, I want to thank you for allowing me to speak and defend myself before you. I'm glad to do it, especially since you are so familiar with the customs and traditions of the Jewish people. Please be patient with me, Your Majesty, and hear me out.

"The Jews know that I lived my religion from the time I was a young man being educated in Jerusalem. I lived the strict life of a Pharisee. Now I'm being judged by these same people. It has to do with the hope I have in the promises God gave our ancestors, to which the 12 tribes clung day and night. It is all about the evidence of this hope. Your majesty, why should it be thought incredible that God can raise the dead?

"At first I didn't believe that God raised Jesus from the dead and used the authority given to me by the chief priests to persecute those who believed this way. I arrested them, sent them to prison, and voted for them to be executed. I visited the synagogues and when I saw them there, I tried to make them renounce their faith in Christ. I did this in Jerusalem and then went after them in other cities, as well.

"One day, about noon, as I and my group were nearing Damascus, suddenly a light from heaven brighter than the sun surrounded us, and we all covered our faces and fell to the ground. Then a voice spoke to me and said, 'Saul, Saul, why are you persecuting Me? You are like a stubborn ox kicking against its master.'

"I said, 'Lord, who are You?' He said, 'I am Jesus, whom you're persecuting. Now get up and stand on your feet. I have chosen you to be My servant, to be a witness that you have seen Me, and to tell of other things that I will yet show you. I will rescue you from your own people and from the Gentiles, to whom I'm sending you. You are to turn them from darkness to light, from Satan to God, so they can be forgiven and have a part in the inheritance with those who are set apart by faith.'

"King Agrippa, I have not been disobedient to that vision from heaven. I have preached repentance and forgiveness, first in Damascus, then in Jerusalem and throughout Judea, and also to the Gentiles everywhere I went. I pleaded with them to turn to God and live lives in harmony with repentance. This is the reason the Jews grabbed me in the Temple and were ready to kill me.

"But God rescued me and that's why I can stand before all of you today and defend myself. I have only preached what Moses and the prophets said would happen—that Christ would come and die, rise from the dead, and be proclaimed as the Light of the World to both Jews and Gentiles."

Then the governor interrupted with a loud voice and said, "Paul, you have lost your mind! Too much learning is driving you insane!"

Paul responded, "Most noble Festus, I have not lost my mind, but I'm saying what is rational and true. King Agrippa knows about these things—that's why I felt I could speak so openly. I can't believe that any of these things escaped his attention, because they didn't happen in a corner somewhere.

"You believe these things, don't you, King Agrippa? I know you do."

Agrippa said, "Paul, are you trying to make me a Christian? Do you think you can do so with just one short speech?"

Paul answered, "I pray to God that you and all those here will believe as I do, except I hope no one would be put in chains for it as I am."

Then Agrippa stood up to leave, as did the governor, Bernice, and all the others who were there. As they were leaving, they said to each other, "This man hasn't done anything that deserves imprisonment and death."

Agrippa agreed and said to Festus, "This man could have been released had he not appealed his case to Caesar" (Acts 26:1-32).

# twenty-three

# On the Way to Rome

After the decision was made that Paul should be taken to Rome, the governor turned Paul and the other prisoners over to Julius, an officer in the Augustan Regiment.

I, Luke, and Aristarchus from Thessalonica decided to book passage and go with Paul. We boarded a ship in Caesarea with the other prisoners, to sail along the coast of Asia Minor and from there catch a ship going to Rome.

At the end of the first day we stopped at Sidon, not far from Caesarea, along the Palestinian coast. Julius was kind to Paul and let him visit his friends so they could give him what he needed for the trip.

We then put out to sea again and sailed just north of Cyprus, because the wind was giving us trouble. We continued along the coast of Cilicia and Pamphilia in Asia Minor until we got to Myra in Lycia. There Julius found a ship from Alexandria going to Italy. We all got on board and headed southwest for the island of Crete. It was slow going, because the winds were not in our favor. We passed the port of Salmone and went on to Fair Havens (Acts 27:1-8).

## A Violent Storm

The owner of the ship and his crew didn't want to stay there, because the port was not as protected from the winter storms as Phoenix was. He decided to sail along the coast and dock there.

Paul knew that from the Day of Atonement on, sailing would be more hazardous. So he talked to Julius and to the owner and navigator and said, "Men, I have a feeling that we're heading for trouble if we leave Fair Havens. We'll get caught in a gale and end up damaging the ship, losing the cargo, and possibly some lives, as well." But Julius agreed with the owner and navigator to go on to Phoenix and wait for better sailing conditions there. When a gentle south wind came up, the men pulled up the anchor, hoisted the sails, stayed close to the coast, and headed for Phoenix.

Shortly after we pulled out, the gentle breeze turned into a gale-force wind. It caught the sails and we were driven out to sea. Soon we lost control and were heading toward the little island of Cauda. There we had some protection from the strong winds and were able to haul the little lifeboat on board, which we had in tow, so we wouldn't lose it. The men lowered the sails, because it was safer to let the ship ride with the wind.

The storm didn't stop and the seams of the wooden hull began pulling apart. The crew slung strong weighted ropes over the front of the ship, pulled them along the bottom, and tightened them around the middle of the ship to keep it from breaking apart. They were able to change the direction of the drift to avoid running aground on one of the hidden sandbars in the shallow waters off the northern tip of Africa.

The next day things didn't look any better. The crew lightened the ship by throwing cargo overboard. The third day they threw the heavy gear and tackling overboard. For days we didn't see the sun or the stars, and we lost all hope of ever being saved.

Many of us were seasick. So after not having eaten regularly for days, Paul stood up and said, "Men, you should have listened to me and not left Fair Havens for Phoenix. If you had, this wouldn't have happened. Now the ship is damaged and you've had to throw a lot of cargo overboard.

"Last night an angel from God, whom I serve, came and said to me, 'Paul, don't be afraid. You will stand before Caesar. God has answered your prayers. All on board will be saved.' So, men, keep up your courage. I have faith in God and believe everything I've been told. We will run aground on some nearby island and will lose the ship."

After being blown across the Mediterranean for 14 days, the sailors sensed we were nearing land. So at midnight they let down a thin rope with a heavy weight on the end to see how deep the water was. It was only 120 feet deep. A little farther on they did it again and it was only 90 feet deep. They knew that we would soon run aground on some rocky shore, so they quickly let down four anchors at the rear of the ship and waited for daylight.

Then some of the sailors decided to save themselves by pretending to lower additional anchors from the front of the ship, when they were actually lowering the little lifeboat. Paul noticed this and said to Julius, "Unless these men stay with the ship, no one will be saved."

Julius ordered the soldiers to cut the ropes and let the lifeboat drop into the sea and drift away.

At the first rays of dawn Paul urged everyone to eat something to gain some strength and energy to survive, because for the last two weeks they had eaten very little. He told them that no one would be lost.

Then Paul took some food, gave thanks to God, and ate. When the others saw him eat, they ate also. Counting everyone, there were 276 people on board.

After they ate, the crew lightened the ship still more by throwing the cargo of wheat overboard.

When it got light enough, they could see land but didn't know where they were. They noticed a beach and decided to let the ship run aground there. So they cut the ropes holding the anchors, loosened the rudder ropes, hoisted the little sails, and headed for shore. The ship took off and hit the beach with such force that it stuck there, while the crosscurrents battered the rear of the ship.

The soldiers wanted to kill all the prisoners before any of them could escape. But Julius didn't want anything to happen to Paul. So he ordered everyone to jump overboard and get to land as quickly as they could. By now the ship was breaking up. Those who couldn't swim grabbed pieces of wood or planks and made it to shore that way. Not one of them was lost (Acts 27:9-44).

### Stranded on an Island

After everyone had abandoned ship and safely reached shore, we learned that the island was Malta. The islanders were very kind to us. They started a fire to keep us warm, because we were wet and cold.

We helped to gather firewood. Paul saw a bundle of sticks and went over and picked them up. As he threw them on the fire, a small venomous snake bit his hand and wouldn't let go. When the islanders saw the snake hanging from his hand, they said, "For sure this man is a murderer or some kind of a terrible criminal. He escaped the sea, but the goddess of justice caught up with him and he will die."

But Paul shook the snake loose and let it fall into the fire. The islanders kept watching, expecting him at any moment to collapse and die. When nothing happened, they changed their minds and said to each other, "He must be one of the gods who has come to visit us."

Nearby was the estate of Publius, the Roman governor of the island. He welcomed Julius and his men, as well as Paul and the two of us, and hosted us for three days until more permanent arrangements could be made.

Now, Publius' father was very sick. He had a high fever and dysentery. Paul went into his room to see him, prayed, laid his hands on him, and he was healed.

When the islanders heard what had happened, they came to be healed, and they were. For the next three months they did all they could to honor and take care of us until the winter was over (Acts 28:1-10).

### Heading for Rome

A ship from Alexandria with the figurehead of the "Twin Brothers," the supposed sons of Jupiter, on its bow had wintered at the island and was now ready to leave for Rome. Julius got us on board, and the islanders said good-bye and gave us all the supplies we needed for the trip.

From Malta we sailed to Sicily and docked at Syracuse for three days, while they were unloading and loading the ship. We then sailed toward Italy, docked at Rhegium for a day, and then headed north. The next day we got to Puteoli, quite a distance from Rome, where we disembarked.

Because Puteoli was a port city, believers had gotten word that Paul was coming as a prisoner. Together with some of Paul's friends and relatives, they went to meet Paul and urged him to ask Julius to let him stay with them for a few days. Julius agreed and we stayed there a whole week before heading to Rome on foot.

During that week the believers in Rome got word that Paul was coming and decided to go to Appii Forum, about 40 miles south of Rome, to meet him. As the prisoners and guards were making their way through the marketplace, a believer recognized Paul and rushed over and hugged him. Then another and another did the same. The Roman guards didn't have the heart to stop it. More believers came to meet him at Three Taverns, 30 miles from Rome. This gave Paul courage and he thanked God for fellow believers.

When we finally reached Rome, Julius turned Paul over to the captain of the Imperial Guard. Because of the good letter about Paul by Governor Festus and Julius' good report, Paul was not thrown into prison, but was allowed to live in a small house by himself not far from Caesar's palace, chained to a Roman guard. (Acts 28:11-16).

### Paul Meets Fellow Jews

Three days later Paul sent a message to the Jewish leaders in Rome to come and see him. When they arrived, he greeted them warmly and said, "Brothers, I have done nothing wrong to be a prisoner. I have not done anything against our people or our faith. While I was in Jerusalem, our leaders handed me over to the Romans. After they examined me, they found nothing to warrant my execution and wanted to let me go, but the Jewish leaders objected. To save my life I was forced to appeal to Caesar. I have no intention of accusing our people of anything."

"I've asked you to come to see me so I can explain to you what happened and why I'm a prisoner. It's because of our faith and the hope we have as a people that I'm in chains."

They replied, "We didn't get word from Jerusalem telling us about you or what you did, so we appreciate your telling us. Also, we would like to know what you think about these people who call themselves Christians. There's a lot of talk about it and it's not very good."

They agreed on a time when they could come back and talk some more. When they returned, a number of others came with them.

From morning till night Paul explained the meaning of the kingdom of God and the hope of Israel. He showed them from the writings of Moses and the prophets that Jesus was the promised Messiah. Some were convinced from Scripture and believed, but others did not.

When they could not agree among themselves, they decided to leave. Before they left, Paul said, "The Holy Spirit was right when He spoke through Isaiah, saying, 'Go tell My people that they keep on hearing but never understand. They keep on looking but never see anything. Their hearts are hard. Their ears are closed. Their eyes are shut. They don't want to see, hear, or understand. So how can I help them?' That's why God sent this message of hope to the Gentiles, because they're willing to listen" (Acts 28:17-29).

### Two Years Later

It was two years before someone came to Rome to bring charges against Paul to appear before Caesar. During this time he welcomed all who wanted to see him, including those from Caesar's palace. He told them about the kingdom of God and taught them about Jesus. He shared his faith boldly, and no one stopped him. (Acts 28:30, 31).

# twenty-four

# Two Brothers: James and Jude

Greetings! This letter is from James, the Lord's step-brother, the leader of the church in Jerusalem, and a servant of God and of the Lord Jesus Christ. It is for those from the 12 tribes of Israel scattered abroad who have become Christians.

My brothers, there is a positive side to the trials you are going through because of your faith. These trials not only test and prove your faith, but they make you stronger. So don't give up, but let these trials do their work, and you'll be a more mature Christian because of what you're enduring.

If any of you lack wisdom, ask God for it. He gives graciously and generously to all who ask and without favoritism. But you have to ask for it in faith, firmly believing that He will give it to you. Those who ask and doubt, going back and forth, are like the waves of the sea driven by whatever wind comes along. If you're like that, don't think that the Lord will answer your prayer, because someone who can't make up his mind is not only unstable in what he believes, but is that way in all the other things he does.

Even though we're poor in this world's goods, we're rich in Christ. Those who are rich and without Christ are like flowers that bloom and fade. Their busy life ends and all they have is gone. But all who make it through the testing time will be glad, because their faith is genuine. And the crown of life that God promised those who love Him will be theirs.

No one should say that God brings on trials and temptations. God never orders persecutions, nor does He use evil people to test us. As far as temptations are concerned, we bring those on ourselves by listening to our desires and feelings. And when we do that, we sin, and the end result of sin is eternal death.

Everything good comes from heaven. The Father is a God of light, not of darkness. He's always the same. He never changes or is inconsistent. He created us to be His children, and through the truth of His Word, He made us new people to be the firstfruits of a great harvest (James 1:1-18).

## Living for Him

Brothers, be slow to speak and quick to listen. Don't be angry, even in your zeal for God. There's no benefit in that. Put away all ill will and unwholesome habits. Humbly hold on to the message God has put in your heart to help save you.

Don't just listen to His Word. Live it! If you just listen to it and don't live it, it's like looking in a mirror and seeing that your face is dirty, then walking away without doing anything about it. But if you look into the mirror of God's law, see what you need to do, and do it, you will surely be blessed.

If anyone among you thinks he's a Christian but doesn't control his tongue, he's fooling himself and his religion is worth nothing. In the sight of God, religion means taking care of orphans, helping widows without income, and avoiding being influenced by the evil in this world (James 1:19-27).

## The Meaning of Love

Brothers and sisters, don't be prejudiced and partial. That's not what our faith in the Lord Jesus is all about. If someone comes to church dressed in an expensive suit and wearing a huge gold ring and you seat him in a prominent place, but you seat a poorly dressed visitor near the back, what have you done? You're treating different people differently and have set yourself up as judge.

Listen to me! Didn't God choose the poor of this world who love Him and are rich in faith to be heirs of the kingdom? But you treat a poorly dressed visitor with less respect than a richly dressed one. It's the rich and powerful who are dragging you into court because of your faith. They are the ones who are against Christ.

The Scripture says, "Love your neighbor as yourself." If you do this, that's good. But if you're partial to the wealthy—or to anyone—you've broken the law. Whoever keeps the whole law but fails on this point is a lawbreaker. God said, "Don't commit adultery" and "Don't commit murder." Now, if you live a pure life and don't commit adultery but murder someone, you have broken the law. So keep the whole law, knowing that you'll be judged by it. In the judgment there is no mercy for those who have been merciless. But mercy triumphs over judgment (James 2:1-13).

## The Meaning of Faith

Brothers and sisters, what good is it if someone says he has faith, yet he doesn't do anything to show it? Will an inactive faith save him? If someone has no food or clothes and comes to you for help, and you pray with the individual and say, "The Lord bless you and may His peace be with you—keep warm and may your pantry always be full," but you don't assist the person in need, what good is your faith? Faith without works is meaningless.

Someone will say, "One person has faith, and another has works." How will I know that you have faith? Let me see it! I will show you my faith by what I do. You say you believe and have faith in God. That's good. The devil and his angels also believe—but look at them.

Let me give you an example from Scripture of what I mean. What does it say about Abraham? He showed his faith in God by going to Mount Moriah to sacrifice Isaac. His faith and his actions worked together. Because of what he did, the Scripture says, "Abraham believed God and his faith was credited to him as righteousness." That's why he is called God's friend. So you can see that we stand justified in God's sight, not just because we have faith and believe, but also by what we do. And what we do actually strengthens our faith.

Another example is Rahab, the Canaanite prostitute. She believed the God of Israel and showed her faith by hiding the Israelite spies and helping them escape. Just as a body that doesn't breathe is dead, so faith without works is dead (James 2:14-26).

### The Power of the Tongue

Brothers and sisters, don't be too eager to become teachers, because teachers will be judged more strictly than others. All of us make mistakes and say things we shouldn't. If someone never made a mistake or said things they shouldn't have, they would be perfect. If someone could do that, they would be able to keep their whole body in check.

Look at horses. We put bits in their mouths and control the whole animal. Look at ships. No matter how large a ship is, the pilot can control it by a small rudder. That's how it is with us. The tongue is a small part of our bodies, but it controls much of how we feel and what we do. A little flame can set a whole forest on fire. And a tongue can set a whole community on fire.

All kinds of land and sea animals have been trained by man, but no human beings have been able to fully control their own tongues. It's a restless evil that can poison everything around it. The same tongue can bless the Lord and curse people. Out of the same mouth can come blessing and cursing. This shouldn't be. Can good- and bad-tasting water come out of the same well? Can a fig tree produce olives or a grapevine produce figs? Neither can a salty spring produce fresh water.

Do you understand what I'm saying? Those who are wise know how to show it by what they do. But if you're jealous and selfish, don't sin by boasting of your wisdom. This kind of wisdom is not from above, but from below. It's earthly, sensual, and demonic. Wherever there's jealousy and selfishness, there's confusion and evil.

The wisdom that comes from above is pure, gentle, peaceable, willing to yield, and full of mercy and compassion; it's impartial and never hypocritical. This is the kind of fruit planted by those who love righteousness and peace (James 3:1-18).

### Pride

Where does all this arguing and fighting among you come from? It comes from you. You're envious and hateful, and even ready to murder to get what you want. You're never satisfied. It's because you don't pray for what you need. You don't get what you ask for because you ask for the wrong reason. You always want things for yourself.

When you're unfaithful to the Lord and behave like the world, you're no longer a friend of God, but His enemy. Don't take the Scripture lightly when it says, "God is jealous for our love and has given us the Holy Spirit to draw us closer to Him." The Scripture also says, "God opposes the proud but gives grace to the humble" (James 4:1-6).

### Humility

Resist the devil by submitting yourself to God and the devil will turn away. Draw close to God and He will draw close to you.

Examine yourself. Is your heart clean? Don't be hypocritical. Repent, mourn, weep, and put aside laughter if you have to, until you feel humble in the sight of God. Then He will lift you up and exalt you.

Don't criticize each other. When you do, you're setting yourself up as judge and going against God's law. God alone can judge, because He's the only one who knows people's hearts (James 4:7-12).

### Business

Those of you in business say, "Today we'll do this; tomorrow we'll do that. Today we'll make a profit here, and tomorrow we'll go there and make a profit." How do you know what will happen tomorrow? How certain is life, anyway? It can be here today and gone tomorrow.

What you should say is this: "If it's according to God's will, we will do this and that today and tomorrow." But you're so proud of everything you do. You love to talk about yourself, your business, and the profits you've made. That's not good and you know it. If you know what's good and don't do it, then it is sin (James 4:13-17).

## Wealth

The time is coming when those of you who are rich and have robbed employees of their rightful wages will weep and mourn. Your riches will be gone and your hoarded gold and silver will mean nothing. Your selfishness and dishonesty will witness against you.

The wages you have kept back from those who mowed your fields and harvested your grain will cry out to God for justice. You have lived in luxury and indulged your every wish. You have feasted and become fat, as though you're getting ready to be slaughtered like a fattened calf. You have persecuted and killed God's people, even though they have done nothing against you (James 5:1-6).

## Patience

Brothers and sisters, be patient. The Lord will come. Notice that the farmer sows, then waits for the spring rains to water the seed and for the fall rains to ripen the harvest. So be patient and encourage one another until the Lord returns.

Don't grumble and complain, because you'll be judged by what you say and do. Look at what the prophets endured when they spoke for the Lord. Yet we honor them for it. Think about Job's suffering. The Lord used him for the purpose of showing the enduring strength of faith against the devil's challenge. And notice how the Lord blessed him afterward. Our God is full of compassion and mercy.

Brothers and sisters, never make a promise, swearing by heaven that you will keep it. You don't need to do that. Just stick to yes or no and then keep your word. Be honest and sincere so you won't be condemned (James 5:7-12).

## Pray

If any of you are in trouble, pray to the Lord and ask Him to help you. To those of you for whom everything is going well, praise the Lord. If anyone is sick, he should call for the elders of the church to come and anoint him with oil and pray for him. The Lord will answer these prayers of faith in His own way. He will definitely forgive the person's sins, and if it's in His plan, He will also heal them.

Admit your mistakes to each other and confess your sins to God. Pray for one another. The prayers of the righteous have great power. Look at Elijah. He was just an ordinary man, but when he prayed for the rain to stop, it did. It didn't rain for three and a half years. Then he prayed for rain and it came, and the land produced a great harvest.

Brothers and sisters, if someone leaves the truth and you win him back, you've saved his soul and covered up a lot of sins that will never be known (James 5:13-20).

## Jude

From Jude, a servant of Jesus Christ and the brother of James, to those who are loved by God and kept safe by Jesus Christ. May mercy, peace, and love be yours.

## False Teachers

Dear friends, I intended to write to you more about our common faith, but under the present circumstances I need to encourage you to stand up for what God has told us.

Certain men have slipped in among you who are twisting the message of God's love and turning His grace into a license to do anything. They're rejecting Jesus Christ as Lord and what He has done for us.

I want to remind you that it was the Lord Jesus who brought God's people out of Egypt. But then He had to let those who didn't believe stay in the wilderness to die off, to be replaced by the next generation that did believe. You know that even angels who didn't stay within the limits of their authority but rebelled against God were cast out of heaven and are destined to be destroyed.

Then you have the example of Sodom and Gomorrah and the towns nearby, where the people thought of nothing but sex and perverting what's natural. They were destroyed by fire from heaven. Yet here are these men who have slipped in among you, claiming to have had visions which condone sin. This is an insult to God and the heavenly angels and a rejection of divine authority.

As you know, one of the names of the Son of God is "Michael," because He's like God and over all the angels, which is what His name means. When He came to resurrect Moses, He didn't argue with the devil or insult him. He simply said, "God rebukes your claim to him."

But these men are more like animals. They don't care whom they insult. They live by instinct. They're going down the same path as Cain did and don't know it. Like Balaam, they'll do anything for money. And they reject God's authority, just as Korah and his friends did when they rebelled against Moses.

They're like spoiled food being served at your *agape* feasts, or like dark clouds driven by the wind which give no refreshing rain. They're like fruitless trees at harvest time, completely dead. They're like wild ocean waves washing dirt ashore, or like meteors streaking across the sky, destined to disappear (Jude 1:1-13).

## The Coming of the Lord

Enoch, the seventh in descent counting Adam, saw the coming of the Lord in vision. He said, "Look! The Lord is coming with thousands and thousands of angels to carry out judgment on all the ungodly, who in their ungodly ways are insulting God by turning against Him." These people are hopeless. They find fault with everything. They never listen and they do whatever they feel like doing. They're full of talk, putting on the charm to get what they want.

You remember what the apostles and the Lord Jesus predicted. They warned us that the time would come, especially in the last days, when people will mock those who believe God. They will do what they think is right and won't listen to the Holy Spirit (Jude 1:14-19).

## Hold On

Dear friends, hold on to your faith. Pray for the power of the Holy Spirit in your lives. Keep your hearts filled with the love of God. And look forward to the coming of the Lord Jesus Christ, who will give you eternal life.

Be kind to those who are having doubts. Pull back to safety those who have fallen into the fire of unbelief. Hate their sins, but love those who sinned. Be kind and merciful to everyone (Jude 1:20-23).

## Blessings

Now to Him who is able to keep you from falling and to present you faultless to God with exceeding joy, to our wonderful Savior be glory and majesty, authority and power, now and forever. Amen (Jude 1:24, 25).

# twenty-five

# First Letter From Prison

While Paul was under house arrest in Rome, waiting for his case to be heard by the emperor, his thoughts turned to the churches and he wrote several letters. The first was written to the members in Ephesus:

"This letter is from Paul, an apostle of Jesus Christ by the will of God, to the believers in Ephesus and to all the faithful in Jesus Christ; grace and peace to you from God our Father and from the Lord Jesus.

"God has given us many spiritual blessings through his Son, Jesus Christ. From the very beginning He planned for us to be holy and stand blameless in His sight. His plan hasn't changed. He does this through Jesus Christ, making us His sons and daughters so we can live in His presence forever.

"It is because of His Son that we have redemption and forgiveness through the riches of His grace, which He lavished on us according to His wisdom and insight. He shared His thoughts and purposes with us through Jesus Christ at the time specified. His plan is to put all things in heaven and on earth under the lordship of Christ. This means that God claims us as His own in harmony with His purpose and plan. It is His will that we should inherit all things.

"So let us praise God because you were among the first of the Gentiles to put your faith in Christ and become God's people. As soon as you heard the truth about God and the good news of salvation, you believed, and God put His stamp of ownership on you through the gift of the Holy Spirit. The Holy Spirit is God's guarantee that we will receive everything He has promised. All the glory goes to Him. Praise His name forever! (Eph. 1:1-14).

## Prayers

"When I heard about your continued faith in the Lord Jesus and your love for all believers, I never stopped thanking God for you and praying for you. May the Father of our Lord Jesus Christ, the God of glory, give you spiritual wisdom and insight as you get to know Him better. May your eyes be opened and may your hearts be enlightened to fully realize the hope you have of the glorious inheritance that's waiting for you. May you feel His power working in you, as it does in all who believe.

"This is the same power that raised Christ from the dead and seated Him on the right hand of God above all rulers, authority, power, and dominion in this age and throughout all ages to come. God put all things under Christ, including the church that is His body, through which He is active in the world (Eph. 1:15-23).

### Grace and Faith

"At one time you were spiritually dead, sinning and patterning your life after the world. You were living the way the unseen ruler of spiritual powers wanted you to live. He energizes all those who are disobedient to live more and more that way. That's the way it was with you. You gave in to the lusts of the flesh, did whatever your heart and mind desired, and were headed for destruction, as are all others who live that way.

"God in His rich mercy and because of His great love for you, even when you were spiritually dead and lived the way you did, gave you a new birth to live a new life. So it's by God's grace that you have been saved, have been spiritually resurrected, and in the person of Jesus Christ are sitting next to God in heaven. God did this for you that you might display His kindness and grace.

"You have been saved by grace through faith in Christ, not by your ability to believe, but because God gave you the ability to believe as a gift. If you were saved by what you can do, you would become proud and boast about it. God made us who we are by what His Son has done for us, that we should walk in the way of Christ (Eph. 2:1-10).

### Don't Forget

"Once you were Gentiles and were referred to by Jews as the uncircumcised. That's when you were still without Christ and not yet part of Israel, because you didn't know about the covenant God made with His people. You were without hope and far away from God, but now you have been brought close to God and made part of God's Israel through the blood of Jesus Christ.

"Christ is our peace, who made Jew and Gentile one. He broke down the wall that separated us and did away with the hostility between us to create a new union of peace. He did this through the cross, putting such hostility to death. When He came, He spoke peace to all, both near and far. And through the Holy Spirit both Jews and Gentiles have access to the Father. So we are no longer strangers, but brothers—no longer foreigners, but citizens and members of the royal family.

"Our faith is built on the prophets and apostles, with Jesus Christ being the Chief Cornerstone that supports the whole structure. And the building continues to grow into a holy temple for the dwelling place of God (Eph. 2:11-22).

## Custodian

"As you know, I'm in prison because I took the good news of Jesus Christ to the Gentiles. I told you this before—how God made me a custodian of His grace. He revealed to me that the Gentiles are included in His plan, along with Israel. I just wrote it out for you. So read it again to make sure you understand the incomprehensible depth of Christ's love, which in the past was not known as it is today. The Holy Spirit first revealed it to the prophets and then to the apostles that the Gentiles should be heirs together with the Jews, and that God's promises and the good news of the gospel belong to both.

"This is what my ministry is all about. It's in harmony with the gift of grace that God gave me when He asked me to exercise His power on your behalf. This gift of ministry was given to me, the least important one of God's people, to share with the Gentiles the unsearchable riches of Christ and to help them understand God's plan, which they didn't know before.

"God's purpose for the church is to model this plan to the angels in heaven so they, too, can better understand His love for us. It is because of what Jesus Christ has done that we have boldness and confidence to come into the presence of God. So don't lose heart while I'm in prison. What I did was according to God's will and for your good (Eph. 3:1-13).

## Gratitude

"For this reason I bow my knees before the Father, to whom the whole family in heaven and earth belongs. I pray that He may strengthen you through the power of the Holy Spirit, and that Christ may dwell in your hearts through faith so that you're rooted and grounded in His love.

"And I pray that you may be able to comprehend with believers everywhere the breadth, length, height, and depth of the love of Christ, which is beyond human knowledge, so that your lives will overflow with the goodness and love of God.

"Now to Him who is able to do for us far more than what we ask or think, to Him be glory in the church through Jesus Christ forever and ever. Amen (Eph. 3:14-20).

# WITNESS: Acts Through Revelation

## Unity

"As a prisoner for the Lord, I urge you to walk worthy of your calling. Do so humbly, as those who have no voice in court but must depend on someone in authority to speak for them. Be gentle and patient with each other in love, doing your best to preserve the unity given by the Holy Spirit, which binds your hearts together in peace. There is one body of believers bound together by one hope. There is one Lord, one faith, one baptism, one God and Father of us all (Eph. 4:1-6).

## Spiritual Gifts

"God has given each of us a gift of grace, according to the riches of Christ, with which to help the church. As the Scripture says, 'When He ascended, He took with Him those who had been raised from the dead at His own resurrection as a sample of the resurrection to come. That's when He gave these spiritual gifts to us.' Does that mean He had to go somewhere on earth to get these gifts for us? Don't be foolish. The point of this Scripture is that He ascended into the highest heaven, from there to give us gifts to complete His mission.

"He gave some the gift of apostleship, some the gift of prophecy, and others the gift to be evangelists, pastors, and teachers. These gifts are to benefit everyone. Such gifts will bring about greater unity in the church and a more mature knowledge of Jesus Christ, and will help us measure up to what Christ has in mind for us.

"God does not want us to be like little children, who can be tossed here and there by the waves of the sea. He does not want us to be blown about by every wind of doctrine crafted by deceitful men to trick people into believing a lie.

"But God wants us to speak the truth in love and to grow up into Christ, who is the Head of the church. The church is His body on earth, knit together by what every part supplies. And with each person doing his share, the body will grow and strengthen itself through these gifts (Eph. 4:7-16).

## New in Christ

"So don't live like the rest of the Gentiles, and don't think like they do. What I'm telling you is from the Lord. They don't understand these things, because they have hardened their hearts against the truth and alienated themselves from God. They continue to be greedy, immoral, and selfish.

"But you're different. You listened to what Christ said and He taught you otherwise. The truth is always found in Jesus Christ. That's why we told you to put aside your former way of life and put on the new man with a new way of thinking, created by God to live a life of right-doing, reflecting His holiness (Eph. 4:17-24).

### The Seal of God

"Stop lying and be honest and truthful to everyone, especially to your fellow members. Don't get angry and end up sinning. Don't end the day like that and give Satan an opportunity to make things worse.

"If you have stolen before, don't keep on doing it, but get a job and share what you earn with those in need. Watch what comes out of your mouth. Talk about what helps the church and encourages people. Don't make the Holy Spirit sad. He brings with Him God's seal of redemption that you belong to Him. So put away all bitterness, anger, bad-mouthing, and arguing. Instead, be kind, tenderhearted, and compassionate, forgiving one another as Christ forgave you (Eph. 4:25-32).

### Imitate Christ

"As children of God, reflect the Father's love, just as Christ did. He gave His life as a love offering to God for you and me. There should be no sexual immorality, filthiness, greed, or jealousy among you. Nor should there be obscene language, coarse jokes, and foolish talking. All this is out of character for followers of Christ. Let your lives be filled with thanksgiving and praise.

"You know that those who do these things will not inherit the kingdom of God. Don't let anyone tell you differently. While God is love, He will carry out justice against those who disobey and live as they please. Don't be one of them (Eph. 5:1-7).

### Walk in the Light

"Once you were in darkness, but now you're in the light. So walk in the light. The light from the Holy Spirit is seen in goodness, right-doing, loving the truth, and doing what pleases the Lord.

"Don't have anything to do with the works of darkness, but expose them for what they are by the way you live. I don't even want to mention some of the shameful things done in secret. But the light will expose them. That's what the Scripture means when it says, 'Wake up, you who are sleeping. Christ is your Light' (Eph. 5:8-14).

### Be Wise

"Be careful how you live. Don't be a fool. Be wise. Live out the will of God. Don't get drunk, but let your lives be filled with the joy of the

Holy Spirit. Meet together. Sing together. Make melody in your heart to the Lord. Be thankful for everything God has done for you through Christ. Give in to each other for the sake of Christ (Eph. 5:15-21).

## Marriage

"Wives, honor your husbands, just as the church honors Christ. Husbands, love your wives, as Christ loved the church and gave His life for her. He set her apart as special. He gave her the Word of Life to make her a beautiful church without a wrinkle or blemish—totally innocent and blameless.

"This is how husbands should relate to their wives and love them. They should value them as they value themselves. We know that people don't hate their bodies but take care of them. That's how it is with Christ and the church. We are His church.

"As the Scripture says, 'A man leaves his father and mother and is joined in marriage to his wife, and they become one.' How two people can become one is a mystery, but that is the same thing that happens between Christ and the church. He is the Head and we are His body. So a husband should love his wife as his own body, and a wife should honor her husband (Eph. 5:22-33).

## Children and Parents

"Children, obey your parents. In the sight of the Lord, this is the right thing to do. 'Honor your father and mother' is the one commandment connected with a promise. Things will go better when you obey it, and you'll live longer. Fathers, don't discipline your children in anger and make them angry. But discipline them and teach them the way of the Lord (Eph. 6:1-4).

## Employees and Employers

"Servants and employees should respect and obey those they work for, not just to please them, but to show honesty and sincerity as Christ would have them do . They are His servants, obeying Him from the heart, which is the will of God. In this sense they are working for the Lord, not for people. And whatever good they do, the Lord will reward them for it.

"Employers should treat their employees the same way. Don't threaten them. You and they have the same Lord, who does not favor one person above another but loves everyone the same (Eph. 6:5-9).

## Spiritual Warfare

"Finally, brothers and sisters, be strong in the Lord. Put on the armor of God to protect yourself against the subtle attacks of the evil one. Our warfare is not against flesh and blood, but against the spiritual powers and cosmic forces trying to rule this planet.

"You need to put on the whole armor of God: the belt of truth, the breastplate of right-doing, the shoes of the gospel of peace, and the helmet of salvation. Then wear the shield of faith to protect yourself against the arrows of the evil one, and take the sword of the Spirit, which is the Word of God.

"Now, take a stand! Stay awake! Pray together! Also pray for me, that I will not lose my boldness in sharing the gospel of Jesus Christ. I'm His ambassador in chains. Pray that I will speak for Christ as I should (Eph. 6:10-20).

### Farewell

"I have asked Tychicus, my fellow worker and a faithful servant of the Lord, to take this letter to you, tell you about my circumstances, and answer any other questions you might have. I'm sending him because he knows all about me and will comfort your hearts and energize your faith.

"Peace to all of you. May the love of our heavenly Father and the Lord Jesus Christ be with you forever. Grace to all who love the Lord Jesus Christ with all their hearts" (Eph. 6:21-24).

# twenty six

# Second Letter From Prison

Greetings from Paul and Timothy, servants of Jesus Christ. Grace and peace from God our Father and the Lord Jesus Christ to all His people in Philippi, especially the elders and deacons.

"I thank God for you, always keeping you in my prayers. How it cheers my heart to think of you and to pray for you! I praise God for your fellowship in the gospel from the first day until now. God, who has begun a good work in you, will continue to do so until Jesus Christ returns.

"It's right for me to think of you this way, because you're in my heart and are partakers with me of God's grace. You're my partners in the work of the gospel for which I'm a prisoner. I truly long to see you with all the love that Jesus Christ has put in my heart for you.

"I pray that your love for the Lord and for each other may grow stronger and stronger, and that you may increase in knowledge and wisdom to choose what is best for your growth in Christ. I pray that you will be filled with the fruit of righteousness that comes from Christ through the Holy Spirit, for the glory and praise of God (Phil. 1:1-11).

### Ministry While in Prison

"Brothers and sisters, I want you to know that my imprisonment has actually advanced the gospel. The palace guards and all who come and go know that I'm a prisoner for the sake of Jesus Christ. My being in prison has given most of our brothers and sisters greater confidence in the Lord to spread the gospel more fearlessly than ever.

"Now, it's true that some are preaching the gospel with a spirit of competition. But others preach with a heart full of love and goodwill. They know that I've been called to the ministry of the gospel. The former are not really sincere, but are motivated by selfishness and cause unnecessary arguments about Christ. They don't care if their contentious ways and disturbances help to keep me in prison.

"But it's immaterial. Whatever their motives are for preaching, whether in pretense or in truth, what matters to me is that Jesus Christ is being preached. That's the important thing and this is what gives me the greatest joy (Phil. 1:12-18).

### Living for Christ

"I am confident that through your prayers and the working of the Holy Spirit, things will turn out for me to be released. But if not, I hope and pray that I will not fail the Lord. I want to be courageous, no matter what happens, so that Christ is exalted.

"For me to live is Christ—or to die is Christ. What is life all about if it isn't living for Christ? What is death all about if it isn't to see Christ someday? I belong to Him. So if I live, I will live for Him. If I die, I will sleep and after the resurrection be with Him. Sometimes I'm torn between these two. It's a lot better to die and later be with Him than to stay here. But for your sake it's more important for me to live and to rejoice with you over my release and continue to preach the gospel. I plan to come and help you make even more progress in your faith and love for Christ.

"In the meantime, conduct yourselves as worthy of the gospel of Christ. Whether I'm released and able to come to see you or not, I want to hear that you're standing firm for Him and, with one spirit and one mind, working together for the gospel.

"Don't be intimidated by your opponents. Always be upbeat and courageous. This will show them that you're on the winning side and they are not. Remember that you have been given the privilege not only to believe in Christ, but also to suffer for Him. Now you can identify with me and know a little of what I've been through and continue to go through (Phil. 1:19-30).

### Humility

"Your life in Christ has given you courage, made you strong, and comforted you. You have the companionship of the Holy Spirit and kindness and affection for one another. Now complete my joy by being united in heart and mind for one purpose—to glorify Jesus Christ.

"Don't be motivated by selfish ambition so that you can boast about what you're doing for the Lord, but be humble, treating others as better than yourselves. Don't just think about your own interests, but the interests of others. Think like Christ and have the same attitude He had toward people.

"Even though He always had the nature of God, He laid it aside and humbled Himself in order to take on human nature and become a servant. Not only that, but He became obedient unto death, even the death of open shame on a cross.

"This is why God has exalted Him and given Him a name that is above every name, that at the name of Jesus every knee should bow in heaven and on earth, and every tongue should openly confess Jesus Christ as Lord to the glory of the Father (Phil. 2:1-11).

### Light Bearers

"Therefore, my brothers and sisters, just as you first obeyed the Lord when I was with you, and now even more so as you have grown in Christ, don't stop. Continue doing so with awe and reverence, because it's a matter of salvation. It's evident that God is working in you, making you even more willing to obey, which pleases Him.

"Obey without complaining or arguing so you may be God's innocent and harmless children, shining as lights in a dark and sinful world. Hold on to God's Word so I can rejoice with you when Jesus comes and not be disappointed that all the work I have done for you was for nothing.

"Even if I'm executed and my blood flows out like a sacrifice, I want you to think of it as a sacrifice of faith in God. I'm not sad, because I'm looking forward with joy to seeing you in heaven, just as you look forward to seeing me. What a happy reunion that will be! (Phil. 2:12-18).

### Timothy

"I hope the Lord will let me send Timothy to you shortly so he can give me a report on how you're doing. He thinks much like I do and has the same deep concern for you as I have.

"Many are busy and don't feel an urgency for the things of Christ as he does. You know the kind of man he is, for he has proven himself to you. He is like a son to me and over the years has faithfully served side by side with me in advancing the gospel.

"I hope to send him to you as soon as they tell me what's going to happen to me. I'm confident that I'll be released soon and that we both can come to see you.

"I thought earlier of sending Epaphroditus but couldn't. He's my brother in the Lord and a faithful worker, a fellow soldier for Christ. You sent him here to minister to my needs, but he's been very sick and almost died. However, God heard our prayers and he's better now, a blessing for both him and me.

"He was very concerned that you might be overly worried about him. Since he's better, I'm sending him back to you so you can see for yourself that he's alive and well. Welcome him with open arms and praise the Lord! Treat him well, as you would all traveling workers for Christ. He risked his life coming here to minister to my needs, doing what you were unable to do for me (Phil. 2:19-30).

## Righteousness

"Finally, my brothers and sisters, rejoice in your relationship with the Lord. It may be repetitious for me to keep saying this to you, but it's a matter of safeguarding your faith.

"Watch out for those who, like dogs, are ready to bite you. They'll tell you to get circumcised as a sign of true worship and commitment to God. Circumcision is a matter of the heart and not a mutilation of the body. It has to do with the Spirit of God in our hearts and gratitude for what Jesus Christ has done for us.

"Our confidence with God is not in cutting our bodies, but in Jesus Christ. If anyone brags that their circumcision and keeping of other Jewish ceremonies give them standing with God, don't believe them. I could brag even more than anyone on that score.

"I was circumcised on the eighth day and belong to the tribe of Benjamin, the same tribe as King Saul. I was a Hebrew of the Hebrews, living the strict life of a Pharisee. As far as keeping the law was concerned, I was blameless. I was so full of zeal for God that I persecuted all who accepted Jesus Christ as the Messiah.

"I thought all these things would endear me to God, but now I see them as having hindered my spiritual growth. Further, I consider everything that leads me away from Christ as no more than trash. He is more important to me than anything else. I have lost everything for the sake of Christ and have done so gladly.

"I have no righteousness of my own. My righteousness is in Christ. I didn't achieve this standing with God by obeying Jewish laws and customs, but by having faith in what Christ has done for me.

"My sole aim in life is to be like Him. I want to feel His power in my life, to be like Him in death, and some day to be resurrected as He was (Phil. 3:1-11).

## Our High Calling

"I haven't yet reached the goal that Christ has in mind for me and for which He laid hold of me. But I don't look back. I forget the past and keep pushing ahead, focusing on the future and our high calling of God in Christ.

"Keep this in mind. Think about your Christian walk with God and

He will show you what changes you need to make. But whatever growing you need to do, first live up to what you already know.

"Follow my example. Others have left you a good example too. Pattern your life after us and don't listen to those I've warned you about. My heart goes out to you, and I've shed many tears as I've warned you against those who reject Christ's sacrifice on the cross as important. All they think about is themselves and their physical well-being. Whatever they glory in is to their shame and final destruction.

"But our citizenship is in heaven, and we look forward to seeing Jesus Christ, our Savior and Lord. He will transform our humble bodies and make them like His own glorious body. All power in heaven and on earth is His, and all things are subject to Him! (Phil. 3:12-21).

### Unity

"Friends, I really miss you. You are my joy and crown. So stand fast in the Lord and keep your eyes fixed on Him.

"As sisters in the Lord, Euodia and Syntyche need to come to a meeting of the minds. And Brother Syzygus should see what he can do to help them. These women have worked with Clement and me and others in spreading the gospel, and they worked hard. There's no doubt in my mind that their names are written in the book of life.

"Rejoice in your union with the Lord! And again I say, Rejoice! Let your kindness and gentleness be seen by everyone. Don't worry about anything. The Lord will come. Tell God what you need, and do so with a thankful heart. He will hear your prayers. His presence among us, which is beyond understanding, will keep your hearts and minds connected with Christ.

"Keep your minds filled with what is true, right, good, pure, lovely, and honorable. Put into practice what I've told you and what you've seen me do. May the peace of God be with all of you (Phil. 4:1-9).

### I Appreciate You

"After such a long time of not hearing from you, it's a great joy to know that you're still concerned about me. I'm not saying this because I think you've stopped caring for me or because I'm in need of anything, but because you haven't had a chance to do anything until now.

"Over the years I've learned to get along with what I have and to do without. There have been times of need and times when I've had more than enough. No matter what the circumstances, I've learned to be content. Whether I go hungry or have more than I can eat, Christ gives me strength to face all circumstances. Through Him I can do anything.

"It was good of you to share with me what you had when I needed help. Early in my ministry when I had to leave Macedonia, you were the only church that helped me. When I was preaching in Thessalonica, more than once you sent something for my needs.

"I'm not asking for anything now, just thanking you for your continued support. Epaphroditus brought your gifts. To me they are like a love offering, a sacrifice pleasing to God. And He will supply all your needs with the riches of heaven that we have in Jesus Christ. To God our Father be glory and praise forever and ever. Amen (Phil. 4:10-20).

### Final Greetings

"Greetings to all the saints, God's people who set themselves aside for Jesus Christ. Those who are with me send their greetings, especially those who work in Caesar's palace and now belong to Christ. The grace of the Lord Jesus be with all of you" (Phil. 4:21-23).

# twenty-seven

# Third and Fourth Letters From Prison

This letter is from Paul, an apostle of Jesus Christ by the will of God, and from Timothy, to all the faithful brothers and sisters in Colosse. Grace to you and peace from God our Father and the Lord Jesus Christ.

"We thank God for your faith in Christ and for the love you have for your brothers and sisters everywhere. Your faith and love have come from the hope you have and from what God has waiting for you in heaven, which you learned from the gospel. The good news is going everywhere and bearing fruit, just as it has among you from the first day you heard and understood God's love and grace.

"It was Epaphras, a fellow servant and worker, who brought the gospel to you and planted a church in your city. He told me about your faith and love and what the Holy Spirit has done for you.

"Since we heard this, we have never stopped praying for you. We are asking the Lord to give you greater knowledge of His will and to fill your hearts and minds with spiritual wisdom and understanding, so He can be proud of you and you can be fruitful in all your good work for Him.

"We pray that God will strengthen you by His power and give you endurance, patience, steadfastness, and joy. We thank our heavenly Father, who through Christ has qualified you to share in the inheritance promised to all who believe (Col. 1:1-12).

### The Superiority of Christ

"God delivered us from the power of darkness and transferred us into the kingdom of His Son, whom He loves very much. Through Christ we have redemption and forgiveness of sin. He is the perfect reflection of God, holding the rights to all creation, as a firstborn son has to his father's estate. Through Him God created everything in heaven and on earth—visible and invisible—angelic authority and cosmic systems. All things were created by Him and everything exists for Him. He existed before anything was created.

"He is the head of the church and conquered death, which makes Him first in everything. It is God's intention that, through the death of His Son, the whole universe be brought back into harmony, as it was in the beginning (Col. 1:13-20).

## The Gospel

"You were once alienated from Christ and were enemies of God. But now He has reconciled you to God through His death on the cross, to be holy and blameless in God's sight without shifting in the faith. So stay grounded and don't let anyone take away the hope that you have in Christ. This is the gospel, which you already know and which is now being preached everywhere. And this is what my ministry is all about.

"I rejoice even in my sufferings because of what the gospel has done for you. If there is any suffering to be added to Christ's suffering, for His sake and the sake of the church I'm willing to do it.

"God called me into the ministry and has given me the responsibility to help fulfill the promise of His Word, that people everywhere should hear the gospel. That's why I'm writing to you. The mystery of God's love was not as fully understood in ages past as it is now, because He has revealed it to us in Jesus Christ. And it is the will of God that Christ, the hope of glory, live in your hearts, too.

"We preach Christ and with all earnestness teach and warn everyone for the purpose of presenting them complete in Jesus Christ. This is the focus of my ministry, for which I labor according to the strength the Lord has given me (Col. 1:21-29).

## Be Careful

"I want you to know how concerned I am for you, for those in Laodicea, and for all those who believe, even though I've never met them. You need to be one in heart and mind, knit together in love, and full of courage. I want you to be spiritually rich, having the full assurance of Christ and a greater understanding of God's love. That is the greatest treasure you could have.

"I'm telling you this because I don't want anyone to trick you into believing something else, no matter how reasonable it sounds. Though I'm not there personally, I am with you in spirit and rejoice to see your unity and firmness of faith in Christ. Continue this way. Be as committed to Christ now as you were when you first accepted Him. Stay rooted in Him by building your faith each day as I taught you to do, making it stronger and overflowing with thanksgiving.

"Be careful about philosophy, human logic, religious traditions, and a spirituality not based on Scripture. Christ must be the center of your lives. You are complete in Him. Nothing else needs to be added. He is fully God, even though He has taken on human nature, and is above all human authority and power (Col. 2:1-10).

### Christ Brought About a Change

"Through Christ your heart was circumcised by cutting away the sins of the flesh, and you were washed clean by baptism. Spiritually, you were buried in a watery grave and raised from the dead by faith in Him. You are now spiritually alive, having all your sins forgiven. When Christ died on the cross, He paid the debt we owed, nailing that legal note to the cross. He defeated all the powers of evil openly for all to see.

"So don't let anyone judge your faith by the food you eat or by the feasts and ceremonial sabbaths you should keep. And don't let anyone take away your security in Christ by telling you to worship angels, no matter how humble they are. These kinds of people are caught up in what they have supposedly seen, and they can't stop talking about it.

"They are not the head of the church—Christ is. Through Him all things are held together, just as ligaments hold a body together. The strength and growth of the church come from God.

"If you died and rose with Christ and stopped listening to the world, why would you now listen to those who tell you what to do to be religious? These false ideas will perish with those who believe them. They have the appearance of wisdom, but it's a worship of God with a covering of humility based on pride. Such mistreatments of our bodies as they suggest have absolutely no value in curbing sin (Col. 2:11-23).

### Look to Christ

"You died with Christ when you were baptized and raised to a new life. So keep your mind on Him, who is at the right hand of God. Don't focus on things of this world, for your life is in Jesus Christ. When He appears, then He will take you to be with Him, giving you a glorious and everlasting future.

"So do away with whatever belongs to this world: sexual immorality, impurity, shameful passions, evil desires, and greed, which are another form of idolatry. Those who do these things will perish, and these things will perish with them.

"At one time you lived this way, but you have put all these things behind you, including loss of temper, using bad language, and being disagreeable. And remember not to lie, because that, too, is part of the old man of sin.

"You are a new people, every day being renewed by God's grace to reflect His image, which is the purpose for which you were created.

"In God's sight there is no difference between a Jew and a Greek, between a free man and a slave, or between a former barbarian and a believer. We are all one in Christ (Col. 3:1-11).

## Christian Character

"As you are now the chosen of God, put on the character of Christ, which means to be full of compassion, gentleness, kindness, mercy, and forgiveness. Be patient with each other. Instead of complaining about others, forgive them, just as the Lord has forgiven you.

"Above everything else add love, which binds us together. Let the peace of God control your hearts, because you are all one people. Always be grateful.

"Let the Word of God fill your hearts with wisdom as you teach and encourage others in the faith. Sing hymns and spiritual songs as your hearts overflow with gratitude.

"Whatever you say and do, do it all in the name of Jesus, praising God through Him (Col. 3:12-17).

## The Christian Home

"Wives should honor their husbands, which is fitting in the Lord. Husbands should love their wives, as the Lord loves the church. Let there be no bitterness between them. Children should obey their parents—this pleases the Lord. Fathers, don't be angry with your children or you'll discourage them.

"Servants, obey your masters, not just to please them, but to please God. The Lord will reward you for it. Those who do wrong will be paid accordingly, because God is not unjust. Masters, be fair with your servants. Don't forget that you too have a Master, a heavenly One (Col. 3:18-4:1).

## Christian Conduct

"Be persistent in prayer. Let your hearts overflow with thanksgiving. Pray for us, that God will open another window of opportunity for us to continue to share the secrets of Christ, even though I'm in prison for it. Also, pray that I may give the message clearly so it can be understood.

"And conduct yourselves wisely toward others. Take every opportunity to share Christ with them. Let your words be gracious and seasoned with the salt of kindness, so that you can always respond to others in the right spirit (Col. 4:2-6).

## Final Greetings

"Tychicus, who is a beloved brother, a faithful minister, and a fellow servant, will be bringing you this letter and will tell you all about me. This is the reason I'm sending him to you, so that you can know how we're doing and don't have to keep worrying.

"Onesimus, a faithful and dear brother, is coming with him. He's one of your own. The two of them will tell you everything.

"Aristarchus, who is helping me here in prison, sends his greetings. If Mark, the cousin of Barnabas, comes to visit you, welcome him. Joshua, known as Justus, also sends his greetings. These three Jewish converts have been a real comfort to me.

"Epaphras, who also is one of your own and a true servant of Christ, sends his greetings. He is always praying for you, that you may be mature and stand up for Christ as all believers should. He has worked hard for you and for those in Laodicea and Hierapolis.

"Our beloved doctor, Luke, sends his greetings, as does Demas.

"Give my greetings to the brothers and sisters in Laodicea, especially Nympha and the church meeting in her house.

"After you read this letter, have the church in Laodicea read it too. Then read the letter I wrote to them.

"Tell Archippus to take his call to the ministry more seriously and to do the work the Lord has given him to do.

"This last line of greeting is from me and in my own handwriting. Don't forget my chains. Grace to all of you" (Col. 4:7-18).

## A Personal Letter to Philemon

"This letter is from Paul, a prisoner of Jesus Christ, and from Timothy, our brother, to Philemon, a dear friend and fellow worker for Christ. Greetings to our dear sister, Apphia; to Archippus, a fellow soldier for Christ; and to the church that meets in your house. Grace and peace to all of you from God our Father and from the Lord Jesus Christ (Philemon 1:1-3).

## Thank You

"I thank God for you and always keep you in my prayers. I continue to hear about your strong faith in the Lord Jesus and your love for God's people. I pray that you may become more and more effective in sharing our mutual faith, and that you may grow in your understanding of all the blessings and privileges that are ours in Christ.

"Your love and concern for me gives me courage and joy, especially when I think about how you continue to cheer the hearts of our people (Philemon 1:4-7).

## A Request

"As an apostle, I wouldn't hesitate in the name of Jesus Christ to demand that you do what is right. But I would rather appeal to you on the basis of love.

"I'm an old man and a prisoner because of Jesus Christ. So I'm appealing to you for Onesimus, whom I have adopted as my spiritual son while here in prison. Before he gave his heart to Christ, he was a useless servant to you, but now he's very helpful to me and will be to you. So while I'd love to keep him, I'm sending him back to you, and my heart goes with him. It's as if you yourself are here helping me in my imprisonment for the gospel.

"But I wouldn't want to do anything without your permission. I don't want you to feel that you have to take him back. I want you to do it willingly. When he ran away from you, he came here to Rome and shortly after that he gave his heart to Christ. So he's been separated from you for a little while, but now you may have him back, not just as a servant, but as a brother forever in Christ. That's what he is to me.

"So if you see me as a partner in the work of the gospel, accept him as you accept me. If he has wronged you in any way or owes you anything, charge it to me. I'm writing this letter with my own hand and promise to repay you for it. Of course, I could mention what you owe me by bringing you to Christ but I will not.

"Refresh my old heart and bring me some joy in the Lord. I know you'll do what I ask, because you always do so and more. That's why I'm writing this letter and sending it back with Onesimus. Prepare a room for me, because I believe that, through your prayers and the prayers of others, it won't be long and I'll be released and will be back to see you (Philemon 1:8-22).

## Goodbye

Epaphras, who is here helping me, sends his greetings, as do Mark, Aristarchus, Demas, and Luke. The grace of the Lord Jesus Christ be with you" (Philemon 1:22-25).

# twenty-eight

# Paul's Letter to the Hebrews

To my learned Hebrew brothers: This is not an ordinary letter. I've given careful thought to what I'm going to say. As you know, in the past God spoke to our ancestors through the prophets, but in our day He has spoken to us in the person of His Son, through whom He made the worlds.

"The Son is His Father's glory, His exact image, and the rightful heir. He upholds everything by His power. After He died for us, He returned to the Father and sat at His right side, the place of honor (Heb. 1:1-3).

### The Son of God

"He is far superior to angels. To which of the angels did God ever say, 'You are My son'? But to Christ He said, 'You are My Son.' He also said, 'Let all the angels worship Him.'

"Angels are powerful beings. They are God's messengers, who travel faster than the wind. But God's Son is different. God said to Him, 'Your throne, O God, like Mine, will last forever and ever. Righteousness is the rule of Your kingdom. You love what is right and hate what is evil. That's why I rejoice over You and have anointed You with the oil of gladness. You created the heavens and the earth. The whole universe is the work of Your hands. The earth will grow old and wear out like a garment. It will become like an old robe that You fold up and throw away, like a garment that needs to be changed. But You are always the same. Your years will never end.'

"To which of the angels did God say all this? None. However, to Christ He said, 'Come, take Your place of honor at My right side. Your enemies will become nothing but a footstool for You.'

"Angels are God's servants, helping those who are being saved and ministering to their needs (Heb. 1:4-14).

### Be Careful

"Therefore, we need to be careful and give even more attention to what the prophets have said, lest we drift away from our faith.

"If what the angels said to our ancestors was true, that every disobedience had its consequences, how will we escape if we don't listen to what God said, neglecting the salvation He has so graciously provided? God confirmed His plan through miracles, signs, and wonders, and by the gift of the Holy Spirit (Heb. 2:1-4).

### Jesus Christ

"God put Adam in charge of the world when He created it, not the angels. As the Scripture says, 'What is man that you think so highly of him or the son of man that you care so much about him? You made him lower than the angels, but only for a little while. You crowned him with glory and honor and put him in charge of everything.'

We don't see God's original plan being worked out, but we do see Jesus, who became one of us, taking a position lower than angels, then being crowned with glory and honor after giving His life for us. This all took place because of God's grace. So it is only right for God to bring all men together under one Head: Jesus Christ, through whom He created all things.

"Jesus could not be made the Head of our race without suffering. It is through Jesus Christ that men and women are made holy. There are no exceptions. All who are made holy have the same Father. That's why Christ can call us brothers and sisters and say to God, 'I will tell my brothers and sisters about You and praise Your name in their meetings.' And, 'Here am I and those You have given Me.'

"We all have the same flesh and blood. So when Christ came and took human nature, He became one of us. And through His death He set us free from death by destroying the power the devil had over us.

"He did not come to help angels, but the descendants of Abraham, who are his offspring by faith. He had to become like us so that He could be an understanding High Priest and make the necessary sacrifice for our sins. Because He was tempted and suffered, He is able to help us when we are tempted and suffer (Heb. 2:5-18).

### Be Faithful

"Therefore, my learned brothers, consider Israel's calling and our High Priest, Jesus Christ. He was appointed to that office by God and was faithful to it, as Moses was. But Jesus is more worthy of honor than Moses, just as someone who designs and builds a house is more important than the house. There's no comparison. A man can build a house, but it's God who gives him the ability to do so.

"Moses was a faithful servant in God's house and talked about things which would come later. But Jesus Christ is in charge of the house because it is His. What house? We are His house, as long as we continue to have confidence in Him and hold on to the hope we have until the end.

"The Holy Spirit says, 'If you want to hear what God is saying, don't harden your hearts as your ancestors did in the wilderness.' He reminds us that God said, 'My people saw what I did for them when I brought them out of Egypt, but they still didn't believe that I would bring them into Canaan. For 40 years they saw My works and refused to obey Me. They said they knew Me when they really didn't. I was very disappointed with that generation. I promised Myself not to bring these rebellious ones into Canaan.'

"So be careful, my brothers, lest any of you doubt what God says and end up turning against Him. Do all you can to encourage each other to believe what God says. Don't harden your hearts. Those who have confidence in what God says belong to Christ.

"As the Scripture says, 'Listen to God and don't be stubborn like our ancestors were when they came out of Egypt and rebelled.' Which ones caused God so much grief for 40 years? Those who were led by Moses and rebelled and died in the wilderness. They never made it to Canaan because they didn't believe what God said (Heb. 3:1-19).

### God's Promise

"It's frightening to think that after God promised to bring us into the heavenly Canaan we would miss it. The good news of salvation through Christ is not only being offered to us—it was offered to our ancestors. But it didn't do them any good, because they didn't accept it by faith. If we believe God and take hold of His promise, our hearts will be at rest, because the Scripture says, 'I will give them rest and bring them into Canaan.'

"Why is God working so hard for us when He finished His work at the time of Creation? As the Scripture says, 'On the seventh day God rested from all his work.' Now it is obvious that He has some more work to do because He also said, 'Only those who are rebellious will never enter Canaan.' So there are some who will enter.

"If God had only been speaking about literal Canaan when He said to our ancestors, 'Listen to Me and don't harden your hearts,' He wouldn't have had to say that in David's day, and then have to say it again today. If we want our hearts to have rest and enter heavenly Canaan, we need to stop trying to make it there on our own by what we do. We need to rest in God's finished work on Calvary, just as He rested on the seventh day after Creation. Let's not fail for lack of faith as our ancestors did.

"God's Word is alive and powerful and sharper than a two-edged sword. It will cut your heart open and expose your thinking, your motives, and what you really want. Nothing is hidden from God. He knows everything, and it is to Him that we have to answer (Heb. 4:1-13).

## Compassionate Intercession

"Jesus Christ intercedes for us as our High Priest. He ascended and is now at the right hand of God in the sanctuary in heaven. Let's hold on to what we believe.

"He's not a high priest who has no sympathy or compassion for us. He was tempted as we are, and even more, but never sinned. So let's come boldly to His throne of grace. He is merciful and will give us the grace and help we need.

"As you know, a high priest is called to serve God and to offer sacrifices for the sins of the people. He deals gently with those who bring their sacrifices but don't understand spiritual things and make mistakes, because he knows his own weaknesses. He must offer sacrifices for his own sins, also. He doesn't just decide to become a high priest. He must be called by God, as Aaron was.

"Christ didn't just decide to be a high priest, but He was called by God, who said, 'You are My Son and I am Your Father. I have chosen You to be High Priest just as I chose Melchizedek.' Who was Melchizedek? He was a priest of God in the time of Abraham before Aaron was even born.

"During his life on earth Christ prayed earnestly to God, with tears and cries of anguish, not to have to die. But He was submissive and devoted to doing God's will. God heard Him, but Christ had to learn from experience what it meant to be obedient unto death. This is what made Him a perfect High Priest and the Source of salvation to all who listen and obey.

"There is much more we can say about all this, but you have had a hard time understanding spiritual things because you're not really listening (Heb. 4:14–5:11).

## Spiritual Growth

"You really should be teaching others about all this. But here I am teaching you the very basic principles found about Christ in Scripture. You need to drink some more spiritual milk before you're ready for solid food. Those who live on spiritual milk are not skilled enough to teach scriptural principles to others, because they're like newborn babies themselves.

"Solid spiritual food belongs to those who are spiritual adults. They can handle what is being said and know the difference between what is scriptural and what is not—what is good and what is evil.

"So let's leave the discussion of the basic principles about salvation in Scripture and not keep on going over the same ground again and again. I should not have to tell you that works will not get you to heaven, that salvation is a free gift, that you should believe what God says, and that there is a resurrection from the dead and a judgment. Let's move on to maturity; God will help us.

"Can we bring back those who have left the faith? They took hold of the light, tasted salvation, and had a share in the outpouring of the Holy Spirit. They knew from experience that the Word of God did them good, and they tasted the power of God's coming kingdom. It's impossible to bring these people back, as long as they keep crucifying Christ again by turning against Him.

"When a field drinks up the rain which God gives and produces things for the good of everyone, people rejoice. But if a field drinks up the rain and produces nothing but weeds and thorns, people curse the ground and set the field on fire.

"We expect you to be a good field and are confident that you will produce crops that go along with salvation. God will not forget your labor of love—how you've helped your fellow believers and are continuing to do so. Do it with full assurance and hope as you look forward to the coming of Christ. Don't slip into a do-nothing state, but believe and persevere as others have and you'll receive what God promised (Heb. 5:12–6:12).

### Promise Keeper

"When God makes a promise, He keeps it. He said to Abraham, 'I will bless you and multiply your descendants,' and He meant it. He even confirmed it by an oath. Abraham held on to that promise and eventually it was fulfilled.

"We do the same in courts today. We take an oath to tell the truth or swear by some higher authority that what we said is the truth. That's why God confirmed His promise with an oath—to leave no doubt that He meant what He said. And since He couldn't swear by a higher authority, He swore by Himself.

"So God's promise rests on two things—His oath and the fact that He cannot lie. What He said cannot be changed. Faith in Him is the anchor of our soul. No one can pull up that anchor.

"This is what gives us courage to come into the presence of God. Jesus, our High Priest, is already there and He'll live on forever (Heb. 6:13-20).

### High Priest and King

Melchizedek was both priest and king. He was the king of Salem who went out to bless Abraham after his victory over the enemy kings who had taken Lot and his family captive.

"Abraham gave his tithe to Melchizedek, whose name means 'king of righteousness' and, because of Salem, 'king of peace.' In this sense he is like the Son of God. Even though we know little about him, just think how great he must have been if Father Abraham gave him his tithe!

"Our ancestors gave their tithe to the Levites, but as descendants of Abraham, they acknowledged a greater priesthood. We know that the lesser always pays tithe to the greater. So when Father Abraham gave his tithe to Melchizedek, though Levi and Aaron had not yet been born, it was as if they had given their tithe to Melchizedek through him (Heb. 7:1-10).

## A New Priesthood

"If the Aaronic priesthood was sufficient, why would we need a different priesthood, one like Melchizedek's? And if there was a change of priesthood, there must have been a reason for it. You don't change the priesthood without reason.

"Moses never said anything about a priesthood from the tribe of Judah. The priests came from the tribe of Levi. But Jesus Christ came from the tribe of Judah, and God declared, 'You are Priest forever after the order of Melchizedek.'

"This change in the priesthood and the laws that govern it means that the former priesthood was not perfect. And if the new priesthood is forever, it does what the former one could not do. This gives us a much better hope, and this hope gives us courage to come into the presence of God.

"Christ's priesthood was confirmed by an oath; Aaron's never was. Of this new priesthood God declared, 'I have taken an oath, and appointed You to be My Priest forever.'

"A new priesthood means a new and better covenant. Jesus Christ guarantees it. We've had priest after priest because they grew old and died, but Christ lives forever. So we have a priesthood that never changes. Christ is always there. He never stops interceding for us and is able to save all who come to God through Him.

"This is the kind of High Priest we need: one who is holy, without sin, and continuously in the presence of God, not just once a year as Aaron was. And He does not have to offer sacrifices every day, as a Levitical priest had to do, first for his own sins and then for the sins of the people. Jesus did this once and for all when He died on the cross for our sins. Our high priests have been men with human weaknesses, but Jesus is sinless. That's why he was made High Priest by an oath from God and will be so forever" (Heb. 7:11-28).

171

# twenty-nine

# Hebrews: A New Sanctuary

Paul continued:

"The main point of what I have tried to show you so far is that we have a new High Priest, who is seated at God's right side in the heavenly sanctuary. That sanctuary was built by God, not by man.

"Every high priest offers sacrifices, so Jesus also must have something to offer. If He were here on earth, there would be no need for Him to be a priest, because we have priests who do this, as Moses taught them. God said to him, 'Build Me a sanctuary after the pattern I showed you when you were with Me in the mountain.' This included directions for offering sacrifices.

"But now we have a better arrangement, a new covenant, a better priesthood, because it's based on the promise of better things to come. If the first arrangement with a human priesthood had been flawless, there would have been no need for change. As God said, 'The day will come when I will make a new arrangement with My people. It will not be like the one I made with their ancestors when I brought them out of Egypt, because I couldn't depend on them.

'I will put My laws in their minds and write them on their hearts. They will be My obedient people, and I will be their God. There will be no need of priests to teach them, because they will all know Me, from the least to the greatest. I will be merciful to them, forgive their sins, and remember their lawlessness no more.'

"If God has made a more permanent arrangement, a new covenant, so to speak, then the first one is obsolete. And what is obsolete should be discontinued (Heb. 8:1–13).

## Symbolism

"We know that the first sanctuary, the one that Moses built, had rules and regulations. Everything about it was orderly. It had a courtyard, and the sanctuary had two parts to it—the holy place and the Most Holy Place.

"In the holy place were the seven-branched lampstand, the small altar of incense, and the table holding the 12 flat loaves of holy bread. Behind the veil was the Most Holy Place, which had the golden censer, and the ark overlaid with gold. On the inside of the ark were the golden pot of manna, Aaron's rod that had budded and bloomed, and the Ten Commandments written by God. On the lid of the ark, which is God's mercy seat, were two carved angels. We don't have time to go into detail about that right now.

"After the sanctuary was built, the priests went daily into the holy place to perform their services. But only the high priest could go into the Most Holy Place and only once a year. Before he went in, he had to offer a sacrifice for his own sins and the sins of the people, even those sins committed in ignorance.

"The Holy Spirit through Scripture told us that the services in the heavenly sanctuary had not yet begun. The services in the earthly sanctuary were only symbolic. Those sacrifices couldn't take away sin or make people holy. Even the food offerings and washings were necessary only until the time would come for change (Heb. 9:1-10).

### Reality

"When Christ became High Priest, He went into the greater and perfect sanctuary in heaven, not into a sanctuary built by men. He didn't go into this Most Holy Place with the blood of sheep and goats, but with His own blood, which He shed for our redemption.

"If the blood of sheep and goats and the sprinkling of their ashes could make the people ceremonially clean and set them apart for God, how much more can the sacrifice of Christ, who was filled with the Holy Spirit, cleanse us and set us apart to serve God!

"This is the reason why Christ is the Mediator of this new arrangement, which God had promised would come. Even under the old arrangement, it was Christ's *promised* sacrifice that redeemed people (Heb. 9:11-15).

### Legality

"When someone makes a will, he has to die before it can go into effect. As long as he lives, it carries no legal obligation. That's why sacrifices were needed even at the old sanctuary.

"After Moses wrote down everything God told him, he took the blood of sheep and goats, mixed it with water, and sprinkled it on the holy scroll and out toward the people. As he did so, he said, 'This blood seals the agreement that God expects you to live up to.' Then he sprinkled the sanctuary and all the utensils with blood. This showed that everything had to be purified with blood and that without the shedding of blood there is no forgiveness of sin.

"The same applies to Christ's ministry in heaven, except that there had to be a better sacrifice than the blood of sheep and goats. Christ did not go into the sanctuary we built, which is patterned after the sanctuary in heaven, but into the presence of God in the heavenly sanctuary.

"Christ didn't have to offer His blood year after year, as the high priests had to offer the blood of sheep and goats for sin before going into the presence of God. If that were the case for Christ, He would have had to die every year since the entrance of sin. But it is now, in our day and age, that Christ came and offered Himself to do away with sin.

"Just as everyone dies at one time or another and there is one judgment, so also there is only one sacrifice that is needed—Christ's sacrifice. And even when He comes the second time, it will not be to die again, but to take those home who have waited for Him (Heb. 9:16-28).

### God's Plan

"The old sacrifices were only shadows of what was to come, not the real thing itself. The sacrifices offered year in and year out couldn't change the people. If so, they wouldn't have had to be repeated, because the sins of the people would have been paid. But the sacrifices continued, showing that they could not do what needed to be done.

"When Christ was about to leave heaven and come to this world, He said to God, 'It's not more sacrifices and burnt offerings that You want, because they can't take away sin. But You have planned a body for Me, and I'm ready to do Your will, just as it says in the Scriptures.'

"First He said that sacrifices, even if done according to law, can never take away sin. Then He said He would come to do God's will. This sequence will tell you that Christ's sacrifice is more important than the sacrifice of sheep and goats. It is through the sacrifice of Christ that we are made holy, and His sacrifice is enough for all time.

"Priests offer sacrifices every day and many times a day. But, as I said, they can never take away sin, no matter how many sacrifices they offer. Christ made one sacrifice for sin and then sat down next to God. This shows that His sacrifice is good forever. Now He's just waiting for the day when God will put Christ's enemies under His feet.

"The Holy Spirit says the same thing. Speaking for God through Jeremiah, He said, 'I will put My laws in their minds and write them on their hearts.' Then He adds, 'I will forgive their sins and remember their lawlessness no more.' If sins are forgiven through Christ, sin offerings are no longer needed (Heb. 10:1-18).

## Confidence

"So let's come into the holiest sanctuary, which is in heaven, and into the presence of God with confidence because of Christ's sacrifice. Through His humanity Jesus made a new way for us to come into God's presence, by taking away the veil that had separated us from Him.

"Jesus is our High Priest, so let us come into the presence of God with pure hearts, clean bodies, and a sincere faith. Let's hold on to the hope we have in Christ with confidence and full assurance that God is faithful and will do what He promised. Let us help each other to be good, to love one another, and to do things for the Lord. And let's not stop meeting together, but continue to encourage each other even more as we get closer to the coming of the Lord (Heb. 10:19-25).

## Courage

"If we willfully keep on sinning after we know the truth and turn away from Christ, there is nothing to take away our sins. The only thing to look forward to is the judgment and total annihilation.

"According to Moses, anyone who breaks the law dies when two or three witnesses present evidence that would prove him guilty. How much more someone who shows contempt for Christ, rejects God's grace, and insults the Holy Spirit! God said, 'Judgment is Mine and I will carry it out.' It's a terrible thing to face the living God with a rebellious heart.

"Remember the early days of your faith? The sufferings and struggles you went through after God's light came to you? You were insulted and ridiculed, and yet you chose to identify yourself with those of like faith who were also treated the same way. Your heart went out to those of us who were arrested and imprisoned, including me. When evil men broke into your houses and took what they wanted, you let them have it, because you knew you had something much better waiting for you which would last forever.

"So don't lose your courage—it will be rewarded. Keep patiently doing the will of God and He will fulfill His promise. As the Scripture says, 'Just a little longer, and He who said He is coming *will* come and will not keep putting it off.' It also says, 'My people will live by faith. It is not pleasant to see those who should have faith turn away from Me.'

"We are not part of those who turn away and will be destroyed, but we belong to those who go on believing and will be saved (Heb. 10:26-39).

### Faith

"Faith gives us a basis for our hope and evidence of things we can't see. This is the kind of faith God commended our ancestors for having. It is by faith we believe that God created this world out of nothing, as He did all the other worlds.

"It was by faith that Abel offered a lamb, believing that the Savior would come. God accepted his sacrifice because it was offered in faith. Abel's faith in God still speaks to us today.

"Then there was Enoch, who was taken to heaven without experiencing death. He had lived a life of faith and pleased God by what he said and did.

"Without faith we cannot please God. We first have to believe that He exists, trust Him, and believe that He rewards those who live for Him.

"By faith Noah believed what God told him and built a boat to save his family. The world was destroyed by a flood, but Noah was declared righteous and saved, not because he built a boat, but because of his faith.

"It was Abraham's faith in God that led him to obey and leave his comfortable home to follow God's leading into a strange land. He never knew where God would lead him the next day. He was a foreigner in a strange country, living in tents as Isaac and Jacob did. They all were pilgrims looking forward to living in a city built by God.

"It was by faith that Sarah in her old age conceived and gave birth to a son, because she believed God's promise. So from a 100-year-old man and a 90-year-old woman came so many descendants that they're hard to count (Heb. 11:1-12).

### Hope

"These three great patriarchs died with faith that God would do what He said. They took hold of His promises and saw themselves as foreigners passing through and as pilgrims heading home.

"They didn't keep looking back, longing for the country from which Abraham came. If they had, they could have gone back. Instead, they kept looking forward to a heavenly country. That's why God is not ashamed to be their God and has a city waiting for them in heaven (Heb. 11:13-16).

### Continued Faith

"Let's come back to Abraham, whose faith was tested when God asked him to sacrifice his son, Isaac. He was willing to do this based on God's promise that his descendants would come through Isaac. He knew that God could raise Isaac from the dead if He chose to.

"Isaac showed the same faith when he later blessed his own sons, Jacob and Esau.

"Then, before Jacob died, he blessed Joseph and his sons in faith as they worshipped together around his bed.

"And before Joseph died, he looked forward in faith to the deliverance of the children of Israel and asked them to take his bones with them and bury them in the land promised to Abraham (Heb. 11:17-22).

### Heroic Faith

"When Moses was born, his parents hid him for three months to keep him from being killed with the other baby boys. Their faith was rewarded and Pharaoh's daughter saved him.

"The time came when Moses had to decide whether to be faithful to Pharaoh's daughter, who raised him, or to suffer with God's people. He turned away from the pleasures of Egypt, for he saw greater riches in suffering for Christ.

"So by faith he left Egypt. And by faith he returned, not afraid of Pharaoh's threat to kill him. By faith he kept the Passover with his people, believing God's promise that the blood on the doorpost would protect the firstborn from being killed. By faith he led the children of Israel through the Red Sea and watched the Egyptians drown.

"By faith the walls of Jericho fell, because the people believed and circled the city seven times. By faith Rahab hid the two spies and was saved, because she believed in the God of Israel.

"We could talk about the faith of Gideon, Samson, David, Samuel, and the prophets. It was by faith that armies were defeated, justice was done, and the land God promised was made secure.

"It was by faith that the three 'worthies' escaped the fiery furnace, that Daniel was saved from being eaten by lions, that God's people escaped being wiped out by the sword, and that Israel received strength to fight off armies. And it was through the faith of Elijah and Elisha that women saw their children brought back to life.

"But there were other heroes of faith. Some died while being tortured, not giving up their faith in the resurrection. Others were made fun of, chained, imprisoned, stoned to death, sawn in half, and killed by the sword. They were destitute, ill-treated, and persecuted, having nothing to wear except sheepskins and goatskins. They lived in deserts, mountains, and caves.

"All these heroes of faith are to be commended for their steadfastness when they could not see that God's promise would be fulfilled. God's plan is to wait for us so that, together with them, He can complete His family of faith (Heb. 11:23-40).

### Source of Faith

"Since our history is full of such heroes, let us put aside anything that is holding us back from having the same kind of faith they had. Let's push ahead to win this race of faith and endure whatever comes by keeping our eyes on Jesus, who is the source and strength of our faith. He did not give up, but kept looking ahead for the joy that awaited Him. Now He's seated at the right hand of God (Heb. 12:1, 2).

### Discipline of Faith

"Look at the hatred that Jesus had to endure. So don't think that your situation is unique and give up. In all your struggles against wickedness, you have not yet had to resist evil to the point of being willing to shed your blood, rather than sin.

"Have you forgotten what God said to you as His sons and daughters? 'My dear children, don't get discouraged and give up when I correct you. I wouldn't do it if I didn't love you. Everyone accepted into My family has to be disciplined.'

"So think of your suffering as a means to strengthen your faith. Discipline is part of life. What father doesn't discipline those he loves? If God doesn't discipline you, then you're not really His children. When our earthly fathers corrected us, we respected them for it. Shouldn't we respond the same way to our heavenly Father? Our earthly fathers did it as they saw best, but our heavenly Father does it for our good so that we can be like Him.

"No correction feels good when it's given. But when it's over, it gives those who are being disciplined an inner calm, which produces a righteous life (Heb. 12:3-11).

### Courage

"Strengthen those arms and legs. Push ahead. Don't keep dragging your feet. Mark out a clear path for others to follow who are weaker than you are so they won't fall and hurt themselves.

"Do your best to be at peace with everyone and live a holy and acceptable life; without such, no one will see the Lord. Hold on to God's grace and don't let bitterness grow in your heart as so many are doing. Don't become like Esau, who gave up his spiritual birthright to satisfy his hunger. Afterward, he desperately wanted it back and, with tears, asked his father to restore it, but it was too late (Heb. 12:12-17).

### Choice

"You're not standing at the foot of Mount Sinai as our ancestors did.

They couldn't come near it (not even an animal could) because the mountain was on fire. First they heard the sound of a trumpet and then the voice of God. They were so afraid that they begged God to speak to them through Moses. But even Moses said he was afraid.

"You're standing at the foot of Mount Zion, the heavenly hill in the New Jerusalem. The living God is speaking, surrounded by thousands of angels. That's where your name is registered, together with all those who have been born again and have the rights of a firstborn. You have been sprinkled by the blood of Jesus, which is much better than even the blood of Abel's lamb.

"Christ is the Mediator of this new arrangement. So be careful not to close your ears and miss hearing what God says. If our ancestors didn't escape the consequences of not listening to God at Sinai, do you think we'll escape if we refuse to listen to His voice from heaven?

"When God spoke at Sinai, the whole mountain shook. He promised, 'I will shake the earth one more time, and this time also the heavens.' It means He will shake out everything from His kingdom that can be shaken so only those things that cannot be shaken will remain.

"But we are part of God's unshakable kingdom, so let's be grateful and thank Him for what He has done for us. Let's serve Him in ways that please Him. God's presence is like a consuming fire, burning up everything not of His making (Heb. 12:18-29).

### Final Advice

"Continue to love God and your brothers and sisters. Be hospitable. Some, like Abraham, have entertained angels without knowing it. Remember those in prison for their faith as if you were there. Remember those of us who are suffering as if you were one of them.

"Honor marriage. Let husbands and wives be faithful to each other. Don't defile your marriage, because God will judge those who are immoral and commit adultery.

"Don't let the love of money control your life. Live within your means. Remember what the Lord said: 'I will never forsake you, no matter what happens.' That's why we can say with confidence, 'The Lord is my Helper. I will not be afraid of what man can do to me.'

"Remember those who brought the message to you and those who are leading you today. Look back on those men of faith. Notice how they lived, and imitate them.

"But imitating Christ is even better. He never changes. He's the same yesterday, today, and tomorrow. So don't be carried away with all kinds of strange teachings. Get your spiritual strength from God's grace, not from rituals or rules about what to eat and what not to eat. Those who make these rules the most important thing in their lives are not receiving the blessings they're seeking.

"Priests who served at the Temple had to follow rules regarding the sacrifices they offered. For example, on the Day of Atonement the high priest brought the blood of the animal into the Most Holy Place, but the body had to be taken outside the camp and burned.

"This is what happened to Jesus. He is both our High Priest and our Sacrifice. He offered His own blood for our sins and then was taken outside the city to be crucified. So let's leave the old city behind and follow Him, because we have no lasting city here. We look for a city to come.

"What sacrifices are we to bring? Praise on our lips for what Christ has done for us and joy in proclaiming His name. Also, we help each other by sharing what we have. These are the sacrifices that please God.

"Listen to your leaders and do what they ask you to do, because they are held accountable to God for you. Make their ministry a joy and not a burden, for that wouldn't help you or do you any good, either.

"Pray for us. We want to do what's right and have a clear conscience at all times. Especially pray for me that God will soon make it possible for me to be released and come to see you (Heb. 13:1-19).

## Farewell

"May the God of peace, who raised Jesus from the dead after He shed His blood for us, give you what you need to do His will. To our Great Shepherd be honor and glory now and forever. Amen.

"I urge you, my brothers and sisters, to take my letter to heart. Read it carefully, for it is not very long.

"I want you to know that Timothy has been released from prison, for which we thank the Lord. As soon as he finds me and I'm released, we'll both come to see you. If not, I'll come alone.

"Greet all your leaders and all God's people for me. The believers here in Italy send their greetings.

"May God's grace be with each of you" (Heb. 13:20-25).

# thirty

# Letters to Timothy and Titus

From Paul, an apostle by the will of God, who saved us, and by the Lord Jesus Christ, who is our hope, to Timothy, my son in the faith. Grace, mercy, and peace to you from God and His Son (1 Tim. 1:1, 2).

## Released

"I was just released from two years of house arrest and am now in Macedonia. I'm sorry you didn't know. Stay in Ephesus and take care of the problems there. Make sure that no one is teaching contrary to the gospel that I taught them. Some are teaching false doctrines and are all caught up in traditions, myths, and endless genealogies. This is based on a lot of speculation and creates confusion about God's plan of salvation, which is rooted in faith.

"The purpose of sound doctrine is love, purity, a good conscience, and an unshakable faith. That's what we taught. But some have forgotten this and love to get involved in endless theological discussions. They want to be teachers and tell everyone what's right. They talk confidently as if what they're saying is really true, when it isn't.

"We know that God's law is good if it's used rightly. The law was not given for good people, but for those who are lawless, rebellious, ungodly, and profane. It's for kidnappers, murderers, those who kill their parents, live immoral lives, practice homosexuality, lie, cheat, give false testimony, and live as they please. These character traits go against everything I taught them and are contrary to the gospel which God entrusted to me (1 Tim. 1:3-11).

## God's Grace

"I thank Jesus Christ for calling me into the ministry and enabling me to preach the gospel. Why He would consider me worthy is hard to understand, because I not only denied Him and spoke against Him, but even persecuted those who loved Him. I was a very violent man. But I didn't know what I was doing, didn't know what faith was, and He knew that. He was very merciful, pouring His grace on me and filling my heart with faith and love.

"Without a doubt Jesus Christ came into the world to save sinners, of whom I am the worst. But in His mercy He decided to hold me up as an example of His love and grace to all who would believe.

"To God, the eternal King—immortal, invisible, and wise—be honor and glory forever and ever! Amen (1 Tim. 1:12-17).

### Courage

"Timothy, my son, I charge you to fight well. Be of good courage. Stand up for the faith. Do what was predicted about your ministry when you were ordained. And do everything with a clear conscience.

"Some have already turned against the faith, including Hymenaeus and Alexander. I finally had to discipline them, hoping they won't give in to Satan and do things to shame Christ and the church (1 Tim. 1:18-20).

### Prayer

"I urge our people to pray and intercede with God for others, also. They should pray for kings and those in authority so we may live quiet, dignified, godly lives in peace. Such prayers please God, because He wants as many people as possible to come to the truth and be saved.

"There is only one God and one intermediary between people and God: Jesus, who paid for the sins of everyone at the time God appointed. This is why I was called to be an apostle, to preach and take the gospel everywhere. This is the truth—I am not lying. I want men and women in the church to pray to God in faith, without doubting His Word or resenting any who have hurt us (1 Tim. 2:1-8).

### Dress

"Our women ought to dress modestly and avoid wearing gold, pearls, expensive clothes, or hairdos that attract attention. What they should be known for is their good deeds and godly lives.

"They should not assert their authority to the point of wanting to be in charge of everything, including their husbands. Let them be willing to listen and learn in church as the rest of us do. Remember that Adam was created first, then Eve, to work together and form a partnership. It was Adam who brought sin into the world, not Eve. She sinned and broke God's law first, but she was tricked into it. Adam was not.

"In spite of Eve's sin, women have had a part in bringing salvation to the world by bearing children. That was the only way the Messiah could come. Because of this privilege of raising godly families, they should live disciplined lives of holiness, faith, and love (1 Tim. 2:9-15).

### Elders and Deacons

"It's good if someone wants to be an elder to help the church. There's nothing wrong with that. But he should have a good reputation, respect others, and be devoted to his wife. He should be a man of sound judgment, hardworking, hospitable, and gifted to teach. He should be self-disciplined, not addicted to wine, not violent, but gentle, not argumentative, and not greedy.

"He should be able to manage his family well, discipline his children without anger, and be respected. If he can't be a good father and manage his own family, how can he manage things in the church?

"He should not be a recent convert but be seasoned in the faith, or he may become proud as Lucifer did and end up being destroyed. And he should have a good reputation among those not of our faith and not be caught in one of the devil's traps, bringing disgrace to the church.

"A deacon also should have a good reputation and respect others. He should not be two-faced, greedy, or given to drinking. He should be blameless, devoted to his wife, have a clear conscience, and value the faith. He should be tested before he's put into office.

"Their wives, as well as deaconesses, should be women of good character, respectful of others, not gossipers, or self-appointed critics, but honest and faithful in everything. Deacons should be able to manage their households well. Those who serve the Lord with all their hearts will have a good standing among the people. The Lord will help them speak boldly about their faith in Jesus Christ (1 Tim. 3:1-13).

### The Church

"I hope to see you soon. But I thought I would write to you about how a local church should function and how people should conduct themselves in the house of God in case I'm delayed. After all, the church is the mainstay of the truth and has been given amazing revelations.

"Just think of it—God's Son becoming a Man! He was vindicated by the Holy Spirit, ministered to by angels, taken to heaven, preached among the Gentiles, and believed by people everywhere (1 Tim. 3:14-16).

### Looking Ahead

"The Holy Spirit has specifically told us that in the last days some will leave the faith, being deceived by the devil's false doctrines. They listen to these lies until their consciences become hardened against the truth. They tell people it's wrong to get married and wrong to eat certain foods, even foods which God made to be enjoyed. There are no such restrictions in the Word of God. We should be thankful for the food God gave us and bless it with prayer (1 Tim. 4:1-5).

### Ministry

"Point these things out to the people, which is part of being a good minister. Strengthen your own faith by the Word of God, and stay with what you were taught. Avoid legends and myths, which the Ephesians love, and focus on living a godly life.

"Don't neglect exercise. It will help you physically. And godly living will not only help you now, but will also prepare you for the life to come. This is true, so give it your full attention.

"You know how hard we work and how we struggle. It's because our hope is placed in God, who wants everyone to be saved, especially those who already believe. Until I come, concentrate on your sermons, on the public reading of Scripture, on encouraging people, and on using the spiritual gift God gave you when the elders laid their hands on you at your ordination.

"Do these things and devote yourself to them so people will see your growth in the Lord. Be careful what you do and teach. By doing what's right you'll save not only yourself, but also those who listen to you (1 Tim. 4:6-16).

### Members

"Don't speak harshly to an older member. Respect him as if he were your father. Treat the younger men as your brothers. Relate to the older women as mothers and to the younger women as sisters (1 Tim. 5:1, 2).

### Widows

"Respect the widows and help those in need. Now if a widow has children or grandchildren, they should take care of her. They'll only be doing for their parents what their parents did for them. God notices this and is pleased.

"A widow who is alone and continues to love God, puts her faith in Him, and prays for help is considered to be a true widow. But a widow who has thrown herself into a life of sin and pleasure is spiritually dead.

"Follow through on these suggestions to protect the reputation of the church. Those who can support their parents and don't do so are going contrary to the faith and are worse than unbelievers.

"Don't put widows under 60 years of age on the list of those to be supported. List only those older, who were faithful to their husbands and are known for good works, such as raising children, showing hospitality, and helping those in need.

"Younger widows are thinking about romance and getting married. Some don't even care whom they marry. They ignore the vow they took to remain single. They spend their time going from house to house gossiping and talking about others when they should be working. So let the younger widows get married if that's what they want to do. Let them have a family, raise their children, manage their households well, and not be a burden to the church (1 Tim. 5:3-16).

## Elders

"Elders who do a good job leading the church should be given the honor they deserve, especially those who preach and teach. As the Scripture says, 'Don't keep the ox from eating as it threshes the grain.' Elders who work full-time for the church should be paid.

"Don't take an accusation against an elder seriously unless it's confirmed by at least two or three other witnesses. But those elders who sin openly must be dealt with openly as a warning to others.

"I charge you before God, the Lord Jesus Christ, and the holy angels to carry out your ministerial responsibilities and do so without prejudice or favoritism. Don't be in a hurry to ordain an elder just because you need help. This will make you partially responsible if he falls into sin. Protect your reputation.

"The sins of some people are obvious, for which they'll be judged. Other sins are not so plain. It's the same with good works. Some are more obvious than others. But whatever good is done will come to light.

"Take care of yourself. It's probably the water you're drinking that's making you sick. Buy some unfermented wine, so you'll get well and be able to digest your food again (1 Tim. 5:17-25).

## Employees

"Servants and employees should respect and honor those who employ them, even if they're not Christians, so these unbelievers don't curse God and what we teach because our people are disrespectful. And those of us who have servants and employees, whether they're believers or not, should respect them and treat them as brothers and sisters. Teach our people these things (1 Tim. 6:1, 2).

## Teachers

"If someone teaches things that are different from what the Lord Jesus taught about godliness and claims that it's the gospel, he doesn't know what he's talking about. All he wants is to get into a discussion and argue over words and meanings. If you argue with him, it will only lead into more discussions, arguing, and the twisting of what Jesus said. Such people are confused. They believe that religion will bring them God's blessings and make them rich. Stay away from such people (1 Tim. 6:3-5).

### Godliness

"Godliness and contentment in the Lord are what makes us rich. We didn't bring anything into this world, and it's for sure we're not taking anything out. If we have food, clothes, a place to stay, and the other necessities of life, let's be thankful.

"Those who think of nothing else but making more and more money will fall into Satan's trap and end up being destroyed with him. Loving money more than anything else is the root of all evil. Some have even left the faith over money and ended up in all kinds of trouble (1 Tim. 6:6-10).

### Advice

"If you've set yourself aside for God, don't get caught up in schemes to get rich. Focus on faithfulness, godliness, gentleness, love, perseverance, and doing what's right.

"Compete for the crown of eternal life as an athlete competes for a trophy. When you were baptized, you promised in front of those present to be faithful to Jesus Christ, no matter what. So I charge you in the sight of God, the Giver of life, and Jesus Christ, who was not ashamed to say who He was when He stood before Pilate, to do what you promised. At the right time He will return as King of kings and Lord of lords.

"Remember, God alone is immortal and lives in a light that no one can approach and live. To God be honor, glory, and power forever and ever! Amen (1 Tim. 6:11-16).

### The Rich

"Warn the rich not to become proud and not to put their hope in what they have, but to put their hope in God, who is generous to all of us. Remind them to do good with what they have, that they may be known for their good deeds and generosity. This way they'll be investing in the future by putting money in the bank of heaven, securing eternal life (1 Tim. 6:17-19).

### In Closing

"Timothy, carefully guard what God has entrusted to you. Don't get involved in worthless arguments which supposedly give you more insight and knowledge. This has already destroyed the faith of some. God's grace be with all of you" (1 Tim. 6:20, 21).

## Titus

"This letter is from Paul, a servant of God and an apostle of Jesus Christ, to Titus. I was called not only to preach the gospel, but to strengthen the faith of God's people in the truth and to encourage them to live lives worthy of Jesus Christ. Our hope is in God's promise of eternal life for all who believe. At this time His Word is being spread everywhere by the preaching of the gospel, with which I was entrusted by the command of Jesus Christ our Savior.

"The reason I left you on the island of Crete was to take care of things I hadn't had time to do before and because I needed to see how our other churches were doing. You need to choose men who can serve as local elders, to guide our people in every town where we have churches.

"An elder should be blameless, devoted to his wife, and have children who are not wild or disobedient. He should have a good reputation and not be arrogant, quick-tempered, violent, greedy, or someone who drinks. He is to be hospitable; committed to what's good, sensible, and honest; and in control of himself. He should hold to the message and to what he was taught so he can strengthen the faith of our people and correct those who speak against it.

"There are many Jews and local people who undermine the gospel. They have a rebellious spirit about them and talk a lot but never make sense. They mislead whole families by teaching things which are not true and expect to get paid for their teaching. These people need to be stopped.

"It was a Cretan prophet who said about his own people: 'They're liars, gluttons, lazy, and wicked.' And he was right. The local people there have a lot to overcome. So you need to urge our converts to continue to grow and become strong in the faith. They need to stop listening to Jewish legends and commandments from those who reject the truth.

"Those who are pure in heart and believe will teach what is right. But the teachings of those whose hearts are not pure and who don't believe in God are twisted in their thinking and have a corrupt conscience. They claim to know God, but by their actions they're denying Him. They're rebellious, full of hatred, and not fit for anything good (Titus 1:1-16).

## Behavior

"Teach behavior that goes along with sound doctrine. Older men should be sober, sensible, dignified, and self-controlled. They should be solid in the faith, full of love, and committed to the church.

"Older women should live lives that testify to their faith. They shouldn't gossip, drink, or criticize, but should talk about what's good. This way they can be an example to young women by teaching them to love their husbands and children, and to be sensible, good housekeepers, and kind so they won't bring reproach on the church.

"Encourage young men to behave themselves and be good examples in all they do. You yourself should be an example of what it means to be good. When you teach and preach, do so honestly, sincerely, and out of a pure heart. Choose the right words so the message can't be criticized and so your critics will be at a loss as to what to say.

"Servants should obey their masters and do their best to please them without talking back. They should not steal, but be honest and trustworthy in all they do, bringing honor to God and credibility to the teachings of Jesus Christ (Titus 2:1-10).

## Discipleship

"God's grace is for everyone. It teaches us to reject godless indulgence and not live lifestyles patterned after the world. We should live righteous lives as we look forward with hope to the glorious appearing of our God and Savior, Jesus Christ.

"The Lord Jesus died to set us free from the captivity of sin and the addictions of this world. He wants us to be His own special people, eager to do good.

"Teach these things. Speak with authority and don't let anyone look down on you. Tell our people to be subject to the authorities, obey the law, and be good citizens. They should not slander other people, but should be peace-loving, gentle, humble, and courteous.

"Before we knew Christ, we were like everyone else—breaking the law, dishonest, giving in to our passions and lusts, full of envy, and hating those who hated us. But when Jesus Christ came, He showed us how much God loves us. He gave His life for us, not because we were good, but because of His mercy. We were born again and made new by the power of the Holy Spirit, which God poured into our hearts through Jesus Christ. So we stand justified in our claim to righteousness because of His grace. We are heirs of heaven, confidently looking ahead to eternal life.

"I want you to teach these things and be persistent about it so that those who have faith in God will continue to do good to everyone. Tell the people to stay away from arguments over the importance of heritage, fights over the law, and other useless discussions. If anyone keeps arguing over these things, give him one or two warnings, and if he doesn't listen, have nothing more to do with him. His thinking is twisted and his attitude and actions tell you that he's wrong (Titus 2:11–3:11).

### One Final Word

"When I send either Artemus or Tychicus to help you, do your best to come to Nicopolis, where I decided to spend the winter. It will be good to see you again.

"Before you come, do everything you can to help Zenas, the lawyer, and Apollos get ready for their mission trip. Make sure they have everything they need. This is another way our people can do good. There's much work to be done and many places in need. Helping to spread the message will make them even more fruitful for the Lord Jesus.

Everyone here sends greetings. Greet everyone there, especially those faithful supporters who love what we're doing. God's grace be with you" (Titus 3:12-15).

# thirty-one

# Another Letter to Timothy

Paul, an apostle of Jesus Christ by the will of God, called to spread the promise of eternal life in Christ everywhere, to Timothy, my beloved spiritual son. Grace, mercy, and peace from God and from our Lord Jesus Christ (2 Tim. 1:1, 2).

### Arrested Again

"Make every effort to come and see me as soon as you can. I was hoping we could go to Jerusalem together. But I've been arrested again, and they've taken me back to Rome and put me in this damp, cold dungeon.

"Demas left me. He loves this present world more than he loves God and went back to Thessalonica. I sent Crescens to Galatia, Titus to Dalmatia, and Artemas to Crete to replace Titus. Luke is the only one with me. Try to bring Mark with you when you come. He's developed into a good missionary and would be a big help to me. I've sent Tychicus to Ephesus to take your place.

"When you come, bring my winter cloak that I left at Carpas' house when they arrested me and hurried me off to Rome. Bring the scrolls and parchments along with you, too. I really miss not having the Scriptures.

"Alexander, the coppersmith, was involved in getting me arrested. He's been against me ever since I first preached in Ephesus. Watch out for him, because he hates what we believe.

"At my appearance before Caesar, no one stood up to defend me. They were afraid to do so. May God not hold this against them! But the Lord was with me and gave me strength to defend myself in such a way that everyone in the courtroom could hear and understand what we believe. Caesar didn't give me the death sentence as I expected he would, but sent me back to the dungeon. The Lord delivered me from the lion's mouth and will bring me into His kingdom. To Him be glory forever and ever (Titus 3:12; 2 Tim. 4:9-18).

## Timothy's Faith

"I thank God when I think about you. I serve Him with a clear conscience, just as some of my ancestors did, and I know you do too. I pray for you day and night. I recall how you cried when you had to leave me last time. I can't wait to see you again. I remember your faith and how sincere you have been since we first met. You have the same faith I saw in your mother, Eunice, and in your grandmother, Lois.

"Keep the flame of your faith alive, and don't lose the gifts God gave you at your ordination when I set you apart for the gospel ministry. God does not give us the Holy Spirit to be afraid, but to think clearly, to speak powerfully for Him, and to love people.

"So don't be ashamed of the Lord Jesus or of me, his prisoner. But, by the power God has given to you, be willing to suffer for Him too. He is the One who has saved us and called us to Himself, not because of anything we have done, but according to His grace and His purpose for all of us before time began. His purpose has now been made clear by the coming of Jesus Christ, who broke the power of death and brought the certainty of immortality to light through the gospel.

"It was this gospel for which I was made an apostle and told to preach and teach. I have suffered a lot for this. But I'm not ashamed of the gospel. I know in whom I have believed and am totally confident He will see to it that the gospel work in which I had a share will be carried on until He returns (2 Tim. 1:3-12).

## Loyalty

"Hold on to what I taught you, and do so in faith and love for Jesus Christ. The gospel is precious. Don't let go of it. It was entrusted to you by the Holy Spirit, who is in us and in all who believe.

"As I mentioned before, all those from the churches in Asia Minor who were here with me have left, including Phygelus and Hermogenes. But the Lord bless Onesiphorus, who came from Ephesus to do what he could for me and was not ashamed of my chains. When he first arrived in Rome, he kept looking for me until he found me. You know how helpful he was to my ministry in Ephesus. May the Lord be especially merciful to him when he stands before Him (2 Tim. 1:13-18).

## Be Strong

"As for you, my son, be strong in the Lord and be filled with His grace. What you heard me publicly teach the people in Ephesus, make sure your leaders teach others when you're gone.

"Endure hardness as a soldier of Jesus Christ. No soldier on active duty involves himself in business, but obeys his commanding officer and does whatever he is asked to do. The same is true with an athlete. He'll not be declared the winner unless he listens to his coach and follows the rules. And a tenant farmer who has worked hard gets the first share of the owner's crops.

"Think about what I'm saying. The Lord will help you apply these principles to your own life and will help others apply them, as well.

"Never forget what Jesus Christ did for us on Calvary and that He was raised from the dead and is alive today. This is the good news of the gospel that I've preached, for which I've suffered, and for which I'm chained and treated as a criminal. I endure all things for the sake of God's people so they will be strong in the Lord and bring glory to His name.

"This is a true saying: 'If we are willing to die for Him, we will live with Him. If we endure for Him, we will rule with Him. If we deny Him, He will deny us. If we're unfaithful, He will always remain faithful, because He can't go against who He is' (2 Tim. 2:1-13).

### False Teachers

"Remind our people of the faithfulness of the Lord, and tell them to stop fighting over the meaning of words. This doesn't help anyone, but harms those who listen to it. Do your best to be approved of God, a worker who isn't ashamed to teach the message, explaining the truth as it is in Scripture.

"Stay away from foolish discussions, which only drive people away from the truth. Once things like this get started, they spread like a cancer. Hymenaeus and Philetus love to get people involved in senseless discussions, saying that the resurrection of their loved ones has already taken place and that they're in heaven. This sort of thing destroys people's faith in what we taught them.

"But God's truth is built on a solid foundation. The Lord knows those who believe and they won't get involved in such discussions.

"In wealthy houses there are dishes and bowls of gold and silver and also those made of wood and clay. The gold and silver ones are used for special occasions, the others are used for everyday, and some are even used to take out the garbage.

"If someone lives a clean life, he's like an expensive dish ready to be used by the owner for special occasions. So tell our young people not to get involved in worldly passions, but to concentrate on being faithful, doing right, being loving and peaceable, and asking the Lord to help them.

"As I said before, stay away from foolish arguments, because they only generate more misunderstandings and fights. Besides, those who serve the Lord are not fighters, but are gentle, kind, and patient, correcting others only when necessary.

"I sincerely hope that those who like to argue will come to their senses, see the truth, and change their ways. They need to get out of the devil's trap. He has caught them and makes them do what he wants (2 Tim. 2:14-26).

### Importance of Scripture

"But you're different. You have followed my teaching, taken on my lifestyle, and adopted the same purpose in life that I have. You have seen my faith, patience, and endurance under persecution in Antioch, Iconium, and Lystra. I lived through those persecutions because the Lord was with me. All who live for Christ these days will be persecuted. Wicked people and religious impostors are getting worse and worse, deceiving others and being deceived.

"As for you, continue in what you have been taught and in what you believe. You have known the Scriptures since you were a child, and they have given you insight into the salvation that is ours through faith in Jesus Christ.

"All Scripture is inspired by God and is given for teaching, correcting, and instruction for right living, so those who have dedicated themselves to God may know what is good and be equipped to do it (2 Tim. 3:10-17).

### The Last Days

"I want you to know this—the last days will be difficult. People will be selfish, in love with themselves, proud, arrogant, cursing anything that goes against their wills, disobedient to parents, unthankful, unholy, and loving money more than anything else. They'll be critical, unforgiving, hard to get along with, and even brutal. They will have no self-control or love for people and will hate those who are good.

"They will have an outward appearance of religion but will know nothing of its power to change lives. Stay away from people like that. They talk their way into people's houses and with their charm gain control of those living in sin and not thinking right. Some are always learning, but never take hold of the truth.

"Just like Jannes and Jambres, Pharaoh's magicians who opposed Moses, these impostors, with their warped minds, oppose the truth and are not really in the faith, no matter what they say. In time their influence with our people will end, just as the magic of Pharaoh's magicians did (2 Tim. 3:1-9).

# WITNESS: Acts Through Revelation

## Solid Teaching

"I charge you before God and Jesus Christ, who will judge the living and the dead when He comes. Hold on to the message. Preach it whether it's convenient to do so or not. Do your best to convince people of the truth, rebuke sin if you have to, encourage those who believe, and do all with kindness and patience.

"The time will come when people can't take straight talk or handle sound doctrine. They like to listen to what they want to hear, so they hire teachers who tickle their ears and make them feel good. They turn away from the truth, hold on to their traditions, and love legends and fables.

"Keep your mind on the things you know are true. Endure hardships. Preach the gospel. Do the work of an evangelist. Fulfill your ministry (2 Tim. 4:1-5).

## Caesar

"I know it won't be long before Caesar pronounces the death sentence. I'm ready to pour out my blood, as a lamb being sacrificed as an offering to Him who died for me. I know the time of my departure has come. I have fought a good fight, have finished the race, and have kept the faith.

"I know that a crown of righteousness is waiting for me, which the Lord, the righteous Judge, will give me one day, and not to me only, but to all who love Him and look forward to His coming (2 Tim. 4:6-8).

## Greetings

"Give my greetings to Priscilla, Aquila, and the family of Onesiphorus. Erastus is in Corinth and Trophimus is in Miletus. Greetings from Eubulus, Pudens, Linus, Claudia, and all the brothers and sisters here in Rome.

"Do your best to come before winter. The Lord be with you and strengthen your spirit. Grace to you always" (2 Tim. 4:19-22).

# thirty-two

# Peter in Rome

This letter is from Peter, an apostle of Jesus Christ to the believers in Galatia, Cappadocia, Pontus, Bithynia, and the rest of Asia Minor. You are pilgrims chosen by God and set apart by the Holy Spirit to obey Jesus Christ and be purified by Him. May God's grace and peace be multiplied to you (1 Pet. 1:1, 2).

## Faith

"Let's thank God, the Father of our Lord Jesus Christ, for His great mercy in giving us a new life and a living hope through the death and resurrection of His Son. This means we can look forward to receiving the inheritance that God has promised, which will not perish or fade away. It is kept safe in heaven to be given to us at the end of this world's history.

"This should make you glad, even though you have to suffer for a little while down here. These tough times you're going through will reveal whether your faith is real or not. Even gold is tested by fire for its value, but its value won't last. Your faith is much more precious than gold, and you will be praised by Jesus Christ when He comes.

"You love Him, even though you didn't get to see Him as we did. You believe in Him, even though you can't see Him now. That's why you have this inner joy and peace that others can't understand—because of your faith in Him who is your salvation.

"The prophets carefully investigated this salvation, which God promised through Jesus Christ. They studied to find out the exact time the Messiah would come, when the Holy Spirit foretold that Christ would suffer and die, and the glory that would follow.

"What the prophets said was not for their own benefit, but for ours. This is the good news that you heard from those who brought the gospel to you, that gospel which angels long to understand (1 Pet. 1:3-12).

## Hope

"Set your hope on the blessing that will come to you when Jesus returns. Keep your mind on Him. Be obedient and don't live life controlled by the urges you had before you knew Him. Reflect the holiness of God. As the Scripture says, 'Be holy because I am holy.'

"When you pray, you call God your Father. You know He loves you. But He also judges everyone and does so impartially, according to what they have done. So live your lives out of respect for God and in reverence for Him. You know that it cost an awesome price to set you free from the grip of this world. God didn't pay for your freedom with silver or gold, but with the precious blood of Jesus Christ, who was killed like an innocent lamb.

"Before the creation of this world, God decided that if we sinned, He would redeem us. This was shown to us by the death of Christ, who gave His life for you and me. We know this is so because after that God raised Him from the dead and gave Him the glory He had before. That's why our faith and hope rest in God (1 Pet. 1:13-21).

## The Word

"Now that you have purified your lives and are obeying the truth, love your fellow believers and do so with all your hearts. You have been born again, not by human seed but by the living Word of God. As the Scripture says, 'People are like grass, and man's glory is like a flower that blooms and fades away. But the Word of the Lord lasts forever.' This is the same Word that we have preached to you.

"So put away all evil, lying, hypocrisy, jealousy, slander, and bad language. Like new babies who long for milk, reach out for spiritual milk so you can grow up and be saved. As the Scripture says, 'You know how good the Lord is. You have tasted His kindness' (1 Peter 1:22–2:3).

## The Stone

"The Lord is a living Rock, rejected by men but chosen by God and precious. And you are living stones used by God to build a spiritual temple. In this temple you are to serve as priests and offer acceptable sacrifices.

"The Scripture says, 'I lay in Zion a chosen, priceless Cornerstone, and whoever believes in Him will not be disappointed.' But those who do not believe are like the builders of the Temple, of which the Scripture says, 'They rejected a perfectly good stone and then found out that it was the only one suited to be a cornerstone.' The Scripture also says, 'People will trip on this Stone and stumble over it.' This Stone is Christ. And the reason people stumble over Him is because they don't believe the Word of God (1 Pet. 2:4-8).

## The Purpose

"But you're different. You're a chosen race, a royal priesthood, a holy nation, God's special people to proclaim the name of Him who brought you out of darkness into light. There was a time when you were not God's people as you are now. Once you didn't know His mercy, but now you do.

"So conduct yourself accordingly. You're pilgrims on your way to heaven. Stay away from things that hurt the soul. Live in such a way that those who talk against you will see all the good you do, change their minds, and thank God for you (1 Pet. 2:9-12).

## Be Good Citizens

"For the sake of the Lord, obey the government, from the king on down to the governor and the local authorities. Those who enforce the law are out there to arrest evildoers and to protect those who are good.

"God's will for you is to silence the ignorance of foolish people who talk against you and the good things you do. You're a free people. Live that way. But don't use your freedom in Christ as a cover to do anything you please. You're God's servants. Be good to people. Love your fellow church members. Honor God. Respect the government (1 Pet. 2:13-17).

## Be Good Employees

"Listen to your employers, not only those who treat you well, but even those who are hard on you. God will bless you for it because you're doing your best for Him. It's better to suffer and have a clear conscience than having to be reprimanded. If you continue to do good even when things are hard, it recommends you to God.

"Christ was mistreated and suffered unjustly, and He left us an example to follow in His steps. He was not deceitful, nor did He sin. When He was mistreated, He did not retaliate, and when He was falsely accused, He did not respond with a threat. He committed Himself to God, who makes the final decision. Christ took our sins on Himself and carried them to Calvary so that we would die to sin and live for Him. Because of His wounds, we are healed.

"You were like sheep that had gone astray. But now you're where you should be, back in the fold with the Shepherd who guards your soul (1 Pet. 2:18-25).

## To Wives and Husbands

"Wives, respect your husbands and be good witnesses to them by the way you live. Even those who don't believe as you do may be won to

Christ. Your conduct, your respect for God, and your not wanting to offend Him will do more than many words.

"Your inner beauty is more important than what you wear. Don't let the latest fashions, hairdo, and glittering jewelry detract from who you are in Christ. The beauty of a kind and gentle spirit is what is precious in God's sight. That's the kind of beauty women of faith had in ancient times. How about Sarah? She respected Abraham and looked up to him. You are her daughters when you have the same spirit she had and are not afraid to be different from other women.

"Husbands, love your wives. Be kind and gentle, and treat your wife with respect. She's your partner, as by grace you both live for God. If you're this kind of husband, God will certainly hear your prayers (1 Pet. 3:1-7).

### Be a Blessing

"Finally, brothers and sisters, be of one mind. Love and respect each other, be compassionate, tenderhearted, and courteous. Don't return insult for insult, or evil for evil, but forgive and bless. And the Lord will bless you for it.

"As the Scripture says, 'He who wants to enjoy life and see good days must watch his tongue and not lie. He must stop hurting others and do good. He must try with all his heart to be at peace with everyone. The Lord notices the righteous and is open to their prayers. But the Lord is against those who do evil' (1 Pet. 3:8-12).

### Do Good

"Who will oppose you for doing good? But if you do have to suffer for doing good, you are still the Lord's special people. As the Scripture says, 'Don't be terrified or let your suffering shake your faith.'

"Keep Christ in your heart, and always be ready to give a reason for your faith and hope to those who ask about it. Be courteous and respectful, doing good with a clear conscience, so that those who slander you may feel ashamed of what they have said about you. If God allows suffering, it's better that it comes from doing good than from doing evil (1 Pet. 3:13-17).

### Live for Christ

"Christ also suffered—for you and me. He did this to bring us back to God. As a human being, He died and was resurrected and taken to heaven, and now He is with us through the Holy Spirit.

"It was through the Holy Spirit that He tried to reach people who were locked in sin in the days of Noah. He did this through Noah's preaching while the ark was being built. But when the Flood came, only eight people were taken into the ark.

"Their experience is a symbol of coming to Jesus, being baptized, and doing so with a good conscience. Baptism has nothing to do with what's on the outside, but what's on the inside. It makes a statement about Christ's death and resurrection and His place at the right hand of God. And we know that all the angels and authorities of heaven are subject to Him.

"Never forget that Christ suffered and died for you. So be ready to do the same for Him. Those who are willing to suffer for Christ have turned their backs on sinful living. They're not interested in living for themselves, but in doing what God wants them to do.

"This is what the gospel is all about. It changes us. Once, you did what everyone else was doing. You went to wild parties, drank, gave in to your passions and lusts, and were entertained by human idols.

"Your friends are shocked that you don't want to go with them anymore. They scorn you for turning down their invitations to such parties. But they will have to answer to Jesus Christ for what they did when He returns to judge the living and the dead.

"The reason the gospel came to you was to bring you to Christ. Men may condemn you and even put you to death, but God is our Judge. And as surely as He lives, He will give us and those who died in the faith eternal life. So let's live Spirit-filled lives and fulfill the purpose for which God called us (1 Pet. 3:18–4:6).

## Glorify God

"For many of us the end is near. So take your faith seriously, practice self-control, and keep praying. But above all, love one another. As the Scripture says, 'Love covers a lot of sins.'

"As stewards of God's grace, use the gifts God has given you to help each other. And don't complain. Be friendly and hospitable.

"Whoever is assigned to preach, let him preach from the Word. Whoever serves, let him do so with the strength and ability God has given him.

"May we glorify God in all we do because of what Jesus Christ has done for us. To Him belong the power and the glory forever and ever. Amen (1 Pet. 4:7-11).

## Don't Be Ashamed

"Dear friends, don't be surprised that going through a trial by fire is something strange. Suffering for your faith in Christ is similar to what He did for you. When He returns, you'll be overjoyed to see Him and be given a share in His glory.

"If you're insulted for what you believe, bless your hearts. The Holy Spirit is with you and will give you the strength you need. I hope that none of you will be arrested and have to suffer because you engaged in some criminal activity, such as murder, robbery, stealing, embezzlement, or even being a troublemaker. But if you suffer because you're a believer, don't be ashamed of it. Thank God that they call you a Christian, which is part of Jesus' name.

"When the judgment comes, it will begin with the members of God's family. So if it starts with us, what will it be like for those who turned against God? As the Scripture says, 'If those who believe and do what's right have to be judged, what will happen to those who disobey and continue living in sin?'

"So let those of us who are suffering for Christ place our souls in the hands of our faithful Creator and continue to do good  (1 Pet. 4:12-19).

### Elders

"As a fellow elder and someone who has witnessed the sufferings of Christ and will share in His glory, I urge you to take care of the flock of God. Don't do it because you're getting paid for it, but do it willingly and gladly.

"Don't lord it over those entrusted to you, but be an example to them. Then when the Chief Shepherd comes back, He'll reward you and give you a crown that will never fade away.

"This also applies to those who are young. Listen to your elders. Be humble. As the Scripture says, 'God is against those who are proud but gives extra grace to the humble.' When the time comes, He will exalt you. Meanwhile, be patient and place all your cares on Him, because He cares about you.

"Discipline yourselves to stay spiritually awake. Your enemy, the devil, is like a hungry lion on the prowl looking for prey. Don't be afraid to face him and resist his attacks. Your faith that Christ will help you will make a difference. Remember that your brothers and sisters all over the world are experiencing the same thing.

"May the God of grace, who called you to share His glory through Jesus Christ, strengthen your faith and help you stand. To Him be glory, power, and dominion forever and ever. Amen (1 Pet. 5:1-11).

### Greetings

"Silas, a faithful brother, is helping me write this letter. You can be certain that what we have taught about God's grace is true. And I want to encourage you to stand up for it against those who deny it.

"The church here in Rome sends its greetings. And Mark, my spiritual son, who came here to do what he could for me after I was arrested, also sends his greetings.

"Greet each other with Christian love and a brotherly hug. Peace to all of you who are in Christ" (1 Pet. 5:12-14).

### Peter's Second Letter

"From Simon Peter, a servant and an apostle of Jesus Christ, to those who have been credited with the righteousness of Jesus Christ through the love of God. You have the same precious faith we have. May grace and peace be multiplied to you as you grow in the knowledge of Jesus Christ, our Lord.

"It is through His power that we have been given everything necessary to live a holy life to His glory. And He has given us precious promises, that through these we would partake of His divine nature, which will help us overcome the corrupting influences and powers in the world (2 Pet. 1:1-4).

### In Addition to Faith

"Add to your faith virtue, knowledge, self-control, endurance, godliness, brotherly kindness, and love. If you add these qualities to your life and continue to grow in Christ, you will always be fruitful for the Lord.

"But those who do not include these qualities in their lives are blind. They can't see ahead. They look only at the present and have already forgotten what Jesus Christ did for them.

"So make sure you know what you believe, and put forth every effort to stay close to the Lord. If you do this, you will never leave the faith or return to sin, and a rich welcome awaits you in the kingdom (2 Pet. 1:5-11).

### Peter Arrested

"This is most likely my last letter. There are some things I need to mention to you, even though you already know them and are firmly grounded in the truth. While I'm still alive, I want to point these things out to you to stimulate your thinking.

"I don't think it will be long before I'll be arrested and Caesar will sentence me to death. The Lord told me I would be crucified.

"I wanted to put some things in writing so that after I'm gone, you won't forget what I said (2 Pet. 1:12-15).

## The Word

"What we told you about Jesus Christ is the truth. It's not based on hearsay or on stories that we made up, but on what we actually saw. We were given a glimpse of His majesty and power when He took us up the mountain and was changed in front of our eyes. We even heard God say, 'This is my dear Son, with whom I am very pleased.' This wasn't a dream or hallucination. It was what we actually saw and heard.

"This confirmed the prophecies to us so that we are more sure than ever that the Word of God is true. What was prophesied about Jesus Christ has happened.

"The Word of God is like a light shining in a dark place. It will continue to shine until the day when Christ breaks through the clouds, and as the Morning Star fills your hearts with joy.

"No prophecy in Scripture was written by someone's whim or according to what he thought about future events. But holy men of God spoke and wrote as they were moved and directed by the Holy Spirit (2 Pet. 1:16-21).

## False Teachers

"Just as there were false prophets among God's people in the past, so there are false teachers among us today. They will quietly begin teaching viewpoints that are not biblical, even undermining what the Lord said. They're bringing damnation on themselves.

"Their lifestyle doesn't help the truth, either. With their smooth talk and deceptive words they surely know how to take advantage of people. God condemned such teachers long ago, and He will destroy them. He didn't even spare the angels who sinned, but expelled them from heaven. They too will be destroyed.

"And in the Flood only Noah and his family were saved. The rest were destroyed. What happened to Sodom and Gomorrah? Only Lot and his two daughters were saved, and they had to be rescued. The fire that destroyed those cities is an example of what will happen to the whole world at the end of time. Lot was so disturbed by the lawlessness and violence he saw and heard every day that the Lord had to step in and save him.

"The Lord knows how to deliver His people. But He will punish the wicked, especially those who despise His authority and follow their passions and lusts. They denounce and curse anyone who opposes them. Even angels, who are much more powerful, don't act that way.

"But these men act more like animals than like rational human beings. They're arrogant and don't care whom they insult. They sin in broad daylight and don't care. When they go to parties, they think of nothing but adultery. Their destiny is destruction, the wages of sin.

"They're full of selfishness and controlled by greed, as Balaam was when he became a false prophet. He loved money more than righteousness. God had to use a donkey to rebuke him and then restrain him in his rush to get rich.

"False teachers are like wells without water and misty clouds driven by the wind. Their future is dark indeed. They sound educated, but their words are empty. They promise believers greater liberty, while they themselves are slaves to sin. A person is a slave to whatever masters him. It doesn't set him free—Jesus Christ sets people free.

"We were set free from being slaves of sin. But some have turned away from Christ and gone back to the world. They are worse off than before. It would have been better if they hadn't given themselves to the Lord than to have known Him and then turn away from Him.

"These proverbs are true: 'A dog turns back and licks its own vomit' and 'After a pig is washed, it goes back and wallows in the mud' (2 Pet. 2:1-22).

## God's Promises

"Dear friends, in these two letters I've been trying to remind you of certain things. I don't want you to forget what the prophets said or what we, the apostles, have told you.

"You need to understand that there will always be those who scoff at what we believe. In the last days they will even scoff about Christ's second coming. They'll say, 'Where is He? He promised to come but no one has seen Him. People live and die, and nothing much has changed since the beginning of time.'

"What they forget is that God created this world out of nothing and covered it with water. In the days of Noah He destroyed the world with water. The time is coming when He'll destroy it again, but this time by fire. And the wicked will be destroyed, just as they were in the time of the Flood.

"Don't forget these things. Time means nothing with the Lord. For Him a thousand years is like one day. He always keeps His promises. And the reason He's so patient is because He wants to save as many as He can.

"But the day of judgment will come. It will come as suddenly as a thief at night. There will be a loud noise and God will roll back the sky as easily as a scroll. Everything on earth and in the sky will be burned up.

"Knowing that this will happen, what kind of people should you be? You should live holy lives and conduct yourselves as men and women who are looking for the return of Christ, doing everthing you can to hasten His coming.

"When Christ comes, the heavens will be on fire, and everything on earth will melt in the intense heat. But after that, there will be a new heaven and a new earth, just as God promised. All evil will be gone and the righteous will live forever (2 Pet. 3:1-13).

## A Final Word

"My dear friends, as you look forward to the coming of Christ, do your best to live in peace and in such a way that when you see Him, you'll be blameless with nothing to hide. Think about the patience of God as giving people a chance to be saved.

"Brother Paul, who has now been executed, wrote to you these same things in his letters, based on the wisdom God had given him. Some things he wrote are difficult to understand. And those who are spiritually unstable twist these things to their own hurt, as they do the rest of the Scriptures.

"Both Paul and I have warned you not to listen to those who try to undermine your faith. Be on guard so you won't lose your spiritual footing. Focus on growing in grace and in your knowledge of Jesus Christ, our Savior and Lord. To Him be glory now and forever. Amen" (2 Pet. 3:14-18).

# thirty-three

# Letters From John

This is John. I want to write to you about the One who is the Word, the One who has existed from the beginning. We have heard, seen, and touched Him. He walked among us and what we're telling you is true. The One who was with the Father and has life in Himself came to be with us. We tell you this so you can have the same kind of relationship with the Father and His Son, Jesus Christ, as we have. That would bring real joy to our hearts.

"What He told us we're passing on to you—that God is light and there is no darkness in Him at all. If we say we know God and yet keep walking in darkness, we're lying. But if we walk in the light as Jesus walked in the light, then we'll bond to Him and to each other, and His blood will purify us even more.

"If we say there's no sin in us, we're deceiving ourselves and not telling the truth. But if we confess our sins, Christ, who is faithful and just, will forgive us our sins and cleanse us from all unrighteousness. If we insist there's no sin in us, we're making Him a liar and have not taken His words seriously.

"I'm telling you these things because I don't want you to keep on sinning. Christ is our Defense Attorney. He is in the Father's court protecting us against the claims of Satan. He died for us—not only for us, but for the whole world (1 John 1:1–2:2).

### Knowing Him

"The only way you can know that you know Him is by obeying Him. Those who say, 'I know Him,' but don't live by His commandments, are lying. There's no truth in what they're saying.

"But whoever lives by what Jesus taught us loves God. This is how we know that our relationship with God is genuine. Those who say they love God ought to live as Jesus did.

"Brothers and sisters, I'm not telling you anything new, but only what you have known since the message first came to you. On the other hand, I do want to give you a new commandment of love. We have seen it in Christ and in some of you.

"The darkness of sin is passing away because the light of truth has come. Those who say they have the light, yet don't love their brothers and sisters, are in the dark. But those who love their brothers and sisters are living in the light and will not cause them to stumble. They're not a stumbling block to others.

"Those who don't love their brothers and sisters are not only in the dark, but they can't see where they themselves are going because they're blind (1 John 2:3-11).

### Being Spiritual

"I'm writing to you, my spiritual children, because you belong to Christ, your sins have been forgiven, and you know the Father. I'm writing to you fathers because you also know Him and know what I'm talking about. I'm writing to you young people because the Word of God is in your hearts and you have overcome the wicked one.

"Don't love what the world offers you. If you love the world more than you love Christ, the love of the Father is not in you. Everything that belongs to the world, with its sinful cravings and pride, does not come from God, but from things of the world. This world and the people in it will one day be no more, but those who love God and do what He says will live forever (1 John 2:12-17).

### Deceptions

"My dear children, you know that in the last days the antichrist will come. Little antichrists are here already, teaching things contrary to what Christ taught. They were one of us but then they left. If they had truly been one of us, they never would have left. But they did, so it shows that they were never really one of us after all.

"You know this because Christ has given you the Holy Spirit so you can tell who is one of us and who isn't. I'm not saying this because you don't know the truth—you do, and you know who is lying and who isn't.

"He who says that Jesus Christ is not the Messiah, is lying and has the spirit of antichrist. He's rejecting both the Father and the Son. Whoever turns against the Son is also turning against the Father.

"Hold on to Christ and who He is, whom you've known from the beginning. If you do this, you'll have fellowship with Him and the Father and be given eternal life just as He promised.

"I'm telling you these things because you're my children and I don't want you to be deceived. The Holy Spirit, whom you received from Christ, will teach you what is true. As long as you have the Holy Spirit in your heart and listen to Him, you'll have union with Christ.

"Stay connected to Jesus Christ so that when He comes you won't have to be ashamed but can meet Him with joy and confidence. You know that Christ is righteous and everyone who does what is right is a child of God (1 John 2:18-29).

## Sons and Daughters of God

"Look at what love the Father has given to us—He calls us His sons and daughters! And since we are God's children, the world can't understand us because it does not know Him.

"Yes, we are the sons and daughters of God. We don't know exactly what we'll look like when Jesus comes, but we know we'll look like Him, and we'll see Him as He really is. Everyone whose hope is centered in Him patterns his life after Him (1 John 3:1-3).

## Lawlessness

"Whoever continues to live in sin is lawless, because that's what sin is—lawlessness. You know that Jesus came to take away our sins by taking them on Himself. He could do this, for in Him there is no sin. Whoever has Christ in his heart does not keep on living in sin. Whoever lives in sin does not know Him.

"My dear children, don't let anyone deceive you. Whoever does what is right, God considers righteous. Jesus did what was right. Those who continue living in sin are of the devil, because he is the author of sin. Jesus came to put an end to sin and the devil. The children of God will have nothing to do with sin. God is their Father and they've been born into the family of God (1 John 3:4-9).

## Love

"There is one way to know the difference between the children of God and the children of the devil: The children of God do what's right and love their brothers and sisters.

"We were created to love each other. But look at Cain. He murdered his own brother! Why? Because what he was doing was wicked and he hated his brother, who was doing what was right.

"So don't be surprised if the world doesn't like you. We know we have passed from a world of death and dying into a world of light and life because we love God and our brothers and sisters. Those who don't are still in the world of death. Whoever hates his brothers and sisters has murder in his heart. And you know that no murderer has eternal life.

"We know what love is like by looking at Jesus. He loved us and gave His life for us. That's how much we should love each other. How can those who see their brothers and sisters in need and are able to help them but don't, say they love God? Let's not just say that we love Him, but say it by what we do. That's how we will know that the truth is in our hearts and that our conscience is clear before the Lord. If our conscience condemns us, there's something wrong. If our conscience is clear, then we can ask God for things and He will help us, because we want to keep His commandments and do what pleases Him.

"He told us what to do—to believe in His Son Jesus Christ and to love our brothers and sisters. Those who love God and keep His commandments have God in their hearts. We know God is in our hearts because the Holy Spirit is encouraging us to obey (1 John 3:10-24).

### The Holy Spirit

"My dear friends, don't listen to everyone who claims to have the Holy Spirit. Test what they say by the Word of God. That will tell you what spirit they have. There are false teachers and preachers everywhere.

"One way to know whether someone has the Holy Spirit or not is what they say about Jesus Christ. Do they believe that He is the Son of God or not? If they don't, then it's not the Holy Spirit speaking through them, but the spirit of antichrist, which is already at work in the world.

"You belong to God and have overcome the spirit of antichrist. The reason is that the Holy Spirit in you is more powerful than the spirit that is in the world. The world listens to these false teachers because they belong to the world. We belong to God, and those who listen to what we have to say belong to God. But those who don't listen don't belong to God. This is how you can tell the difference between those who have the Holy Spirit and those who have a false spirit (1 John 4:1-6).

### Knowing God

"Dear friends, let's love one another. Everyone whose heart is full of love has been born again, for love comes from God. Those who don't love, don't know God, because God is love.

"Here is how we know that God is love: He sent His Son into the world to save us. It's not because we loved God. No! God loves us so much that He sent His Son to save us even when we didn't love Him (1 John 4:7-11).

### Seeing God

"No one has actually seen God. But we know that God is here because His love is in our hearts. He lives in our hearts through the Holy Spirit.

"Besides that, we have seen His Son, whom the Father sent into the world to represent Him. Whoever accepts Jesus Christ as the Son of God has God in his heart.

"God is love. And when we love God and others, we don't have to be afraid of the judgment, because we live as Christ did when He was here.

"There's no fear in love; in fact, perfect love eliminates fear. So no one who loves God should be afraid of Him. Those who fear God don't know Him. But we know Him and love Him because He first loved us (1 John 4:12-19).

### Obeying God

"If someone says, 'I love God,' but hates his brother, he's lying. If he can't love his brother whom he can see, how can he love Someone he has never seen? Jesus told us that if we really love God, we will love our brother also.

"Whoever believes that Jesus is the Son of God has been born of God. And anyone who loves the Father will love those who are born of God. We know we are the children of the Father if we love Him and keep His commandments. To love God means to live by His commandments, and it's not that difficult.

"We have been born of God, which is why we can overcome the world. What gives us the strength to do so is our faith. Only those who believe that Jesus is the Son of God can overcome the world (1 John 4:20–5:5).

### Believing God

"We have evidence who Jesus Christ is from both His baptism and His death. When He came out of the water, the Father spoke about Him. When He died, it was for us that He shed His blood. The Holy Spirit confirmed this at Pentecost, and He says only what is true. So we have three Witnesses: the Father, the Son, and the Holy Spirit. They all agree.

"If we accept human witnesses to settle cases in our courts of law, why shouldn't we accept Witnesses from heaven? If we don't, we're saying that God is a liar. God doesn't lie. Besides that, He has promised eternal life to all who believe, and this life comes to us through His Son. Those who cling to the Son of God have eternal life, and those who don't, don't have it.

"I'm putting these things in writing to help you hold on to Jesus Christ and to your belief that He is the Son of God. When you do that, you can be sure that you already have the gift of eternal life (1 John 5:6-13).

## Confidence in God

"We have confidence that if we ask God anything that's according to His will, He will hear us. And if we know He hears us, we also know that He will give us whatever is best for us.

"If you see your brother sinning and you pray for him, God will hear your prayers and do all He can to bring him around and give him eternal life. But there is a sin that leads to death. It is the sin of stubbornly continuing to sin. All wrongdoing is sin, but this kind ends in eternal death.

"Whoever is born of God does not live in sin but is always careful what he does. God will watch over him and the devil won't be able to touch him. We know that we belong to God, even though the world is controlled by the wicked one.

"The Son of God gave us a glimpse of what God is like. That's why we have such confidence in God and why we are in union with Him and with His Son, Jesus Christ. This is the true God, the One who gives us eternal life.

"My dear children in the Lord, be on guard against false doctrines, which some have made their idols. Blessings. Amen" (1 John 5:14-21).

## John's Second Letter

"From John, the old disciple, to a dear lady, one of God's own, and to her children, whom I love very much, as does everyone else who knows the truth. The truth about Jesus Christ stands forever. Grace, mercy, and peace to you from God the Father and from His Son, Jesus Christ (2 John 1:1-3).

"I'm so happy to know that your children are walking in the truth, just as our heavenly Father has asked us to do. We should all do that, and we should also love one another.

"This is nothing new. We've known that from the beginning. And what you have heard from us, all of you should do (2 John 1:4-6).

## Don't Be Deceived

"Deceivers are everywhere. If they don't believe that the Son of God became a human being, don't listen to them. They're not for Christ—they're against Him, no matter what they say.

"Be careful that you don't lose the faith you have or all our work for you will be lost, including your eternal reward. Whoever is not faithful to what Christ has taught us doesn't know God. But those who continue in the faith have the Father and His Son in their hearts.

"If someone comes to see you and you know that he isn't faithful to what Christ taught, don't let him in. If you do, you're having a part in the evil he does (2 John 1:7-11).

## Final Greeting

"I have a lot of other things to write about, but I'd rather come and talk to you face to face. That way we can rejoice together in what Christ has done for us and in what He has taught us.

"Your sister and her children send their greetings" (2 John 1:12, 13).

## John's Third Letter

"From John, the old disciple, to Gaius, my brother in Christ, whom I truly love.

Dear friend, I hope all is well with you and that you're in good health, just as your soul is. What a thrill it was to listen to your brothers in the faith telling us how loyal you are to Jesus Christ and what a witness you are to the truth! (3 John 1:1-4).

## Commendation

"You're so faithful in all you do for your fellow believers, as well as for strangers visiting your church. We were told how much you love people and what you have done for missionaries who stopped by, giving them what they needed so they could be on their way. This kind of love pleases God.

"These travel-weary missionaries were not well received by unbelievers. This means we should do all we can for them, and in that way we have a part in their mission work (3 John 1:5-8).

## Two Different Men

"I wrote a letter to the church, but the head elder, Diotrephes, refused to read it. He doesn't listen. When I come, I'll try to take care of the situation and show that he has no business being head elder. I'll tell the church how he has twisted what we've said and even lied about us.

"Not only that, but he has no use for traveling missionaries and even threatened to remove from membership those wanting to help them! Don't listen to him, but keep on helping these missionaries. Those who do good are born of God, but those who do nothing to help others will never see God.

"I'm sending Demetrius to you. Everywhere he goes people speak well of him, and we feel the same way. That's why we're sending him. And what we're telling you is true (3 John 1:9-12).

### Final Greeting

"I have so much more to write, but I plan to stop by shortly and we can talk about it. God's peace be with you.

"Your friends send their greetings. Greet our friends for us" (3 John 1:13-15).

# thirty-four

# Another Arrest

I, John, an apostle of Jesus Christ, am sending this message to the seven churches in Asia Minor. Grace to you and peace from God the Father, who always was, who is, and who is coming, from the Holy Spirit by God's throne, and from Jesus Christ, the Faithful One. He is the One who rose from the dead and has all the rights of a firstborn son.

"He is the rightful ruler over all the kings and authorities of this world. He is the One who loved us and gave His life for us to set us free from the holding power of sin. He has made us into a kingdom of priests in the service of God the Father. To Him be glory and power forever and ever. Amen.

"I am your brother and fellow sufferer. Even though I was arrested and sentenced to death, the Lord intervened and I have been exiled to the prison island of Patmos. All this happened because I believed the Word of God and proclaimed the truth about Jesus Christ (Rev. 1:4-6, 9).

## Revelation

"This book is about Jesus and the things God told Him to share with us concerning the future. He appeared to me and spoke to me through His angel, and I wrote down everything I saw and heard.

"Blessed are those who read this book. And blessed are those who listen to what is read and who do what it says. The time is near when all these things will begin to happen.

"The Lord will come in the clouds of heaven and everyone will see Him, including those who killed Him. People from every nation will grieve because He's coming to carry out judgment against them. And so it will be.

"He said, 'I am the Alpha and the Omega, the Beginning and End, the All-powerful One who always was, who is, and who is coming (Rev. 1:1-3, 7, 8).

# WITNESS: Acts Through Revelation

## A Vision

"I was alone worshipping on the Lord's Day, the Sabbath, when I heard behind me a loud voice like a trumpet, saying, 'I also am the Beginning and the End. Write what you will see and hear in a little book and send it to the congregations in Ephesus, Smyrna, Pergamos, Thyatira, Sardis, Philadelphia, and Laodicea.'

"I turned to see who had spoken to me, and I saw seven golden lampstands, and the Son of God was walking among them. He wore the same daily dress that the high priest wore when he ministered in the sanctuary—a long, white robe and a golden belt. His hair was white as snow, and His eyes looked as if they were on fire. His feet looked like polished brass, and His voice sounded like the roar of a waterfall. He had seven stars in His right hand. When He spoke, a laser sword flashed from His mouth. His face was as bright as the noonday sun.

"I closed my eyes and fell at His feet, as lifeless as if I were dead. He touched me with His right hand and said, 'Don't be afraid. I am the First and the Last. I am the One who was dead and is alive. I will never die again but will live forever and ever. I have the keys to the prison house of death and the grave.

"'Get up and write what you saw and what I will show you. Some things apply to both the present and the future. The seven stars you saw in My right hand represent the leaders of the seven churches, and the golden lampstands are the seven congregations' (Rev. 1:10-20).

## History of the Christian Church

### Letter to Ephesus

"From John to the leader of the church in Ephesus:

"This message is from the One who walks among the churches. He says, 'I know all about you. I know your commitment, how hard you work for Me, and that you can't tolerate duplicity and evil. You have tested those who claim to be apostles and found them to be frauds and liars. You are to be commended for your perseverance and loyalty to what's right.

"'But I need to point out something to you. You have lost the ardent love you once had for Me. So turn around and go back to when you first met Me. Be motivated by that love or I'll have to take away your lampstand. Yet there is a lot of good about you. You hate how the Nicolaitans twist the gospel and undermine your faith, which I hate too.

"'You have ears, so listen to what the Holy Spirit is telling you. Whoever holds on to Me I will give the right to eat fruit from the tree of life which is in the middle of the Garden of God' (Rev. 2:1-7).

### Letter to Smyrna

"From John to the leader of the church in Smyrna:

"This message is from the One who is the First and the Last, who was dead and is alive. He says, 'I know your troubles and distress. I know your sufferings and poverty. But you are rich because of your faith and love for Me. I know how those who claim to be My people slander and accuse you of evil. They're doing exactly what Satan wants them to do.

"'Don't be afraid of what's coming. Some of you will be arrested and thrown into prison. Your faith will be severely tested. This persecution will last for some time. Be faithful to Me, even if it means you have to die. I will resurrect you and give you the crown of life.

"'You have ears, so listen to what the Holy Spirit is telling you. Those who die for Me now will not have to die the second death' (Rev. 2:8-11).

### Letter to Pergamos

"From John to the leader of the church in Pergamos:

"This letter is from the One who has a laser sword in His mouth. He says, 'I know where you live. I know that Satan has set up his temporary headquarters there. But you continued to hold on to Me, even after you saw Antipas arrested and killed for refusing to worship Caesar.

"'Yet I need to point out something to you. Some among you act like Balaam. He got the people of Israel to compromise their faith by luring them into adultery and idol worship. And you—you're listening to the Nicolaitans, who are twisting the gospel and undermining your faith. You need to repent and change or I'll have to use the sword in My mouth and take action against your church.

"'You have ears, so listen to what the Holy Spirit is telling you. Everyone who is loyal to Me will eat the manna of heaven and will be given a new name engraved on a white stone' (Rev. 2:12-17).

### Letter to Thyatira

"From John to the leader of the church in Thyatira:

"This message is from the One whose eyes look like they're on fire and whose feet look like polished brass. He says, 'I know your faith and love, your perseverance and good deeds, and that you're doing more for Me now than ever before.

"'But I need to point out something to you. You have let false doctrines come in among you, like those Jezebel brought in to Israel. She called herself a prophetess. She encouraged actual adultery as part of idol worship. I gave her time to repent, but she didn't.

"'Those who worship idols will suffer terribly unless they repent. And those who follow her teachings will be killed as she was. Then the church will know that I search hearts and minds and reward each one according to what he has done.

"'But for those of you in Thyatira who have not listened to Satan, all I ask of you is to hold on to your faith. When I come, I will share My power and authority with those who have been faithful, and they will help decide the fate of nations. This is according to My Father's will. As the Scripture says, "The Lord will sit in judgment on the nations and break their power as easily as if it were a clay jar."

"'You have ears, so listen to what the Holy Spirit is telling you. When sin is no more, you will shine as the morning star' (Rev. 2:18-29).

### Letter to Sardis
"From John to the leader of the church in Sardis:

"This message is from the One who, through the Holy Spirit, holds the seven stars in His hand. He says, 'I know what you're doing. You have a good reputation, and it looks to others like you're all for Me when you're not. Wake up! Strengthen the love for Me you do have so it doesn't die. God is not pleased with what you're doing.

"'Remember what you were taught and do it. If you don't wake up and change, I'll have to take control. You won't know when I will do this, but it will be as unexpected as a thief in the night.

"'A few in Sardis have not soiled their clothes. They will walk beside Me in white because they're worthy. All who overcome will be dressed in white, and I will not take their names out of the book of life but will acknowledge them as Mine before the Father and the angels.

"'You have ears, so listen to what the Holy Spirit is telling you' (Rev. 3:1-6).

### Letter to Philadelphia
"From John to the leader of the church in Philadelphia:

"This message is from the Holy One, the One who is true, who has the keys of the kingdom of David to open and close doors, which no one else can do. He says, 'I know what your good deeds are and that you love Me. I have opened a door for you, but you don't have enough strength to go through it on your own. Yet you have kept My word and not turned away from Me.

"'Those from the synagogue of Satan who listen to his suggestions are not real Jews, no matter what they say. I will stop them from speaking against you and will make them see that I love you.

216

"'Because you have kept my Word and remained faithful, I will be with you during the testing time that will come upon the whole world. I am coming soon, so hold on and don't let anyone take away your faith and cause you to end up losing your crown of life.

"'Those who are faithful will be pillars in the temple of My God. You will never have to leave. I will write My name on you, along with the name of My God and the name of His city, the new Jerusalem, which will come down from heaven.

"'You have ears, so listen to what the Holy Spirit is telling you' (Rev. 3:7-13).

**Letter to Laodicea**

"From John to the leader of the church in Laodicea:

"This message is from the 'Amen,' the Faithful and True Witness, who created all things under the direction of God. He says, 'I know the good things you do, but you're neither cold nor hot towards Me. I wish you were one way or the other so people could tell where you stand. You're like stagnant water because you keep talking about how spiritually rich you are and how much money you have. You think you don't need anything. But you don't realize that you are spiritually poor, blind, and naked. You are to be pitied.

"'I urge you to buy the gold I'm offering you, which has been refined in the fire. That is what will make you rich. I'm also offering you a white robe to cover your nakedness so you won't have to be ashamed. And I have ointment for your eyes, to help you see things as you should.

"'I discipline those I love because I care about them. So be in earnest and change your attitude. I'm knocking at your heart's door. When you hear Me calling, come and open the door. I'll be happy to come in and we can eat together.

"'Don't give in to the world, and I will give you a place to sit with Me on my throne, just as I didn't give in to the world and am sitting next to My Father on His throne.

"'You have ears, so listen to what the Holy Spirit is telling you' (Rev. 3:14-22).

### The Throne Room

"After I got the letters off, I had another vision. I saw an open door in heaven. And I heard a voice that sounded like a trumpet, calling, 'Come on up! I will show you things that will happen in the future.'

"The Holy Spirit took hold of me, and the next thing I knew, I was in heaven. There was an open door, and I saw a throne and Someone sitting on it. I knew it must be God. A light sparkling like diamonds covered His face, and a rainbow was above the throne.

"In a semicircle in front of the throne were 24 smaller thrones and on them sat 24 elders dressed in white with golden crowns on their heads. Lightning flashed around God's throne, and there were sounds of thunder and the roar of a coming storm. Seven burning torches were in front of the throne, representing the Holy Spirit. There also was an open courtyard before the throne that looked like a large sea. It was as clear as crystal and as smooth as glass.

"There were four angel guards standing near the four corners of the throne. The first represented the power of a lion, the next the service of an ox, the third the intelligence of man, and the fourth the speed of an eagle. They were dressed in robes which were covered with eyes from front to back. Each one had six wings, and they never slept day or night. They were singing, 'Holy, holy, holy is the Lord God Almighty, the One who always was, who is, and who will come!'

"When the four angels gave glory and honor and thanks to God, the 24 elders laid their crowns in front of Him, fell on their knees, and worshipped the One who lives forever and ever, saying, 'You are worthy, O Lord our God, to receive glory and honor and to exercise Your power, because You created all things and by Your will they continue to exist' (Rev. 4:1–11).

### The Lamb

"The One who sat on the throne had a scroll in His hand. It was written on both sides, front and back, and sealed in seven sections.

"A powerful angel called out: 'Who is qualified to break the seals and open the scroll?' No one was. When I saw that no one could, I cried. One of the elders said to me, 'Don't cry. The Lion from the house of David out of the tribe of Judah is qualified. He will break the seals and open the scroll.'

"Then I saw a Lamb standing in the middle of the elders, facing the throne and the four angel guards. It looked as if it had been killed. It had seven eyes and seven little horns which represented His wisdom and power, working through the Holy Spirit all over the world.

"The Lamb was the Son of God. As High Priest, He stepped forward and took the scroll out of the hand of the One who sat on the throne. When He did, the four angels and the 24 elders fell on their knees, bowed before the Lamb and worshipped Him.

"As they stood, I saw that each elder had a harp and a golden bowl holding the incense of the prayers of God's people, and together they sang,

'You are worthy to take the scroll and break the seals, because You gave Your life for us and bought our redemption by Your own blood. You took us from different tribes and nations and made us kings and priests, to serve God and to rule with Him on the earth made new.'

"Then I heard the voices of many angels join the four mighty ones and the elders, singing, 'Worthy is the Lamb that was sacrificed to receive power and riches, wisdom and strength, and honor, glory, and praise!'

"Voices from all over heaven and earth, and voices from the sea joined in singing: 'To the One who sits on the throne and to the Lamb be praise, honor, glory, and power forever and ever!'

"The four angels shouted, 'Amen!' and the 24 elders fell on their knees and worshipped God and the Lamb" (Rev. 5:1-14).

# thirty-five

# History of Spreading the Gospel

### The First Seal

"When the Lamb broke the first seal and unrolled that section of the scroll, the first angel guard said, 'Come! See what's happening!'

"I looked and saw a white horse, and the One who sat on it had a bow in His hand and arrows strapped to His back. I saw a crown of victory placed on His head, and He rode across the earth, spreading the gospel for God (Rev. 6:1, 2).

### The Second Seal

"When the Lamb broke the second seal and unrolled that section of the scroll, the second angel said, 'Come! See what's happening!'

"I looked and saw another horse. This one was red, and the one who sat on it had a huge sword in his hand and was given permission to take away peace from the earth. Then persecution came and many of God's people were killed (Rev. 6:3, 4).

### The Third Seal

"When the Lamb broke the third seal and unrolled the next section of the scroll, the third angel said, 'Come! See what's happening!'

"I looked and saw a black horse. The one who sat on it had a scale in his hand. Then I heard a voice coming from among the four powerful angels, saying, 'Food will be scarce. It will cost a day's wages just to buy a quart of wheat or three quarts of barley. But this will not hurt the spiritual oil and wine' (Rev. 6:5, 6).

### The Fourth Seal

"Then the Lamb broke the fourth seal and unrolled that section of the scroll. When He did, the fourth angel said, 'Come! See what's happening!'

"I looked and saw a pale horse, and the one who sat on it was called 'Death.' Wherever he rode his horse, graves popped up in his tracks. He swung his sword and brought violence, hunger, disease, and death to one fourth of the earth (Rev. 6:7, 8).

### The Fifth Seal

"Next the Lamb broke the fifth seal and unrolled that section of the scroll. I looked and saw an altar, and next to it lay the bodies of those who had been killed because they were true to the Word of God and held to their testimony.

"Their bodies cried out, 'How much longer, Lord? You are holy and true. How much longer before You come and judge those who shed our blood?'

"Then white robes were given to them, and they were told to wait a little longer until the death decree against their brothers and sisters was stopped (Rev. 6:9-11).

### The Sixth Seal

"When the Lamb broke the sixth seal and unrolled this section of the scroll, there was a huge earthquake. The sun turned dark and the moon turned red. The sky was full of falling stars, dropping like figs from a tree blown by a strong wind.

"After that the sky rolled back like a scroll, and every mountain and island was moved out of place. The kings of the earth, the generals, the rich and powerful of the earth, and every free man and slave fled to the mountains to hide in caves or among the rocks, saying, 'Cover us and hide us from the face of the One sitting on the throne and from the Lamb! The day of judgment has come! Who can survive?' (Rev. 6:12-17).

### The Sealing

"Then I saw four angels assigned to hold back the winds of judgment from blowing across the land or destroying the trees of the Lord. A fifth angel came from the east with the seal of God in his hand. He called out to the four angels, 'Don't let go of the winds until we have sealed God's people for eternity.'

"I heard the number of those who were sealed—12,000 from each of the tribes of spiritual Israel, a total of 144,000, which is a symbolic number of all of God's people. Then I saw a sea of people too large to count, from every nation, tribe, and language, standing before the throne in white robes with palm branches in their hands. They broke out in songs of praise, singing, 'Salvation comes from our God, the One who sits on the throne, and from the Lamb!'

"Then the angels formed a circle around the throne, the four guards, and the 24 elders. They fell on their knees and bowed to the ground in worship. Then they stood up and sang: 'Praise and glory, wisdom and thanksgiving, honor and power to our God forever and ever. Amen!'

"One of the elders asked me, 'Who are these people in white robes? Where did they come from?'

"I answered, 'I don't know, but I'm sure you do.'

"He said, 'These are the ones who have washed themselves in the blood of the Lamb and have gone through the troubles of the last days. That's why you see them standing before the throne. God has given them a special place of honor. He will be among them, and they will serve Him continuously.

"'They will never go hungry or thirst again, nor will they have to suffer the scorching heat of the sun. The Lamb will be their Shepherd and will lead them to springs of living water. And God Himself will wipe away all tears from their eyes' (Rev. 7:1-17).

### The Seventh Seal

"Then I saw the Lamb break the seventh seal and unroll the last section of the scroll. When He did, there was a silence of anticipation in heaven awaiting the arrival of the saints (Rev. 8:1).

### History of Wars

#### Seven Trumpets

"Next I saw seven angels come up to the throne, and God gave each one a trumpet. I saw a small golden altar before God's throne and another angel with a censer standing there. He was given large amounts of incense, which represented the prayers of God's people. He offered them on the altar, and the smoke of the incense rose up in front of the throne.

"Then the angel filled his censer with fire from the little golden altar and threw the censer down to earth. There were flashes of lightning, peals of thunder, and a powerful earthquake. This alerted the seven angels, and they got ready to blow their trumpets (Rev. 8:2-6).

#### The First Trumpet

"The first angel blew his trumpet, and fire and hail the color of blood came down on the earth. One third of the trees and the green grass were burned up (Rev. 8:7).

#### The Second Trumpet

"Then the second angel blew his trumpet, and an erupting volcano, together with the whole mountain, was thrown into the sea, and one third of the ocean turned to blood. A third of the fish died and many ships were destroyed (Rev. 8:8, 9).

### The Third Trumpet

"Next the third angel blew his trumpet, and a huge burning meteor fell from heaven. It hit a third of the earth's rivers and sources of water. The name of the meteor was 'Bitterness' because a third of the waters turned bitter and people died from drinking it (Rev. 8:10, 11).

### The Fourth Trumpet

"When the fourth angel blew his trumpet, the sun, moon, and stars lost one third of their brightness. There was no light for one third of the day and one third of the night. An angel flying overhead cried out, 'Woe! Woe! Woe! Terrible times are coming when the next three angels blow their trumpets' (Rev. 8:12, 13).

### The Fifth Trumpet

"Then the fifth angel blew his trumpet, and this brought on the first terrible woe. I saw an angel come down from heaven with a key to the demonic pit. When he opened the pit, smoke shot up as if coming out of a huge furnace. The smoke was so thick that it blocked the rays of the sun and poisoned the air.

"Out of the smoke came an army of locusts. They were told not to harm any growing grass or green tree or plant, but only those who did not have the seal of God. They were given power to sting but not to kill. This lasted for some time. It was so terrible that people wanted to die rather than live.

"These locusts were huge—more like horses ready for war. On their backs were strange-looking riders who had something like crowns on their heads, and their long hair looked like women's hair. Each rider had an iron breastplate, and when they gave the battle cry they looked as vicious as attacking lions.

"They rode into battle as if they had wings, and the thunder of their horses' hooves sounded like thousands of chariot wheels. The horses had tails like scorpion stingers with which to hurt people. This went on for some time. The king over them was in charge of the demonic pit. His name in both Hebrew and Greek means 'Destroyer.'

"The first woe is past, but two more are coming (Rev. 9:1-12).

### The Sixth Trumpet

"After this, the sixth angel blew his trumpet, and the second woe began. I heard a voice coming from the direction of the little golden altar before the throne of God, saying to the sixth angel, 'Tell the four angels holding back the river Euphrates to let go.'

"The four angels let go, and the river overflowed for some time, killing a third of the people. The number of mounted troops who attacked the people over days, months, and years numbered in the millions. Their breastplates glistened in the sun, making them look like they were on fire. A third of the people were killed by the fire, smoke, and fumes that came out of the horses' mouths.

"The people who survived did not turn to God for help, but continued worshipping idols of gold, silver, bronze, stone, or wood, which cannot see or hear. They did not repent, but continued their murders, witchcraft, immorality, and stealing (Rev. 9:13-21).

### The Little Scroll

"During this time the Son of God came down from heaven in the form of a powerful angel. He was wrapped in a cloud and had a rainbow over His head. His face was as bright as the sun, and His legs looked like pillars of fire. He was holding a little scroll in His hand.

"He set His right foot on the sea and His left foot on the land. He called out in a loud voice that sounded like the roar of a lion. Then I heard seven voices as loud as thunder respond with frightening words. I was ready to write down what I heard, but a voice said to me, 'Don't write it down, because for now these words are sealed.'

"Then the Son of God raised His hand to heaven and, in the name of God who created heaven and earth, took a vow that there would be no long delay, but that during the sounding of the seventh trumpet, the spreading of the gospel would be finished as the prophets had predicted.

"The voice that told me not to write also said to me, 'Go up to the Son of God, and take the little scroll and eat it.' So I went up and asked Him to let me have the little scroll. He gave it to me and said, 'Take it and eat it. It will taste sweet in your mouth, but it will give you a sour stomach.' So I took the little scroll and ate it. In my mouth it tasted sweet, but it gave me a sour stomach, just as He had said.

"Then I was told that God's message must yet be taken to many nations, people, languages, and kings (Rev. 10:1-11).

### The Word of God

"After that I was given a measuring rod and told to measure God's temple, the altar, and those who worship Him. I was told not to measure the outer courtyard, because those who were there have been trampling down holy things and will do so for some time.

"The two testaments of God's Word were like two witnesses. They had power to speak during that time and did so with grief in their hearts. They received their oil from the two olive trees and their light from the two lamps that stood in the presence of God.

"If anyone tried to hurt the two witnesses, they had been given the power of Elijah to call fire down from heaven on God's enemies and to close up the sky so it wouldn't rain. They also had power to turn water into blood and to bring on plagues, as Moses did in Egypt.

"The leader from the demonic pit went to war against the two witnesses, trying to silence them. It looked as if he had succeeded because the people saw the two witnesses lying dead in the streets of the city—a city as sinful as Sodom and as rebellious as Egypt. People continued crucifying the Lord in their hearts.

"This lasted for some time, and people thought it was the end of the two testaments. They celebrated because they didn't have to listen to the witnesses any more or be disturbed by their prophecies. But the Holy Spirit breathed life into the two witnesses, and they stood to their feet. When the people saw this, they became frightened. I heard a voice say to the two witnesses, 'Come up here!' As their enemies watched, they went up in a cloud and stood in the sky.

"Then a great earthquake shook the city, and one-tenth of it was destroyed. Thousands of people were killed, and the rest were afraid and honored God as they had never done before.

"The second woe has passed, and the third woe is coming (Rev. 11:1-14).

### The Seventh Trumpet

"Then the seventh angel blew his trumpet, and there were voices in heaven, saying, 'The kingdoms of this world were given by God to His Son, and He will reign forever and ever.'

"The 24 elders I had seen earlier fell on their knees, bowed to the ground, and worshipped the One on the throne. They said, 'We thank you, Lord. You are the mighty One, the One who was, who is, and ever will be. You have taken your great power and have begun to rule.

"'The nations of the world have turned against You. The time of Your judgment has come, the time to judge the living and the dead. You will reward all those who have served You and honored Your name, whether they were small or great. And You will destroy those who exploited the earth.'

"Another door opened into the temple of God in heaven, and I saw the ark of the covenant containing the law of God. Then there were flashes of lightning, peals of thunder, a global earthquake, and a tremendous hailstorm. The third woe ended, and so did the history of the world" (Rev. 11:15-19).

# thirty-six

# Satan and the Woman

John continued:

"In vision I saw a woman in the sky. She was standing on the moon, dressed with the light of the sun, with a crown of 12 stars on her head. She was pregnant and cried out in pain, ready to give birth.

"Then I saw something else in the sky. It was a huge red dragon. It had seven heads with seven crowns and ten horns. With its long tail it swept a third of the stars out of the sky and threw them down to earth. It had its eyes on the woman, ready to kill her baby soon after it was born. But her Son was destined to rule all nations. So God took Him to heaven to sit next to Him on His throne.

"Then the woman had to flee into the wilderness to survive. God guided her to a place where she would be taken care of for some time to come (Rev. 12:1-6).

## War in Heaven

"Next I had a vision of eternity past and the war in heaven. The huge red dragon, called 'the devil' and 'Satan,' had rejected the authority of the Son of God, who is known as 'Michael.' So Michael and His angels had to fight against the dragon and his angels. The huge dragon, that ancient serpent was defeated and thrown out of heaven, and his angels with him.

"Then I heard a voice from heaven, saying, 'Heaven is now safe. The kingdom of God is secure, and the authority of Christ is no longer challenged. The devil, who falsely accused God's Son, is now accusing the followers of Christ day and night. But they are overcoming him by the power of the blood of the Lamb and by the Word of God, and they are not afraid to die.

"'Let heaven rejoice! But this is not the end of things. The devil is angry with those on earth because he knows his time is short (Rev. 12:7-12).

### The War Continues

"When Satan realized that his activity was confined to this earth, he went after the woman. But God gave her two huge wings, which she used to fly to the place in the wilderness He had prepared for her. There she would be safe from the dragon's intent to kill her.

"Then the dragon decided to flood her out. But God opened the earth and it swallowed up the flood. This made the devil furious, and he attacked the woman's descendants who love God, keep His commandments, and by faith hold on to what Jesus said (Rev. 12:13-17).

### The Final Battle

"Then I saw a terrible-looking animal come out of the sea. It had seven heads and ten horns with crowns. On each of its seven heads was a word that insulted God.

"This huge animal had the body of a leopard, the feet of a powerful bear, and the mouth of a ferocious lion. Satan was nearby and gave this animal demonic power and great authority.

"As I looked, I saw this terrible-looking animal receive a deadly blow to one of its heads. But, amazingly, the wound healed. The whole world marveled at its recovery and began listening to this animal. People said to each other, 'Who can stand up against such a powerful animal and make war with it?' So they worshipped this animal and, by doing so, were worshipping the dragon who gave it its power.

"This terrible-looking animal became very proud and claimed to speak for God. It was allowed to do this and to exercise its authority for some time. What it said and did during this time was an insult to God and to all of heaven.

"It attacked God's people and was soon able to exercise its authority over every tribe, language, and nation. Everyone whose name was not written in the Lamb's book of life ended up worshipping this animal.

"If you have ears, you need to listen to what I'm telling you. Those who take God's people captive and kill them must be taken captive and killed. This will call for a strong faith and special endurance on the part of God's people (Rev. 13:1-10).

### The Battle Intensifies

"Next I saw a huge animal come out of the earth. This one was different. It had two little horns like a young ram, but it had the voice of a dragon. It stood next to the terrible-looking animal and used its authority to force the whole world to worship the animal whose head wound had healed.

"This huge animal with two little horns did many marvelous things. It even made fire come down from heaven in front of people. These things deceived the people and made them listen to what this land animal had to say. It told them to worship the animal who had received a deadly blow, yet lived. Those who refused would be killed. Everyone had to receive an identification mark on his right hand or forehead, whether small or great, rich or poor, free or slave. No one could buy or sell unless he had the worship mark with the name and number of the first animal.

"This calls for special wisdom. Those with spiritual insight will know to whom the name and number belongs. The number is 666, which stands for the authority of a man (Rev. 13:11-18).

### The Lamb of God

"The scene changed and I saw the Lamb of God standing on Mount Zion. With Him were the 144,000 with His Father's name on their foreheads.

"Then I heard a voice from heaven that sounded like the roar of a huge waterfall or crashing thunder. I heard the music of a harp and a new song being sung by those who were with the Lamb. They sang this song in front of the four mighty angels and the 24 elders. No one was able to learn and sing this song of redemption like they could.

"The 144,000 were like the firstfruits of the redeemed from all over the earth. Their faith was pure and they followed the Lamb wherever He led them. In their mouth was no dishonesty, and they stood blameless before God as a sample of God's great harvest of all to be redeemed (Rev. 14:1-5).

### Three Angels

"Again the scene changed and I saw an angel flying high up in the sky with a special message of the gospel for everyone on earth—for every tribe, language, and nation. He announced with a loud voice, 'Honor God and give glory to him, for the time of judgment has come. Worship the One who created heaven and earth, oceans, and springs of water.'

"Next I saw another angel flying high up in the sky. He announced to everyone on earth: 'That great spiritual city called Babylon that men have built has fallen from the truth about God and will continue to fall, because she is making all nations drink its polluted wine.'

"Then I saw a third angel flying high up in the sky, announcing with a loud voice, 'If anyone worships the first creature and the second one and has the identity mark on his forehead or his hand, he will not escape the justice of God. He will face annihilation by fire in the presence of the holy angels and in the presence of the Lamb. The smoke will rise until all is burned up. No relief or hope will be available for those who worship the two creatures and have their identifying mark.'

"What I saw calls for special endurance on the part of God's people who are committed to keeping God's commandments and are faithful to Jesus.

"Then I heard a voice from heaven say, 'Write all this down. Blessed are those who die in the Lord.' 'Yes', says the Holy Spirit, 'they will rest from all their work, and what they did will not be forgotten' (Rev. 14:6-13).

### The Harvest

"The scene changed and I saw a huge white cloud. On it sat Jesus, the Son of Man. He had on His head a crown of gold and in His hand a sharp sickle. An angel came out of the temple in heaven and called to Jesus, 'Now is the time to reap the earth's harvest because it is ripe!' So Jesus swung His sickle and the harvest was reaped.

"Then another angel came out of the heavenly temple and he, too, had a sharp sickle. A third angel came out of the temple with fire in his hand. He called to that angel, 'Use your sickle to cut the clusters of grapes off the vine, because the grapes are ripe for judgment!' So that's what the angel did. Then he threw the grapes into God's winepress outside the heavenly city, and blood came out. It flowed everywhere. This meant the wicked would be destroyed and be gone forever (Rev. 14:14-20).

### The Song of Deliverance

"Next I saw seven angels coming out of the temple. Also, I saw what looked like a sea as smooth as glass with fire underneath. On the sea stood those who had rejected the identifying mark of the terrible creature with its name. They had harps in their hands and sang the song of Moses and the Lamb, a song of deliverance, saying:

Great and marvelous are the things the Lord our God has done!

He is the King of nations!

His ways are right and just!

Who does not stand in awe of what He has done?

Who can refuse His greatness?

Lord, You alone are holy. All nations will bow and worship You because Your justice has been seen by all" (Rev. 15:1-4).

# thirty-seven

# God's Justice

Then my eyes turned back to the seven angels I had seen coming out of the heavenly temple. They were dressed in shining white robes with golden bands around their waists. One of the four angels guarding the throne gave each of the seven angels a bowl of God's justice.

"The temple was filled with smoke from His glory and power. No one could go into the temple until God's justice was carried out (Rev. 15:5-8).

### Seven Angels

"Then I heard a voice calling to the seven angels, 'Go and carry out God's judgments!'

"So the first angel poured his bowl on the earth, and sores broke out on the bodies of those who had the identifying mark of the terrible-looking animal and on those who had obeyed the land animal that imitated it.

"The second angel poured his bowl on the ocean, which turned as red as blood. Every living thing in the ocean died.

"The third angel poured his bowl on the lakes and rivers and springs of water. They, too, turned as red as blood. I heard the angel say, 'Lord, You are righteous. You have always existed and always will. You have judged those who have shed the blood of Your people by turning their water red, reminding them of what they have done.' Another voice out of the temple in heaven said, 'True and right is the justice of the Lord God, the Almighty One.'

"The fourth angel poured his bowl on the sun, and its rays scorched parts of the earth and caused people to feel its intense heat. The people did not repent, but cursed God for letting this happen.

"The fifth angel poured his bowl on the palace of the sea creature that exercised such power. It became so dark that people bit their tongues in pain, but they did not repent. Like the others, they cursed God for what He had done.

"The sixth angel poured his bowl on the river Euphrates and its water dried up. The Holy Spirit was withdrawn from the earth, and the way was opened for the battle between the King of kings and the demonic spirits, which looked like frogs coming out of the mouth of the dragon, the sea beast, and the animal who was a false prophet.

"These demonic spirits went all over the world working miracles to gather people to fight against God and His people. This is the battle of Armageddon.

"The Lord said, 'I am coming quickly. Blessed are those who stay awake and wear the garment I've given them so they don't have to be ashamed.'

"The seventh angel poured his bowl into the air, and a loud voice from heaven declared, 'It is done!' There was lightning and thunder and an earthquake so powerful that it shook the whole world. There was never an earthquake like this before. The cities of the world crumbled, islands sank, mountains disappeared, and hailstones as huge as blocks of ice fell from the sky. The world had become as wicked as ancient Babylon. It was divided in three parts and each part received God's judgment. The people did not turn to God, but cursed Him instead (Rev. 16:1-21).

### The Woman and the Beast

"Then one of the seven angels with the seven bowls said to me, 'Come, let me show you the judgment of the prostitute who sits on the waves of the sea luring people away from God. Kings have gone to bed with her, and the people are drinking her wine.'

"The angel took me to a deserted place, and there I saw the woman sitting on a red beast which had seven heads and ten horns. The beast had insulting words about God written all over it. The woman was beautifully dressed in red and purple and had a golden cup in her hand. She had a mysterious name on her forehead, meaning Babylon the Great, Mother of Spiritual Prostitutes, and Universal False Worship.

"The woman was drunk with the blood of God's people, those she had killed for their faith in Jesus. When I saw this, I was stunned!

"The angel said to me, 'Why are you so shocked? Let me tell you about the mysterious working of this woman and the beast she sits on. People whose names are not in the book of life are drawn by the power of this beast which was, then was not, and now is.

"'The seven heads of the beast represent seven mountains where the woman lives. They also represent seven nations. Five have come and gone. One currently exists and one is still to come. When it does, it will last only a short time. The dragon's kingdom is number eight, but it's really made up of the spirit of the former seven. It's like one kingdom with seven heads, and they will all be destroyed.

"'The ten horns you saw represent ten nations which are not yet united. For a short time they will unite and go along with the dragon. They will be of one mind and will use their power and authority to support the woman. They will fight against the Lamb of God, but the Lamb will overpower them. He is King of kings and Lord of lords, and those who stand with Him will be faithful and true.

"'The sea on which the woman and the beast sit represents people, multitudes, languages, and nations. The woman also represents the city from which the dragon controls the kings of the earth. God will let these kings go along with the woman until the time comes for Him to act. Then the nations will see that the woman has deceived them and will turn on her, strip her naked, and set her on fire' (Rev. 17:1–18).

## Spiritual Babylon

"After this, I saw a powerful angel with great authority come down from heaven. The whole earth was covered with light from his brightness.

"With a strong voice he called out, 'The spiritual city of Babylon has fallen! She has come under the influence of demons! Every evil spirit is there and every hateful thing. The nations are drunk with her adulterous wine, and the merchants of the earth have become rich by supplying Babylon with luxuries.'

"Then I heard another voice from heaven, saying, 'Come out of her, my people! Don't take part in her sins and have God's judgments fall on you. Her sins are piled up to heaven, and the time has come for God to act. He will treat her just as she treated you and pay her double for making you taste her harshness more than once.

"'She has lived a life of luxury and thought of herself as an eternal queen, never having to suffer, never to be a widow. But very quickly God's judgment will come and she will know sorrow, grief, and pain. She will experience famine and will be destroyed by fire. God is strong and powerful. He is the One who will judge her (Rev. 18:1–8).

## Commercial Babylon

"'The nations will weep when they see her go up in smoke. They will watch and say, "That great and powerful city has been destroyed so quickly!"

"'The merchants will cry because their markets are gone. They had traded with her in gold and silver, sold her pearls, ivory, precious stones, linen, silk, rare woods, bronze, iron, marble, incense, spices, oils, wine, flour, wheat, cattle, sheep, horses, and wagons, and had provided her with workers.

"'All the luxuries and splendid things of Babylon are gone. And the merchants who became rich because of her are crying. They're saying, "That great city was dressed in fine linen and silk, wearing gold and precious stones and pearls. She was so wealthy, but in such a short time she has come to nothing."

"'When the ship captains and those who trade by sea and air see this, they will cry out, "There was never a city like this great city!" They will throw dust on their heads, saying, "All of us who traded with her became rich, but now she's gone!"

"'Let all of heaven rejoice and the people of God be glad. The Lord has condemned her for what she has done to His people and to those who spoke for Him.'

"Then the mighty angel picked up a huge rock and threw it into the sea, saying, 'In this same way Babylon will suddenly be thrown into the sea and disappear. Her music will end. Her musicians, flutists, harpists, drummers, and trumpeters will never be heard again. Her artists, craftsmen, farmers, and manufacturers will be gone. Her lights will be out, and in place of celebrations and the happy voices of brides and bridegrooms, there will be silence.

"'She deceived the merchants, the great men, and every nation on earth. She has blood on her hands and is responsible for killing God's people and those who spoke for Him'" (Rev. 18:9-24).

# thirty-eight

# The Wedding

John continued:

"After this, the scene changed and I heard a large multitude in heaven with one voice shouting, 'Alleluia! Salvation, glory, honor, and power belong to our God! His justice is true and right! He condemned the woman who corrupted the earth with her prostitutions and killed God's people.' Again they shouted, 'Alleluia! The rebellious city is going up in smoke!'

"The 24 elders and the four mighty angels by the throne fell on their knees before God, worshipped Him, and cried out, 'Amen! Alleluia!'

"After this, a voice from the throne thundered, 'Praise God, all you who serve Him, both small and great!'

"Then the multitude in heaven spoke with a voice that sounded like the deep roar of a mighty waterfall and as loud as thunder, saying, 'Alleluia! The Lord God omnipotent reigns! Let us rejoice and be glad and give Him the glory that is due His name. The marriage of the Lamb has come! His wife is ready! She is dressed in a clean, white wedding gown given to her by the Bridegroom, embroidered with her kind deeds.'

"The mighty angel who was with me said, 'Write this down: Blessed are those who have received the invitation to the wedding and reception of the Lamb.' Then he added, 'This is what God said and His words are true.'

"I fell on my knees before the angel, but he pulled me up and said, 'Don't worship me! Worship God! I'm just one of God's servants, as you are, and as all those are who hold on to what Jesus said through the gift of prophecy' (Rev. 19:1-10).

## The King Comes

"Then I saw heaven open and the Son of God riding on a white horse, ready for war. He is faithful and true and is coming to carry out God's justice. His eyes looked as if they were on fire, and on His head was a triple crown. His robe was as red as blood. His name is the Word of God!

"The armies of heaven followed, all dressed in clean, white robes, riding white horses. His words were like a laser sword with which to fight the nations. The time for mercy and forgiveness is past. With a rod of iron He will administer the justice of Almighty God. On His robe by His thigh was written: King of kings! Lord of lords! (Rev. 19:11–16).

### Enemies of the Bride Destroyed

"Next I saw a mighty angel standing in the light of the sun. He called to the vultures, 'Come! Get ready to eat the dead bodies of the leaders, the captains with their horses, and all people, small and great.'

"I saw the kings of the earth and their armies come together under the influence of the terrible creature to fight against the One on the white horse and His army. The terrible animal was captured, and so was the huge animal who deceived the people by the great things he did and by making them worship the sea animal and receive its mark.

"Both of them were thrown into a lake of fire, and the people with the identifying mark were killed by the laser sword of the One on the white horse. Then the vultures came and ate their dead bodies.

"After this, I saw another angel come down from heaven with a key to the demonic pit and a large chain in his hand. He took hold of the dragon, the old serpent known as the devil, or Satan, tied him up, and confined him to his demonic pit for a thousand years. Then the angel locked the gate so the devil couldn't get away. After a thousand years he will be released, but only for a little while (Rev. 19:17–20:3).

### Trial by Jury

"During the thousand years the righteous were in heaven, sitting on thrones next to Jesus. Some were martyrs who had given their lives for Christ and for believing the Word of God. Others were there who had refused to worship the terrible animal and receive its mark.

"They are blessed, for they were raised at the first resurrection before the thousand years began and will not have to die again. They have the status of priests and were given power to judge for a thousand years.

"All this time the wicked remained dead, but when the thousand years ended, they were brought back to life, and Satan was released from his confinement. When he saw the wicked who had been raised from the dead, he went all over the earth, gathering them together into an army so large they couldn't be counted. They came from all parts of the globe and surrounded the city of God, which had descended from heaven to earth.

"Then fire came down from heaven and destroyed them. The devil, who had deceived people into thinking they could overpower God, was also destroyed in that fire, along with the sea beast and the land animal who had become a false prophet. They were all destroyed forever (Rev. 20:4-10).

### The Verdict

"Before Satan and his followers were destroyed, I saw God sitting on a great white throne. Heaven and earth seemed to melt at His presence. Those who had been dead, the great and the small, whether they had died at sea or been buried on land, stood before God. The books of heaven were opened, including the book of life. All people were judged by what was written in the books, according to what they had done.

"Anyone whose name was not in the book of life was destroyed by fire. Death and the grave came to an end. This is the second death, which is final (Rev. 20:11-15).

### A New Beginning

"After this, the scene changed and I saw a new heaven and a new earth. The old earth with its atmosphere was gone, and so were the large oceans. I saw the city of God, the New Jerusalem, come down from heaven, looking as beautiful as a bride coming to meet her husband.

"I heard a voice from heaven say, 'Look! God has moved His throne to earth to be with His people forever. They will be with Him, and He will be their God. He will wipe away all their tears, and there will be no more death or crying. And there will be no more pain, because the former things are passed away.'

From His throne, God's Son said, 'Look, I have made all things new. So write down what you've seen and heard because it is true.' Then He said, 'It is done! I am the Alpha and the Omega, the Beginning and the End. The water of life is free. My people will inherit everything I promised. God will be their Father and they will be His children.'

"'But unbelievers, sinners, murderers, perverts, liars, traitors, the sexually immoral, and those who practiced magic and worshipped idols have died in the fire, which is the second death, and it will last forever' (Rev. 21:1-8).

### The City

"Then one of the seven angels who had the seven bowls of God's judgment came over to me and said, 'Come, let me show you the city of God, the New Jerusalem, the bride of the Lamb.' He took me to a very high mountain. From there I could look down on the city of God, which had come from heaven and settled on the earth.

"The city was filled with light from the glory of God. It glistened like a precious gemstone as clear as crystal. It had beautiful, high walls with 12 gates going into the city and an angel at each gate. The names of the 12 tribes of Israel were on the gates, one name on each gate. There were three gates on each of the four sides of the city. The wall rested on 12 foundations, each of which was engraved with the name of one of the 12 apostles.

"The angel who showed me all this had a measuring stick in his hand, which he used to measure the city, including its foundations and walls. The city was laid out as a square and measured 1,500 miles on each side, and it was just as high as it was wide and long. The walls were made of precious stones, and the entire city was made of gold, as clear as crystal.

"The 12 foundations were made of 12 colored gemstones, a different color for each foundation. The 12 gates were made of 12 pearls, each gate of just one pearl. The streets of the city were made of gold, but as clear as glass.

"There was no need for a temple in the city as there had been in Jerusalem, because God and the Lamb are there in person. The city doesn't have to be lighted by the sun during the day or by the moon at night, because God and the Lamb are its light.

"The saved from all nations will live in that city and will give all the glory to God and to the Lamb. The gates will never close, because dark nights never come. No thieves, liars, or immoral persons will be there— only those whose names are written in the Lamb's book of life.

"Then the angel took me inside the city and showed me the river of life. Its water is as clear as crystal, flowing through the city, coming from the throne of God and the Lamb. In the middle of the city is the tree of life. The river flows around it, and its branches reach to both sides of the river. Each month it produces new fruit, and those who eat it will live forever.

"The curse of sin is gone. The throne of God and the Lamb is there. The people see God and talk with Him face to face. They all have the Father's name and gladly serve Him.

"There is no need of lights in the city because of God's presence. From there His people will govern the universe with Him forever (Rev. 21:9–22:5).

## Final Message

"Then the angel said to me, 'Everything I've told you is true!' Just as God sent His angel to speak to the prophets of old, so He sent His angel to me, to show me what will soon take place.

"Jesus said to me, 'I will come quickly. Blessed are those who hold on to the prophecies written in this book.'

"I, John, am the one who saw and heard all these things. So I fell on my knees in gratitude before the angel who showed me these things. He said, 'Stand up! I'm one of God's servants, just as you are and as the prophets were and as those are who believe what's written in this book. Don't worship me. Worship God!'

"Then he said, 'Don't seal the prophecies of this book, because those who live at the end of earth's history will need them. The time will come when those who are unjust will not change, and those who are morally filthy will remain that way. But let those who do right continue to do right, and those who are holy continue to be holy.'

"Then Jesus said, 'I will come quickly and will reward everyone according to what he has done. I am the Alpha and the Omega, the First and the Last, the Beginning and the End. Blessed are those whose sins are washed away and who keep My commandments. They have the right to enter the city and eat from the tree of life. Outside are liars, murderers, those who practice magic, the sexually immoral, and idol worshipers.

" 'I sent my angel to tell you these things so that you can write them down and send them to the churches. I am the Foundation Stone and the Offspring of the house of David. I am the Bright Morning Star!'

"The Holy Spirit says to everyone, 'Come!' The churches say, 'Come!' Let those who hear this message say, 'Come! Whoever is thirsty, come and drink the water of life. It's free!'

"I, John, warn everyone who hears the prophecies of this book not to add anything contrary to them. If anyone does, God will add to his punishment the full weight of judgment described in this book. If anyone takes away from these prophecies, God will take away his right to the city and to the tree of life.

"Jesus says, 'When I come, I will come quickly!'

"Yes, come, Lord Jesus! Come quickly! The grace of the Lord Jesus Christ be with all of you. Amen" (Rev. 22:6-21).